D1128684

4/16/83

Keep working on your
shooting — we may need
a body guard before this is
all over.

Fondly,
Nancy

HOME
GAMES

To N.I.S.

Thanks for your insights
and being a special friend.

Love,
Bobbie

4/10/83

Dear Bobbi —

    Jim told us of your separation
of course, we were sorry to hear of
it. The kinds of lives we have
led aren't terribly conducive to
smooth and peaceful marraiges.
While Mike u   still together,
the straius   th us —

a
th
a
al
th
d
me

agen
Day
enjo
day
but
The
ha
to
m

James Hansen

Fondly
Nancy

HOME GAMES

Two baseball wives speak out

by Bobbie Bouton and Nancy Marshall

With a Foreword by Lawrence S. Ritter

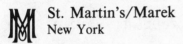 St. Martin's/Marek
New York

HOME GAMES: TWO BASEBALL WIVES SPEAK OUT. Copyright © 1983 by Bobbie Bouton and Nancy Marshall. All rights reserved. Printed in the United States of America. No part of this book may be used or reproduced in any manner whatsoever without written permission except in the case of brief quotations embodied in critical articles or reviews. For information, address St. Martin's/Marek, 175 Fifth Avenue, New York, N.Y. 10010.

Design by Kingsley Parker

Library of Congress Cataloging in Publication Data
Bouton, Bobbie.
    Home games.
        1. Bouton, Jim.   2. Marshall, Mike.
3. Baseball players—United States—Biography.
4. Bouton, Bobbie.   5. Marshall, Nancy, 1942–
6. Wives—United States—Biography.   I. Marshall,
Nancy, 1942–   .   II. Title.
GV865.B69B68   1983   796.357′092′2   [B]   83–2961
ISBN 0–312–38846–2

First Edition
10 9 8 7 6 5 4 3 2 1

For our daughters
    Deborah
    Becky
    Kerry
    and
    Laurie
With love

Contents

Contents

Acknowledgments

Writing this book has almost been easier than deciding how to appropriately acknowledge all the people who in one way or another lent a helping hand.

Special thanks must go to Larry Ritter for saying so succinctly in just a few pages what it took us hundreds to say, and to all of our friends and family who read the rough drafts and offered criticism and advice.

From Nancy, a special thanks goes to C.B. for keeping his date books from years past and thereby refreshing my memory. And, not only my thanks but my love to June Mack for telling me that I was okay so often that I eventually believed it. I know you won't like a lot of what you read in here, but hope you approve of how I ultimately turned out. I'd also like to thank my friend Carol Gallagher, whom I love dearly for letting me have the legs this time around.

Finally, to my daughters. I love you all. Thanks for cooking dinner for yourselves when I was too caught up in my writing to stop long enough to feed you.

From Bobbie, special thanks to Marianne Vecsey who, with her husband George, was always there when I needed help, and to Alice Twombly, who often put off grading English papers to check over the manuscript. Also thanks to N.I.S. for many ideas and quotes. To Phil, for helping, caring, and always being enthusiastic. Finally, love to Michael and David—may you someday understand.

Thanks to everyone for contributing the following titles that we weren't able to use.

Ball Who?
Who's That Sitting in My Seat?
Leeches and Lechers
Breaking Balls

It's Not My Telephone Number
Breakfast with Champions
Extra Innings
Our Turn at Bat

Foreword

This book packs an emotional fastball that explodes as it reaches home plate. On one level, it is about baseball players and their families, and in that respect it illuminates in a very special way life behind the scenes in the world of big-time sports. Bobbie Bouton and Nancy Marshall reveal a human-interest side of baseball that few fans have ever been privy to before. From now on, though, readers of *Home Games* will find it almost impossible to think about ballplayers solely in terms of batting averages and won-lost percentages.

On another level, this is a story of interpersonal relationships. Intense interpersonal relationships, marked by elation, loyalty, lust, betrayal, pride, anger, and revenge. Although the particular people who inhabit these pages are unique, as is every individual, they share feelings that are common to us all. Few readers, whether interested in baseball or not, will be able to keep their emotions on the sidelines as the events recounted here unfold. The story is told through an inventive exchange of candid letters—many created out of later wisdom—that took courage to publish for all the world to see. But it is because of their very candor, their directness and simplicity, that they touch a universal nerve.

And deep down, emerging as the book progresses, runs an undercurrent characteristic of memorable literature for centuries: gradual awareness of the gulf between appearance and reality, between surface and substance, between words and deeds. As life turns sour, unpalatable alternatives have to be faced and bitter choices made. The shock of awakening can be overwhelming and the alternatives frightening.

It does not require a degree in clinical psychology to understand why so many star athletes wind up with broken marriages. Coddled from an early age, pampered through high school and college, applause constantly ringing in their ears, making more in their twenties than 99 percent of the population can ever hope to earn, they are even less equipped than the rest of us to distinguish the permanent from the ephemeral.

In the beginning, star athlete–beauty queen marriages are idyllic.

Universally envied, the partners hold each other aloft as trophies that prove their superiority. They glory in his triumphs, suffer in his defeats, acknowledge the applause of their peers, and share the fruits of stardom and celebrity. If they have no children, and she aspires to no career of her own, they probably have as good a chance of staying happy as any other young couple.

Children or a second career in the family, however, threaten the hero-worship foundation on which the marriage is based. Children introduce new stars into the constellation; a second career requires mutual accommodation in place of automatic privilege. With the spotlight no longer exclusively his, the deposed king finds himself in unfamiliar and hostile territory.

Nonathlete families face similar problems. And many athlete families cope successfully with such complications. But it is singularly difficult for celebrities to share the pedestal, especially those who have been told since childhood how special they are. Few celebrities—whether in sports, acting, music, politics, the business world, or elsewhere—are able to maintain a sense of proportion with respect to their place in the overall scheme of things.

The effects of stardom on satellite family members are often devastating. Children grow up feeling inadequate by comparison with their famous parent. No one ever lets them forget whose children they are. They respond by becoming compulsive overachievers, by withdrawing into their own self-contained cocoon, or by identifying so fully with the hero that they cannot develop personalities of their own.

Wives, burdened by the realities of parenthood, begin to need nurturing themselves. But Daddy is rarely home. Ballplayers are away from home much of the time from March through September, and frequently take off for one reason or another during the off-season as well. When he is home, the athlete wants to receive, not give, the praise and attention he is accustomed to. The result is a growing mutual frustration that breeds antagonism between husband and wife, an antagonism that feeds on itself. Without emotional support, the wife and mother becomes less likely to worship every move the athlete makes. This in turn makes him feel appreciated everywhere except in his own home. Applause junkies feel withdrawal pains as much as narcotics addicts; without their daily ration of adulation at home, they are tempted to seek it elsewhere.

The role of women in the macho world of big-time male sports exacerbates this estrangement. For rock stars and athletes, women are as available as hamburgers and they are less expensive. Both at home and especially on the road, teams attract camp followers who want to share in the action. It is the standard assumption of most ballplayers that any woman who says "hello" wants to jump into bed as soon as possible. Although ballplayers may not think that way in the beginning, they come to that conclusion before too long because that's the way it often turns out. Women become as disposable as Kleenex, sex as casual as hailing a cab.

Athletes generally resolve this in their minds by thinking of women as falling into one of two categories: either vixens or Madonnas. Vixens mean fun and games, Madonnas motherhood and purity. Over time, therefore, an increasing share of many athletes' sexual gratification takes place away from home. As a consequence, the ex–beauty queen begins to question her continued attractiveness. Her fears (and suspicions) are not eased by stories she hears from time to time about what happens when the team is on the road, although her husband always swears he was alone and fast asleep in his hotel room at the time. It would not be surprising if sooner or later she considers turning to someone else for reassurance.

As closeness erodes at home, team camaraderie plays an increasingly important role in fulfilling an athlete's emotional needs. Better than any outsider, teammates understand and appreciate what an athlete does, what he goes through, day in and day out. Teammates are supportive without being demanding or judgmental. They are fun to be with in the locker room and on the town. Home begins to stand for complaining and confinement, while teammates represent relaxation and freedom. Many a ballplayer has expressed his eagerness to quit playing so that he could spend more time with his family, only to turn up next year as a batting or pitching coach. It isn't primarily the money, because most coaches barely make the major league minimum salary of about $30,000. More often than not, it is an emotional need that is being filled, not a financial one.

The fact that an athlete's playing career ends so early in life increases his needs while diminishing his means of satisfying them. Baseball players are usually forced into retirement by their early thirties, football players even younger. When other careers are just working up a head of steam, the athlete's is over. If he defines himself mainly as an athlete, rather than also as a person, a husband, a father, an intelligent human being who can do many things besides play ball, he is in trouble. Thirty-year-old adolescents do not become mature adults overnight.

Except for the greatest, fame and applause vanish within a few months, a few years at most. Soon people hardly remember who they were. Youngsters of nine or ten never heard of them. "Didn't you use to be Lefty Ryan?" can trigger an identity crisis that only the best-adjusted ex-athletes can laugh off.

It is not easy to become an anonymous insurance salesman after years in the spotlight. If you were a ballplayer and aren't anymore, what are you? If you're not a somebody, does that mean you're a nobody? A business suit is no substitute for a uniform with "Giants" proudly displayed across the front.

With public applause gone, the need for private praise is even greater. However, by that time relationships at home have often deteriorated beyond repair. Resentments have become too deep to heal, and being at home so much more than formerly only brings matters to a boil. Alcohol is frequently used as a means of escape. Separation or divorce is common, if it has not occurred already.

Outsiders might conclude that the ex–beauty queen has discarded her husband now that he is no longer rich and famous. Typically, however, it works the other way. It is the ex-athlete, not the wife and mother, who leaves, and the reason, conscious or unconscious, is because he has found someone else who will put him back on the pedestal he needs for emotional security. Leaving also provides an escape from responsibilities formerly ignored or avoided by going off to the ball park.

Not long ago, I was talking with eighty-year-old Bill Wambsganss, hero of the 1920 World Series. We came to the subject of retirement from baseball, and he glanced off into the distance. "One day when I was playing with Cleveland," he said, "we came to New York to play the Yankees. I was on the train going to the ball park and I was reading a newspaper. As I was reading, I came across a poem and before I got to my stop I cut it out and put it in my wallet.

"That poem stayed there in my wallet until it disintegrated. By then it didn't matter, because I'd memorized every line of it. I don't remember who wrote it, and I don't remember the name of the poem, but I still remember every word. It went like this:

> "Now summer goes
> And tomorrow's snows
> Will soon be deep,
> And the sky of blue
> Which summer knew
> Sees shadows creep.
>
> As the gleam tonight
> Which is silver bright
> Spans ghostly forms,
> The winds rush by

With a warning cry
Of coming storms.

So the laurel fades
In the snow-swept glades
Of flying years,
And the dreams of youth
Find the bitter truth
Of pain and tears.

Through the cheering mass
Let the victors pass
To find fate's thrust,
As tomorrow's fame
Writes another name
On drifting dust."

Bill Wambsganss was perceptive enough to realize that there is a difference between the ephemeral and the permanent. He tried to get his values straight and his priorities in order before he had to make the transition from star to human being. "Even so," he recalled, "having to leave the game was a very difficult adjustment to make, and that goes for every single ballplayer. Don't let any of them tell you different."

It bears repeating that many athlete families cope successfully with such problems. They try to accommodate one another's needs during the playing career and then slide gracefully—or awkwardly, as the case may be—into a more or less normal life thereafter. To accomplish this, however, requires awareness, foresight, and no small amount of preparation on all sides.

Long-range financial planning is very big among athletes today. They spend a lot of time with their accountants, agents, and lawyers planning for lifetime security through tax shelters, deferred salary payments, and annuities. A fraction of that time spent reflecting on who they are and who they will be after the cheering stops would pay even larger dividends. If this book makes just a small contribution toward that end, it will serve a most worthwhile purpose.

LAWRENCE S. RITTER

HOME
GAMES

FROM THE
AUTHORS

From Nancy Marshall

I'm currently a very gray-haired mother of three teenage daughters, one hundred pounds heavier and forty years older than I was when I was born on July 21, 1942, in Adrian, Michigan. On that day the doctor turned to Don and Evelyn Matthes and said, "Look, folks, I only deliver them, I don't explain them."

I had the misfortune of being born second. My brother, Tim, was a good athlete, respectful to our parents (he even got the good citizenship award his senior year in high school), president of his high school class each year, smart enough to be accepted at Purdue and West Point, and, worst of all, he never violated his curfew.

Someone forgot to tell me I was a girl. Instead of playing with dolls, I played football—tackle—in my backyard in the middle of winter in two feet of snow. It wasn't all my fault, however. There were no girls in my neighborhood. I had a horde of cousins, but most of them were boys. The only girl cousin my age didn't like me much then. In fact, she still doesn't like me. That used to bother me, but now I consider it a compliment.

I attended St. John's Lutheran grade school for eight years, but I think from very early on my teachers knew my religious training wasn't sticking. Junior Walther League was what you went to on Sunday night so you could sneak out halfway through and cruise the local teenage drive-in restaurant or maybe paint railroad trestles.

It wasn't that I was a troublemaker, just a bit of a rebel and a touch irreverent. I was a feminist at a very young age, ever since I voiced very loudly my disgust at having to wear a dress in twenty-below-zero weather while the boys got to wear pants to school. After all, why should I freeze my ass off, folks?

My irreverence got me into trouble more than once in those days. One Sunday night when I was in eighth grade, our church had a gathering in the school gymnasium to welcome our new minister, a rather quiet, stoic, conservative man. That night some of the boys were playing basketball. One of my teachers, who was sitting next to the new minister on the opposite side of the gym from me, hollered across: "Nancy, why aren't you playing basketball with the boys tonight?" I yelled back: "I wanted to, but they wouldn't let me be skins."

When I think back on my childhood, I think of family gatherings with my dad's side of the family. You could count on my being with the uncles because that's where the light banter and jokes were. I learned at my father's knee always to have a quick comeback ready. To this day, when my dad gets on the phone, the first thing we do is tell each other our latest jokes.

I'm not sure my mother always appreciated my sense of humor. Long after I had left home she sent me a book called *God's Psychiatry*. (She doesn't give up easily!) I wrote back that I was sending her a book called *The Joy of Sex*. I told her I wanted to make sure Dad got some piece and quiet in his old age.

My almost used-to-be husband, Mike, never forgave my dad for encouraging my fast retorts. He maintained that strong as he was he could never overpower my mouth.

Speaking of Mike, I met him in ninth grade, so I've known him ever since he was a boy. Actually, I don't think he was ever young. Even his mother said he's always been a little old man.

We fought our way through high school and two and a half years of college (he was at Michigan State University and I was at Eastern Michigan University studying social work). We eventually got tired of that long-distance battling and so we got married. We stopped fighting long enough to have three kids within the next four years. Who had the time or energy to fight with that crew around?

Unfortunately, the girls grew up, and Mike and I had too much time on our hands, so now I'm a single parent who spent the last year writing a book and going to law school, which is why I weigh only one hundred pounds more than I did on July 21, 1942.

From Bobbie Bouton

From 1962 to 1981 I was married to Jim Bouton. We met when we were freshmen in college and married the year after I graduated. In 1962 Jim had just crowned his rookie season by becoming a world champion New York Yankee. Next year much of my time was spent watching games in Yankee stadium, loving every minute.

Twenty years have quickly elapsed, and I still enjoy watching baseball. But with a different perspective. Back in the 1960s it was nerve-racking and exciting to watch my husband's team perform, and nail-biting time if Jim was pitching.

Now it's the eighties, and the last time I went to a game, it was relaxing and fun. Not only was I watching the action from the right-field seats (in the old days my seats would have been reserved boxes near first base), but I was there because someone special had never seen Fenway Park and I wanted to share it with him.

Some of the names were the same. Yaz (Carl Yastrzemski) is still going strong. The ageless Louie Tiant pitched and unfortunately was tagged. (I find myself rooting for everyone over thirty-five now.) Rod Carew, who is probably the best hitter I've ever watched, and Reggie Jackson, one of the most magnetic, both played.

The coaching staff had one of our old teammates from the Seattle Pilots, the once speedy Tommy Harper. Lee Stange, who had vied with Jim as a top pitcher in the minors, was now Boston's pitching coach. Ralph Houk, Boston's skipper, was Jim's first major league manager. For a while, Jim had almost worshiped the dirt Ralph kicked. Today, with the Sox winning easily, Ralph didn't even appear on the field. I was hoping for at least a spit of tobacco juice or a puff of dust for old time's sake.

Fortunately, in Fenway, little has changed. That's partly why I wanted to revisit this field. It's old-fashioned and fun. The "Green Monster" is exciting—especially when your car is parked underneath, as mine accidentally was. Every time a ball went over this short left-field fence, I strained to hear glass shattering.

The grass is the real stuff at Fenway. I still can't get used to

5

"pretend grass," as my daughter used to call Astroturf. There's something special about real grass; the fake stuff is like an aluminum Christmas tree. Since I was raised on a farm in Michigan that cultivated Christmas trees, an artificial tree is a real affront to me. The two things I associate most with growing up are Christmas trees and blueberries.

To this day, I cannot eat a raw blueberry. Cooked, fine, blueberry pie is terrific, but picking berries was the way I earned money as a kid.

When you grow up in a farming town, population 4,777, there are plenty of fruit-picking jobs available, and I picked everything native to southwest Michigan. Peaches are a pain. Rubbing the sweat off your brow with peach-fuzzy hands makes you want to pick a different fruit. Raspberries are worse because the prickers are not very cooperative. Apples weren't bad, but continually having to move the ladder and the weight of the apples make it tough for a small kid. Strawberries gave you permanent backache. So blueberries it was.

Out early in the morning, hoping to pick a good amount before it turned too hot, you could feel the dew drip down your arm and drop off the end of your elbow.

A hat was a necessity for protection from the sun. I had a blue straw that at one time had been my grandmother's Sunday best. To this day, I do not like to wear hats.

Taking your full carrier to the packing shed was a pleasant break. It seemed to me that the women who worked in the packing shed had the glamorous job. Sorting the berries and placing cellophane over neatly rounded pints seemed infinitely superior to slaving away in the fields under the hot sun.

The second best part of going to the shed—the first being to add pints to your daily total—was to stop for a drink from the cooler. Today's plastic tops can't compare to the metal lids on the ones I sipped from as a kid. There was something extra cool conveyed from the metal that's missing from plastic.

This was for me what the Canadian writer Margaret Laurence called "Where the World Began" in her book *Heart of a Stranger.* The blueberry patch was also my introduction to baseball. Here I heard the boys talking about their favorite players and learned from them. At lunch I'd admire their bubble-gum cards; I became hooked on baseball.

Later, I could rattle off statistics with the best of them while we stripped the defenseless bushes of their booty. At night I could relax by listening to a Tiger game, and I'd discuss it in detail the next day. This whiled away many an otherwise dull day. Is it any wonder I graduated to become a real fan?

It's also possible I learned about baseball to have something to help give me confidence in relating to males. Since my parents were divorced when I was in grade school, the attention I received from adult males wasn't as much as I craved. My grandfather and uncles helped, but I found that by being knowledgeable about baseball, it was easier to relate to friends' fathers, to neighbors, etc. Maybe I was just trying to please—God, I hate to think that was it. Perhaps that was a small part of it, but baseball can grow on you for many reasons. Maybe it's the way the field is laid out or the dramatic confrontations or the time to plan strategy. There's just something special about the game.

My love for baseball continued and I was official scorekeeper and statistician for my high school team for two years. In college, I met a baseball pitcher. He had been a high school standout and was going to try out for the freshman team. I was not impressed by his baseball knowledge but did find him cute, sincere, sweet, and determined to pitch well.

He did pitch well, so well that he signed for a $30,000 bonus with the New York Yankees in his sophomore year. Jim Bouton continued at Western Michigan University during the fall semester and played ball during the spring and summer. During the ball season we almost kept the U.S. Postal Service out of the red.

I had been crushed that the Detroit Tigers didn't offer him enough bonus money. Being an old Yankee hater, it was hard to switch and root for them. But switch I did and change. Some changes were slow and some were abrupt; it was never dull.

We married in December of 1962, after Jim had played with the major league Yankee team for one year. He eventually played with the Seattle Pilots and Houston Astros. He wrote a book called *Ball Four* and appeared as a TV sportscaster. Then he did something I think no one else has ever done. After seven years away from the game, he returned to major league ball.

After the Braves' comeback, our marriage ended. For a while I was mad at Jim because he had ruined my memories, but now I realize that wasn't so. The memories are there, and as the song title goes, "I wouldn't have missed it for the world."

From Both of Us

We met when our husbands played together on the Seattle Pilots in 1969. The following year we were also together with the Astros. Even though years would go by without our seeing each other, we had the kind of friendship that was easily renewed.

Nancy had the idea for a book several years ago and started writing about Mike and his controversial career. She knew from the start that it was not going to be an "Isn't it wonderful?" book and so she titled it *One Long Trail of Toilet Brushes.* And as she started writing, the content of the manuscript slowly changed. It became less and less a book about Mike and more and more a philosophical treatise on the lifestyle in general.

Finally she thought, why not write with another wife and use a letter format? This is when Nancy called Bobbie. Bobbie had also kept journals and had thought about writing a book, but she was using all her energy just going through an unpleasant divorce. Even though she is a private person, she decided the book would be a good catharsis.

We decided to keep the continuity of letters even for the period before we met. We feel it is easier to read and the facts are not changed in any way. So Part I, 1963–69 is what we *would* have said to each other. Later years include actual letters with added explanations for our readers, plus the many letters we wrote in our minds but never sent!

What we really wanted to accomplish is to show the lifestyle and how it affects the women who are married to professional athletes. Outsiders see the glamour, and it's true that the glamour is there. But people read only about what it's like to be Mickey Mantle's wife. They don't know that another wife on the same team, a seven-months-pregnant Maxine Kunkel, washed her clothes by hand to save money.

We recently heard a lawyer say that there is no such thing as perjury: it's just that sometimes people recollect things differently. These recollections are our truth. But we also know Virginia Woolf was right when she wrote, in *A Room of One's Own:* ". . . when a subject is highly controversial, and any question about sex is that—

8

one cannot hope to tell the truth. One can only show how one came to hold whatever opinion one does hold. One can only give one's audience the chance of drawing their own conclusions as they observe the limitations, the prejudices, the idiosyncrasies of the speaker."

No doubt there will be readers who feel some things are better off unsaid. We feel that sharing our private thoughts and exposing our weaknesses as well as our strengths will show our growth and help us and the readers learn from these experiences.

We're reasonably sure our truth won't coincide with our husbands' and, for that matter, with that of some of the other women in baseball, but, on the other hand, there will be a lot of women nodding their heads when they read this.

One of the objectives that we set for ourselves in writing this book was to show the growth of two women who started out being dominated by two very strong, controversial men and ended up by becoming two very self-sufficient and, we hope, well-put-together ladies.

We see our generation of women being to the women's movement what Buddy Holly was to rock 'n' roll. So when anyone asks us why we wrote this book, we tell them we wrote it for all the women who wished they could and for our daughters so they won't have to.

When you're married to a controversial baseball player, you get to move a lot. And when you take along with you only what will fit into the trunk of your car, you get to borrow all kinds of items, like your next-door neighbor's husband—but just long enough to open that stubborn jar lid.

Since it is our book, we figure we can take a few liberties. So, to all the people in the following cities who let us borrow your vacuum cleaners, thanks again.

The Towns We Lived In

NANCY

1963: East Lansing, Michigan; Twin Falls, Idaho (Phillies)

1964: East Lansing, Michigan; Chattanooga, Tennessee (Lookouts)

1965: East Lansing, Michigan; Chattanooga, Tennessee; Eugene, Oregon (Emeralds)

1966: East Lansing, Michigan; Montgomery, Alabama (Rebels)

1967: East Lansing, Michigan; Toledo, Ohio (Mudhens), Detroit (Tigers)

1968: East Lansing, Michigan; Toledo, Ohio; Adrian, Michigan; Mayagüez, Puerto Rico (Indians)

1969: East Lansing, Michigan; Seattle, Washington (Pilots); Adrian, Michigan; Toledo, Ohio

1970: East Lansing, Michigan; Oklahoma City, Oklahoma (Eighty-niners); Houston, Texas (Astros), Winnepeg, Canada (Whips)*; Adrian, Michigan; Montreal, Canada (Expos)

1971: East Lansing, Michigan; Montreal, Canada

1972: East Lansing, Michigan; Montreal, Canada

1973: East Lansing, Michigan; Montreal, Canada

1974: East Lansing, Michigan; Los Angeles, California (Dodgers)

1975: East Lansing, Michigan; Los Angeles, California

1976: East Lansing, Michigan; Atlanta, Georgia (Braves)

1977: East Lansing, Michigan; Atlanta, Georgia; Arlington, Texas (Rangers)

1978: East Lansing, Michigan; Minneapolis, Minnesota (Twins)

1979: East Lansing, Michigan; Minneapolis, Minnesota

1980: Minneapolis, Minnesota

*Cities where Mike lived without the family.

1981: Minneapolis, Minnesota; New York, New York
(Mets)*

Spring Training Towns (Grapefruit League)

Dunedin, Florida (Phillies)
Dade City, Florida (Phillies)
Lakeland, Florida (Tigers)
Tempe, Arizona (Pilots)
Cocoa Beach, Florida (Astros)
West Palm Beach, Florida (Expos and Braves)
Vero Beach, Florida (Dodgers)*
Orlando, Florida (Twins)

BOBBIE

1962: Ridgewood, New Jersey; New York, New York
(Yankees)
1963: Ridgewood, New Jersey; New York, New York
1964: Ridgewood, New Jersey; New York, New York
1965: Ridgewood, New Jersey; New York, New York
1966: Ridgewood, New Jersey; New York, New York
1967: Wyckoff, New Jersey; New York, New York; Syracuse, New York (Chiefs)
1968: Wyckoff, New Jersey; New York, New York; Seattle, Washington (Angels)
1969: Wyckoff, New Jersey; Seattle, Washington (Pilots);
Vancouver, Canada (Mounties); Houston, Texas
(Astros)
1970: Wyckoff, New Jersey; Houston, Texas; Oklahoma
City, Oklahoma (Eighty-niners)

Tryouts and Semipro Teams during Hiatus
1970–76

Ridgewood Barons, New Jersey, Met League
Teaneck Blues, New Jersey, Met League
Englewood Rangers, New Jersey, Met League

*Cities where Mike lived without the family.

11

Clifton Tigers, New Jersey, Met League
Pittsfield, Massachusetts (Rangers), Eastern League AA
Calgary, Canada (Jimmies), Canadian Tournament
Portland, Oregon (Mavericks), Northwest League A

Comeback

1977: Knoxville, Tennessee (White Sox); Durango, Mexico
(Alacranes-Scorpios); Portland, Oregon (Mavs)
1978: Richmond, Virginia (Braves);* Savannah, Georgia
(Braves); Atlanta, Georgia (Braves)

Spring Training Towns (Grapefruit League)

Fort Lauderdale, Florida (Yankees)
Cocoa Beach, Florida (Astros)
West Palm Beach, Florida (Braves)
Sarasota, Florida (White Sox)
Orlando, Florida (Worked out with a college team)
Mesa or Tempe, Arizona (Pilots). (I'm not sure about the
town. I do remember the players talking about killing
rattlesnakes in the outfield.)

---

*Jim was pitching only batting practice—not on roster.

Baseball Terms

Baseball Annie or Camp Annie or Flies
A baseball groupie or camp follower.

Beaver shooting
Ranges from being a Peeping Tom (complete with drills) to peering out of the dugout to look up dresses in the stands.

Biggies
The big, or major, leagues. Antonym: *bushes.*

Bombed
A pitcher is bombed when a majority of his pitches are hit hard and the opposing team runs up an impressive score. Being bombed on the field is often followed by getting bombed (drunk) off the field.

Boot
Error.

Bullpen
Area where the relief pitchers can sleep, warm up, or shoot beavers.

Bunt
Holding the bat so that the ball will go only a short distance. Often used as a sacrifice to advance a runner.

Bushes
The minor leagues. Antonym: *biggies.*

Cactus League
Spring training games in Arizona or the Southwest.

Cup
A hard protective insert that fits into a jockstrap.

Cup of coffee	Short stay with a big league team.
Cy Young Award	Yearly award given by the sports writers to the best pitcher in each league.
Disabled list	When an injured player is placed on this list, another player may be temporarily added to the roster.
ERA	Not the Equal Rights Amendment but earned run average. Gives the number of earned runs allowed by a pitcher for every nine innings.
Fireman	An effective relief pitcher (he puts out the blaze). Antonym: *Whale shit.*
G.M.	General manager. Only slightly lower than God in the baseball hierarchy. The manager (field manager) runs things on the field. The G.M. buys, sells, and trades warm bodies to play in the field. Only the owner has more power, and some owners defer to their G.M. Often recognized by a stogie, slicked-back hair, and shiny-seated polyester suit.
Grapefruit League	Florida spring training games.
Greenies	Amphetamines, or uppers, often used to delude pitcher into thinking his 70-mph fastball is really 100 mph. Pitchers probably use them less than the players that have to perform every day.
Holdout	When a player doesn't sign the contract management sends and misses spring training until they can come to terms.
Knuckleball	Difficult-to-control pitch, thrown with the fingertips. The object is to release the ball without any spin. Then the air cur-

14

rents take over and cause it to move erratically.

Laugher	Game won by a large margin.
Mop-up	The job of getting the last outs in a game that your team is losing badly. This thankless role is usually saved for the lowest-rated pitchers or whale shit.
Relief Pitcher	Pitcher who replaces the starting pitcher or another relief pitcher.
Screwball	Difficult pitch to throw and control. Hard to hit because it's a reverse curve.
Showboat	A player who adds an extra flair to his job; often guilty of making a standard play look difficult. Synonym: *Hot dog.*
Smoke	A fastball thrown so fast that it is almost invisible.
Whale shit	In the bullpen, it is the pitcher down at the very bottom, the pitcher used to mop up.

Part 1

TRUE BELIEVERS
1963-69

DEAR NANCY,

It seems impossible how life has changed for me in the past year. Last year at this time, I was working at a home for delinquent girls outside of Philadelphia. I worked in the "locked-up" cottage and hadn't been there long when a girl broke out of her room and started bashing my door down to kill me. She was going to carve me up with a broken Coke bottle, then take my keys and escape. After what seemed like ages, and gearing myself to jump out of my second-story window, help finally arrived.

Needless to say, I was happy to turn in my "career" for marriage. Jim and I had been dating for four and a half years and waited until he was in the big leagues to marry. Jim thought that being married while he was playing in the minors would have been too tough on a wife.

Being married to a big league ballplayer is quite a jump from being a college student and neophyte social worker. Western Michigan University didn't have any classes to prepare me for this life.

I spent most of my salary last year buying clothes so I wouldn't be quite so out of place at the stadium. The other wives always dress so well and know where to shop for nice outfits. Then here am I—one year removed from the Sears Roebuck catalog. Some of the wives that live nearby have taken me to places where they receive special discounts. I bought some really nice suits that greatly improved my wardrobe.

Actually, my wardrobe will take a drastic change soon because I'm pregnant. This year really couldn't be better: The pregnancy agrees with me—haven't been sick a minute—and Jim is pitching better than ever.

In fact my twenty-fourth birthday present next week will be to go to the All-Star Game in Cleveland. Hopefully, to see Jim pitch. Wow! Am I ever excited. All those years I rooted for the Tigers, and now

—at least for one day—Jim is on a team with Al Kaline. It really is a dream come true.

I go to every game that Jim pitches and many of the other ones, too. The Yankees have such a wonderful team and are exciting to watch. Jim likes me to keep score and count the pitches in his games; it helps him recap the game later.

How do you like fixing dinners at midnight? I'm getting used to the crazy schedule, but when the baby comes, sleeping late may be a problem. I sort of like the midnight dinners, but I sure hate being alone during the road trips. Jim calls a lot and that helps. Also we bought a five-room Cape Cod not far from Jim's folks, and fixing it up takes much of my spare time.

You know, sometimes I have to pinch myself and wonder, "What's a girl from a little town in Michigan doing being married to a big league ballplayer?" Having the time of her life, that's what! You're next.

Good luck,
BOBBIE

East Lansing, Michigan
DEAR BOBBIE,   October 10, 1963

After reading your letter about your first year in baseball, all I can think of is what a contrast it was to mine. I think I like yours better!

We'd been married only a few months when Mike flew to Florida by himself for spring training. I reluctantly stayed in Adrian, Michigan, with my parents. There was no money for me to fly to Florida, and since Mike was late reporting to camp because of his classes at Michigan State, there wasn't time to drive.

After having had a good year in Bakersfield, California, in 1962 (Mike was chosen as the All-Star shortstop in the California League), I know he was disappointed when the Philadelphia Phillies sent him to their Class A team in Twin Falls, Idaho.

But Twin Falls is a small, friendly farm community. Mike and I spent most of our spare time golfing, baking rhubarb pies from scratch, and picnicking alongside the Snake River with the Shoshone Falls cascading behind us. It was so peaceful that when Mike was on the road I would go there by myself and read.

There were some rough spots for Mike baseball-wise. About halfway through the season, while warming up before the start of the game, Mike hurt his arm. The field was a quagmire and the game shouldn't have been played, but there was a doubleheader that night, and I suspect management didn't want to give up the gate receipts. During the first game Mike sat on the bench. The manager wanted him available to pinch-hit. However, during the second game, Mike realized that his arm was stiffening up, and since he couldn't even lift the bat, he came home and started treatment on his arm. Apparently, someone—maybe the manager—felt that he had not hurt his arm warming up but had injured it while doing some pitching on the sidelines before the game. At any rate, they were quite angry with him and told Mike that under no circumstances was he to get medical treatment.

Mike wasn't about to take any chances with an injury to his arm, so the next day he went to a doctor. The physician diagnosed it as an injury to the ulnar nerve and put his arm in a cast.

When Mike went to the ball park that day, the general manager called him into his office, handed Mike some papers, and said, "Here, sign these." Mike never signs anything without reading it first. The team was suspending him for insubordination. Mike made confetti out of the papers and headed for the field. I wasn't there to see it, but one of the players told me that the only thing that kept Mike from making confetti out of the manager was that the backstop was between them.

Two nights later Mike and I were sitting behind home plate watching the game. The team was leaving for a road trip that night, and I thought that despite the fact that he couldn't play, Mike was going to have to travel with them. Like a real ninny, I sat there and cried half the night. I really missed Mike when he was gone, and the thought of his having to go along just to ride around on the bus for a week really upset me. After the game was over, the manager told Mike he could stay home. We had a marvelous week enjoying each other.

Rough spot number two occurred when Deborah was born. She arrived August 17 around three in the afternoon. As it turned out, the manager's wife delivered her daughter later in the day. The nurses thought it would be nice to room us together. Unfortunately, a couple of days later that decision turned out to be a rather uncomfortable one for both of us.

Mike told me at the time that he had asked the manager if he could stay home for a couple of days if the team was on the road when I had Deborah. I don't know if Mike did or didn't ask, but he did stay and take us home from the hospital. He didn't have any choice in the matter. Other than a few wives, I knew absolutely no one in Twin Falls. My dad would have gladly picked me up, but it was a bit of a drive from Adrian to Twin Falls.

The day after Deborah was born, Mike came to the hospital, and

I could tell from the look on his face that something was wrong. The general manager had left a note on our front door informing Mike that the team was fining him $50 a day for each day he wasn't with the club. Mike made only $500 a month. Divide that by thirty, and you find he was making about $17 a day. I could have understood them docking him the seventeen bucks, but they took three times as much as he was being paid. I asked Mike how they could do that, and he informed me that management can do just about anything they want to a minor league ballplayer.

The really ironic twist to this story is that each day Mike stayed in Twin Falls, he went over to the manager's house to fix the fire for his wife and make sure she had everything she needed. I was rather proud of him for that.

Mike eventually took an eight-hour bus trip and rejoined the team. However, the manager sat him on the bench for the remainder of the trip. They didn't want him to stay home with me, but paid for him to ride a bus for hours and then didn't use him.

One night after Mike returned from that trip, one of the local civic groups sponsored a "lucky number" night at the park. If a fan's number was drawn, he got to dip his hand into a barrel of loose change. That night Mike hit a home run to win the game, so they let him dip into the barrel, too. Only he used his baseball cap. He came away with nearly fifty dollars. Considering his recent fines, I thought a small act of justice had occurred.

After the season was over, we drove back to Michigan via Yellowstone Park and the Grand Tetons. The clubhouse man told Mike about a good place to stay in Yellowstone, near the Old Faithful area. By the time we got to the park it was late at night. We drove for what seemed like hours and didn't pass a single car. It was so dark and deserted that it gave me a very eerie feeling. Finally we saw lights, and Mike stopped to get a room. When he got back in the car I asked him how much he'd paid and he said, "Eight dollars . . . plus two dollars for the wood." He said the part about the wood *very* quietly! I said, "What's the wood for?" Dumb question.

Our room turned out to be a one-room cabin that had one electric bulb hanging from the ceiling, a wood-burning stove, and a sink with a cold-water faucet. The johns were down the road a ways! I did what any grown woman with a two-week-old baby would do. I laid down on the bed and cried.

No restaurants were open, but we were lucky enough to have some cans of food in the trunk of the car. Mike heated up some soup in the teakettle. By this time he had a fire going and the room was warm; I had regained my sense of humor, so I could laugh as he poured the

22

alphabet out of the spout of the teakettle. However, after seeing the bear rummaging in the garbage can outside the cabin, there was no way I was walking to the johns, and I chose to balance precariously over the sink instead.

If I ever drive through the Tetons with Mike again, it will be too soon. When Mike is through with his baseball career, he'll no doubt take up racing. Mike has a theory that if you drive real fast, you'll get through the mountains quicker and therefore not be in danger nearly as long as if you drive slow. Most of the road had no guardrail along it, and it seemed as if the cliffs were always on my side of the car so I could continually see where I was going to die.

Despite being terrified, I couldn't help but enjoy the magnificent gorges of the Tetons. We also stopped to see breathtaking Mount Rushmore. The rest of the trip home, however, was not nearly so scenic. Since we didn't have much money, we drove until two or three in the morning and stopped only when we found a motel that would give us a room for half-price. I've discovered that baseball is full of convoluted logic. The unmarried players get a plane ticket home. The married players who drive home with their families receive a check equal to the cost of a bus ticket. Makes sense to me!

I've had some real problems adjusting to being back at Michigan State. Even though Mike was on the road half of the summer, when he was in town, we were with each other all the time. Now that Mike is back in school, he spends all his time in class or at his desk studying. Since Mike attends school only two terms a year, despite the fact that this will be his fourth year in college he's only beginning his junior year. Because he's behind schedule, he takes extra classes each term, which means he has very little free time.

We're living in married housing, which has some advantages. First of all, it is cheap, and the rest of the people who live here in the same financial situation as we are—broke.

Last year at this time I was single, attending Eastern Michigan University, managing the dorm office, sitting up until two in the morning laughing with my roommate and partying on the weekend. Now I'm stuck in an apartment that doesn't even have curtains at the windows, and I have this two-month-old baby that no one has trained me to take care of. Mike certainly has changed his lifestyle too, but he still walks out the door a whole lot more often and easier than I do. He still plays racquetball with his buddies and still has touch football practice several times a week. I don't resent his being able to do those things, but I'm feeling very penned in right now. If I want to do anything, I have to find out first if Mike will stay home and take care of Deborah. There's no walking out the door for me and no money for baby-sitters. I'm regretting now that I didn't do the paperwork necessary to transfer from Eastern Michigan to Michigan State.

I hope this doesn't sound as if I'm being critical of Mike. He's carrying an extra-heavy work load, and he is at home most of the time. It's just that the change in the way we live has been so drastic.

If baseball doesn't pay off, Mike wants to teach and coach. I know we have to sacrifice so that he can do both careers, but it sure is taking some getting used to at the moment.

Keep in touch.

NANCY

Co-Owners Barbara and Jim Bouton
announce the signing of the Littlest Yankee
MICHAEL GEORGE ("Baby Bulldog"),
a right-handed spot starter and short man (17½″),
reported into training camp three weeks early,
weighing 5 lbs. (solid muscle)

He threw out his first bawl on October 26, 1963

Ridgewood, New Jersey
December 1963

DEAR NANCY,

After reading your letter, I understand why Jim didn't want to get married while he was playing in the minors. Being in the major leagues makes a big difference. Fortunately, we don't have the money problems. We were especially lucky because the Yankees were in the World Series, and the extra money meant we could buy a new car.

It was very exciting seeing the first two Series games. It's too bad the Yanks lost, but Jim really pitched well despite losing 1–0. I didn't go to the Series games in L.A. It would have been expensive, and being eight months pregnant isn't a good time for a long trip. I watched

Jim's game on TV with his family and a reporter who came to cover my reactions. I felt a little awkward with the press there, but they have their jobs to do and I try to cooperate.

The players' wives really dressed beautifully for the Series. Even I splurged and bought a good maternity suit (one that can be taken in later). Most of the wives have rings and charm bracelets from previous Series. Most of them also have mink stoles. Although I'm not the fur-stole type, I felt I looked pretty good in my gray suit, considering my approaching motherhood.

Being with the Yankees has really been fun in the off-season too. We've been invited to some great places. Recently, a bunch of the players went to Grossinger's, a Catskills Mountain resort. We are treated like royalty—it takes a bit of getting used to—but now I can pretty much relax and enjoy myself.

Now on to the really good stuff. Michael is wonderful! He was supposed to be born the middle of November, but . . . on October 25 Jim and I were painting the living room, getting everything ready before the baby arrived. We were still working late at night when I started getting cramps. I was in the middle of painting a door and told Jim I felt crampy and was going to lie down.

He said, "Why don't you finish the door first?" So I did. Because the cramps kept getting worse, I suggested we time the pains. We timed them; they varied—ten minutes, seven, nine, etc. Jim said it must be false labor because it wasn't clockwork. So I tried to sleep but couldn't and finally called the doctor. He said that since we were so close to the hospital, I could wait until the pains were three minutes apart, or if the pain became too bad, to go sooner. Although I was uncomfortable, I opted to stay home. During the wait, when I turned to ask Jim to rub my back, I discovered that he had fallen asleep—so much for my timer.

Michael was born less then two hours after we went to the hospital that morning. Jim apologized all over the place for doubting that I was serious.

Unfortunately, Michael's weight dropped under five pounds, so we couldn't take him home. I couldn't even hold him, and, boy, did that hurt. But we were lucky; some babies in the room with him were under three pounds, and some didn't make it home at all. Fortunately, Michael came home two weeks after he was born. Being separated from your new baby is even worse than having your husband away on a long road trip.

We're all going to Florida for the full time this year. If Jim doesn't have to hold out, that is. It doesn't look good and after a terrific year, a year beyond our wildest dreams. At the beginning of the season we just hoped he'd have a good year, and maybe break into the starting rotation and win 12–15 games. But he had a 21–7, 2.53 ERA season and they only want to give him $15,000, a $5,000 raise. It seems like a lot of money, but, compared to other players, it isn't. The other 20-game winners make twice as much.

Jim has been nicknamed "the Bulldog" because he is tenacious and digs in there. So the Yankee front office isn't dealing with a pushover in this salary hassle. However, I know deep down he enjoys pitching so much that if he had to he'd pay them!

Are you keeping a scrapbook? I really enjoy doing ours. I also help Jim answer his fan mail. He gets some interesting letters. The Yankees would send out a stamped photo, but Jim likes to read the letters and answer them personally, so it's a fair amount of work. I address them and sort the letters that need special replies. It's fun and I do it when he's on the road. Just wish there weren't so many from women saying how great he is, etc. I agree, but enough is enough.

Hope you have a good year. I follow the *Sporting News* but keep me posted. Also send a picture of Deborah. I've enclosed one of Michael.

Good luck in 1964,
BOBBIE

The charm bracelets worn on a baseball wife's wrist typically included: the husbands uniform number; a charm for each team he played on; All-Star or World Series mementos—if you were one of the lucky ones.

Mine also had a model of the Astrodome and some amateur baseball souvenirs. The pièce de résistance on my bracelet was a golden jockstrap with a ruby chip (my birthstone).

The less impressive charms were for your children or school. Later, Jim gave me a TV camera and a book engraved with the title Ball Four.

After Jim left the Yankees, I rarely wore the bracelet. I did wear the book on a chain around my neck. Now the bracelet sits in a safe-deposit box with a World Series ring. A provision in my will leaves both to our daughter Laurie. Jim demanded this provision in our divorce contract. At first I rather resented his controlling me even after I was dead, but Laurie is welcome to it all. Ironically, she couldn't care less.

B.B.

Dear Nancy,

This has been another terrific year, and it's only half over. . . . I got to meet Sandy Koufax, Bill Russell, and Jimmy Brown. Being a sports fan, it's really cloud nine being introduced to these stars.

The fun stopped when the general manager, Ralph Houk, called on Jim's birthday (March 8) and threatened to fine him $100 for every day of spring training that he missed after March 10. Jim didn't want to hold out, but after winning twenty-one games last year, he certainly deserves a generous raise. Unfortunately, the Yankee front office didn't agree with our idea of a good raise hike, so while the other pitchers reported to spring training camp, we stayed at home.

Houk's fining Jim reminded me of Mike's fine when Deborah was born. If you figure that Jim works from March 10 to September 30, it's about two hundred days, and if he gets $18,500, that's $95 a day. Even major league baseball management will fine a player more than he makes.

Maybe they figure he makes more than $100 a day during the season, since players aren't paid for spring training. I can't understand why their salary doesn't start when they start working out. Money for meals and transportation expenses for the player only doesn't help much when he has a family. Saving money during the winter till the first paycheck takes a lot of good planning.

I guess this system saves the teams money because if they cut someone they've saved six weeks' salary. And players who didn't save during the winter are over a barrel and can't hold out. I can't imagine any other professional working for six weeks with an option that he might be dropped without pay.

We decided a $100-a-day fine was too much to fight, and Jim agreed to sign and end his two-week holdout. A couple of days later we flew to Florida.

We rented a nice, clean little house with a pool. Since I can't swim and Michael would have to be watched every second, I really didn't want a pool, but the price was right. Not everyone was so fortunate to find such a clean place. I was visiting the wife of another Yankee pitcher, Roland Sheldon's wife Rhonda, when she screamed and ran out of the room, frightened by a roach. This was the first time I had ever seen a roach, one of the hazards of renting. I don't know about you, but even when we rent a place that looks clean, I'm just not comfortable until I've gone over everything with Lysol. It's a pain in the neck doing this extra cleaning, but after that I know the dirt is mine and am not so fussy.

Getting to the park wasn't a problem because the Yankees have some agency that lends them free cars. When you're a Yankee ballplayer, it seems there are always plenty of people who want to pick up the tab. I guess they like to tell their friends: "Hey, I bought Whitey Ford [or even Jim Bouton] a drink." Often the players are given free merchandise for no other reason than that they're ballplayers. The people who provide the freebies are often known by their products: the "meat man" or the "shirt man." Sometimes they are treated to a tour of the Yankee clubhouse. Once in a while someone complains about these intruders but not too loudly; it's been going on a long time.

We are also often moved up in line and treated to special tables, etc. For example, if we go to Toots Shor's restaurant, we join his table. This whole scene makes me uncomfortable, and one of the things I really don't like is the "kissing." It seems phony to me, maybe because I don't remember this open display of affection back home.

Sometimes people get carried away after all this attention. Some players were complaining to Bruce Henry, the traveling secretary, that the friends they left free tickets for were unhappy that the seats were in the mezzanine. Bruce asked, "How did they like the price?" Jim and I use this line a lot.

In July, I took an interesting trip to Washington, D.C., with Jim's folks. We saw the games and went to visit Jim's Great Uncle Peter who lives on a farm in Virginia. It's a gentleman's farm, not like the one that I grew up on in Michigan. They raise horses and have servants and a historical house. Needless to say it was a treat.

But I must admit that I felt a bit out of place sitting around after dinner with drinks (I still don't like liquor) discussing what a wonderful president Goldwater will be. I would have felt more comfortable in the kitchen with the maid who was my age and had a baby girl. A hospital had told her to take the baby home even though she weighed only 3½ pounds. Then the mother had taken special care, fed her around the clock, and she survived. What a contrast to my experience. I would have been petrified!

How long do you think it will take before I feel comfortable in rather "grand" social situations? It's fun and I'm certainly not an embarrassment, but I feel like an observer and more than a little shy. Maybe if I learn to like liquor, I won't even notice my lack of confidence.

Hope you're having a good year. I've always wanted to see Chattanooga. Next to Kalamazoo, I think that's the neatest name for a U.S. town.

Best to Mike and Deborah,
BOBBIE

East Lansing, Michigan
October 10, 1964

DEAR BOBBIE,

Once again we're back at Michigan State for fall and winter term. And once again Mike is carrying an extra-heavy load at school.

After the Phillies sent Mike to their AA minor league team in Chattanooga, Tennessee, last summer, he had a good season with the Lookouts—even made the Southern League All-Star team. I have to qualify this statement by explaining that just before the selections were made, Birmingham's shortstop, Campy Campaneris, was called up to the major leagues by the Kansas City A's. Doubt Mike would have made it if that hadn't happened. Still, I was proud of him. I actually got to go to the game with him. Because Mike's parents were visiting us, I sat apart from the rest of the wives at one of the games. The people who were sitting in front of us, Aaron and Margaret McMahon, overheard me say that I wasn't going to be able to go with Mike because I didn't want to take Deborah with me and didn't know anyone to leave her with.

I hadn't met the McMahons before that night, but I had noticed that they brought their two sons to nearly every game. It didn't take me long to realize that they were a lovely family, and eventually Deborah stayed with them. Having friends like Aaron and Margaret sure made being in a strange city a lot more tolerable when Mike was gone. I used to while away some hours by driving to the top of Missionary Ridge and strolling with Deborah along the road that ran along the ridge. It was full of historic plaques of the Civil War. That area just reeked of American history. However, after meeting the McMahons, I practically lived with them during the road trips. I learned to enjoy fried okra, yellow squash, and green tomatoes. Margaret's vocabulary rubbed off on me. I now "mash the light button," "fix to do things," and "carry people to the store."

We are expecting our second baby in December. I'm not too proud to admit to you that I'm not terribly excited about it. In fact, I was downright depressed for the first four months. Then one night I had some horrible pains and thought I was going to lose the baby. I realized I didn't want that to happen, either. Still, I hardly got used to being married when Deborah was born. Now I'll have another one

29

just sixteen months later. Mike made only $550 a month this season
—we have no health insurance—and since I went back to school this
term, we have double tuition due. Financially, it's scary. No doubt
that is one of the other reasons Mike is carrying so many classes.

I don't know how long we can hold this thing together when he
works only four months out of the year. We have to keep track of
every penny we spend. Our entertainment allowance consists of a
three-dollar pizza once a month. I toyed with the idea of getting a job
instead of going back to school, but Mike doesn't want me to work,
and with the baby due in just a couple of months, it really doesn't
make much sense.

Although it's an added expense, I'm glad to be back in school, even
if it's only part-time. I'm taking night classes so that Mike can be
home to take care of Deborah. Now, instead of taking a nap along
with Deborah, I do homework.

In the majors you get to sit at Toots Shor's table, huh? Well, in the
minors you hope there is a man who owns a meat market who will
sell you food for what it costs him. There was one such kind man in
Chattanooga, and he also made the best baked beans and barbecue
sauce in the whole world. He sold his meat wholesale to policemen,
firemen, just about anyone he knew who didn't make much money.
And, to the best of my knowledge, he got nothing in return. Mike
offered him passes to a game, but he never took them.

Cross your fingers that this baby doesn't arrive on time, or I won't
be able to take my finals. Keep in touch.

NANCY

*During our divorce negotiations Mike sent a letter to my attorney
stating that when he married me he had $30,000 and expected to get
that back off the top. I was flabbergasted when I read that. Had I
known we had that much money, I would have ordered mushrooms on
the pizza.*

N.M.

Ridgewood, New Jersey
DEAR NANCY,   December 1964

This past year has certainly been above and beyond anything we
could have hoped for again. Jim really finished strong. I remember

a newspaper headline in early August saying BOUTON BATTERED when he lost to Baltimore 2–0. Mind you, he gave up only 4 hits and 1 run in 7 innings but was "battered." It makes one respect the power of the press. (Good thing Communications 1 taught critical reading.)

The next time out, he beat Jim Kaat and Minnesota 2–0. When I was the baseball statistician back home in Allegan High, we played against Kaat. He beat us and was impressive even then. Being sentimental, I still sort of root for him—but not against my Jim.

Jim finished with a 18–13 win-loss record and a 3.02 ERA. Then he topped off a terrific year by winning two games in the World Series.

I was really nervous for Jim's first Series start at Yankee stadium. My mother flew out, and we were waiting in line when I recognized Stan Musial in front of us. Somehow I got up enough nerve to introduce myself; he was very nice. Later, when Mickey Mantle hit the homer to win the game 2–1, I had trouble keeping my feet on the ground.

A lot of celebrities came to watch the games and sat in the "family section." Buddy Hackett's seats were nearby, and I met Ed Sullivan. The regular family section is between first base and home plate, but during the Series, the seats were moved slightly to the left of home plate and down at the box level. When I was a kid, I never would have even dreamed about seats like these.

Jim also pitched the sixth game in St. Louis. I didn't go because Jim thought it would be too much of a hassle. I wanted to go but not enough to argue, so I watched the game on TV with Jim's family. We almost fainted when Jim singled in the tying run. He can bunt, but like most pitchers, he isn't much of a hitter.

It's too bad that Mel Stottlemyre didn't win the last game. He's had a good year and is such a nice kid. When Mel was called up in August, his wife Jean and the baby, who's Michael's age, stayed with me while she looked for a rental. (The team was on the road.) She reminds me of myself two years ago—really in awe of the Yankee team and scene. I'm still impressed but at least I can *appear* cool and collected.

We've been meeting more sports figures at banquets. Jim became friendly with a handball player, Jimmy Jacobs, and we really enjoy his company. Frank Gifford (he's gorgeous), Kyle Rote, Jack Dempsey, and Gene Tunney were at a dinner we attended; I've also met Howard Cosell. Jim does a good imitation of Cosell that even Howard seems to enjoy.

I was happy to hear that Mike made the All-Star team. You should be in the "biggies" soon, and I won't have to feel funny telling you how wonderful it is because you'll know.

Let me know when the new addition arrives.

Stay well,
BOBBIE

Thank goodness back then they didn't turn the TV camera on the wives when their husbands were in crucial situations. It was nerve-racking enough without knowing that thousands of viewers were watching you. I remember watching Tug McGraw's wife a couple of years ago and thinking it's not fair: She didn't bargain for this attention. Get Tug's reaction; he's the pro and emotional—that should be enough. Let the poor wife, who's all knotted inside and can't do anything about it, have some privacy. Being so into the game, I found it hard even to be cordial when Jim was pitching—unless it was a "laugher."

Usually I had to go to the bathroom and would try to hold it for when Jim was off the field and the best hitters weren't due up. It seemed that I was always in the ladies' room when the loud cheering or the suspended "Oooooh" could be heard echoing under the stands. I'd try to hurry and, with trembling hand, put on my lipstick, skip combing my hair, and rush back, sure that I'd missed the play of the game.

B.B.

Eugene, Oregon
June 15, 1965

DEAR BOBBIE,

Rebekah Lynne Marshall was born December 19, 1964. Uglier kid I've never seen. She was long and skinny, had a nose the size of an adult, and was covered with black hair from her forehead to her eyebrows. She even had hair on her ears. To make matters worse, she was born with an immature stomach and threw up all the time. Fortunately, she molted and has finally stopped upchucking. I think she might turn out to be a looker someday. It's a good thing she was two weeks late, as I finished my finals just two days before she was born.

So far, 1965 has not been what you would call a wonderful year. When Mike got his contract in February, the Phillies had given him a $50 raise and assigned him back to Chattanooga. Since he led the team in hitting last year, Mike thought they would at least give him a shot at the Triple A team.

If we didn't need the money to get Mike through one more year of school (he has only two terms left until he gets his B.A.), I'm sure Mike would have quit. But since he couldn't do that, he decided to foul up the organization and return as a pitcher instead of a shortstop. When I questioned him about his motivations for making this decision, he said, "Why should I bust my ass playing shortstop every day when I can just go out there and pitch every fourth day? This will no doubt be my last year in baseball. I may as well enjoy myself."

I don't know why the Phillies didn't give Mike the ultimatum of playing shortstop or being released. Certainly Mike didn't have any real club to hold over their head. I guess a warm body, no matter how obstinate, is of value to a baseball team. Part of the inventory maybe.

The ironic part of the story is that when Mike finally got to spring training, he found that both of the Triple A shortstops were no longer in the system. One had retired, and the other had been drafted by another major league team. The Triple A shortstop job was Mike's for the taking if he just said the word. But he stuck to his decision to pitch.

You and I both know that spring training is a time to prepare for the season, to get into shape gradually. Apparently, the Phillies didn't agree because they did everything they could to make it difficult for Mike. One time, after Mike had pitched on three straight days, they took him along on a road trip. At the time Mike thought he was going along as a batboy. When they got to the game, the manager informed him that he was the starting pitcher. He left the game after six innings, losing 1–0. Clay Dennis, the farm manager of the Phillies, called to Mike and said, "Congratulations. You lost your first game today. It is the first of many you will lose." Obviously Clay didn't think Mike had any chance of ever being a quality pitcher.

We were both surprised when they sent Mike back to Chattanooga. I think they hoped he would eventually change his mind about pitching and revert to being a shortstop. Mike fouled up their thinking, though, by pitching quite well. In fact, Andy Seminick, the manager in Chattanooga, told Mike he would be starting in one of the games of a doubleheader. Unfortunately, the domino theory caught up with him before that could happen. The Phillies sent three players to the AAA team, and AAA team sent three to Chattanooga, and Chattanooga assigned three guys to other teams, and that is how we ended up in Eugene, Oregon!

The Phillies gave us four days to drive from Chattanooga to Eugene. After that, they would fine Mike for each day he was late. I'm beginning to realize what baseball is all about—threats, ultimatums, and fines.

We got the McMahons out of bed at midnight, and they helped us

33

pack. We were on our way to Eugene by six in the morning. Four days and four flat tires later, we arrived. That night Mike lost his first game as a Eugene Emerald.

But, surprisingly, it's been a fun year out here. Mike plays shortstop sometimes, right field others, and occasionally pitches. One night he played right field for eight innings, then, without warming up, came in to pitch to one man, got out of a jam, went back to right field, and hit a home run to win the game in the ninth inning!

There are several older players on the team who are here for what will probably be their last year in baseball. There is no pressure on any of them, so they are just having a good time.

Mike got a little too nonchalant for me a couple of nights ago. He loves to watch David Janssen in "The Fugitive," so on Tuesday nights he takes a shower before the game. If he doesn't pitch he can just change into his street clothes and dash home. The other night he had his shirt unbuttoned, pants loose, and shoes untied before he even left the field. He quickly changed clothes and ran to the car. He got home in time to see his show, but I had a bit of a problem, since Deborah, the baby, and I were still at the ball park! Mike was out of the parking lot before we could even get out of the stands.

Things aren't all rosy here, however. In my spare time I occasionally taxi one of the wives around town so that she can look for her husband. Guess she doesn't believe the scratches on his back came from that barbed-wire fence he told her about.

One of the other wives (a newlywed) seems a lot happier. She keeps telling me that her favorite place to make love is on her ironing board. I suggested that was as good a place as any to get the wrinkles out.

We don't get the paper regularly but have occasionally noticed that things have not gone particularly well for Jim. Is there anything wrong with his arm?

Write when you can.

NANCY

While at age forty I'm glad my children are teenagers at a time when I'm young enough to really enjoy them, I sure paid the price in the early years and, ultimately, so did my marriage.

In those years, I had no self-confidence and no direction. By the time I was twenty-two I had two children who were only sixteen months apart, neither of them planned, as far as I was concerned. Shortly after Becky was born I realized I resented having someone else (namely

Mike) controlling my body and announced that I was going on the pill.
Mike in turn said he wouldn't allow that. And I gave in without any
thought that perhaps he was wrong or that he didn't have the right to
make that decision unilaterally. Years later I recognized that this was
when I started stacking up, very quietly, my resentment chips.

I made the mistake for a while of thinking I was angry with Mike.
But somewhere along the line, around 1978, I recognized that I was
really furious with myself for not having the guts to take more control
over my own life. The really good part was when I forgave myself. That
happened in early 1979 when Mike and I were in counseling with a
wonderful man named Arnold Werner.

In one of our sessions, Arnie said, "Nancy, why did you wait until
now to come to me? You had a lot more reason to be here when you
were twenty-five than you do now. Where were you then?"

I became very angry and said, "I was twenty-five, had three children
under the age of four, no visible means of support, and not a lot of
self-confidence. I sure as hell wasn't up to rocking the boat."

I don't think I even recognized how discontent I was back then. Just
getting through the day required all the energy I had. There wasn't time
to think about "relationships" or "self." Mostly, I just reacted. The
baby cried in the middle of the night; I got up. The clothes basket filled
up; I went to the Laundromat. The clock said five o'clock; I fixed
supper.

When Mike and I were first married, we agreed that we were always
going to make time each day to be alone. And we did that. The girls
were always in bed by seven o'clock. The problem was that, owing to
our hectic schedule, we were alone—sometimes in the same room—but
we weren't together. We'd both have our noses in a book. There just
wasn't time to sit and talk. We were so busy getting ahead that we ended
up moving backward.

N.M.

Ridgewood, New Jersey
June 30, 1965

DEAR NANCY,

Congratulations! But too bad we couldn't trade babies right now.
You are swamped and I've been trying to get pregnant so that we
could have a baby in the off-season. It's been hard to hit on my good
days because the road trips are spaced wrong for us. I'd love to have
a girl.

Sixteen months apart like yours would be a real handful, but I like the idea of two years between them so they can be good playmates. I'm also lucky because we've found a terrific baby-sitter that we can afford. I don't know how you can take care of Deborah and Becky and go to school at the same time without a baby-sitter. Even with a full-time sitter you'd have your hands full.

We really don't go out all that much. Mostly just friends and family come over. We're basically homebodies. And I must admit that spending time with Michael is a treat, especially reading to him. (Plus, he enjoys it as much as I do.) Some night I'm afraid I'll turn over to Jim in bed, kiss him, and say, *"Good-night, Moon."*

Michael is on a crazy schedule, so he can see his dad more often. His naptime is 6:00 to 8:00 P.M. and bedtime 11:30 P.M. That way he sleeps late in the morning. If he were on a regular baby schedule, Jim wouldn't be able to see him at all. We plan to keep him with these hours until he starts school.

I wish we didn't have to organize our life around the baseball schedule. When we get the home dates, I first look to see if Jim's home for my birthday, then holidays, etc. It would also be nice to be able to go with others to the beach or picnic with friends in the summer.

Unfortunately, Jim hasn't been doing well. He pitched opening day in Minnesota when it was freezing. But you know how having a lot of people in the stands means that a game will be played unless there's a monsoon. To make matters worse, it went into extra innings. I remember thinking after each inning, "Please, take him out." We suspect that pitching this game weakened his arm.

The team has been hurt by major injuries, but Jim feels responsible for a big chunk of the Yankees' failure. He feels sorry for Johnny Keane, the new manager, because he's such a decent man. We were impressed last year by Keane's quote on why he let Bob Gibson finish pitching the last World Series game, even though he was tiring. "I had a commitment to his heart." That's Jim's type of manager. We didn't understand why the Yankee brass let Yogi Berra go, but at least they replaced him with another good man.

Being a manager's wife when the team is losing must be as bad as being a losing pitcher's wife.

A pitcher's wife has it really tough. It's so nerve-racking that I sometimes think I'll get an ulcer—old easygoing me, no less. My stomach gets into knots when Jim's in a crucial situation. A shortstop can make up for a boot by getting a double later, but a pitcher can only throw and hope for the best. . . .

Fondly,
BOBBIE

Most working people have about twenty-eight days off during the summer. A baseball player normally will have fewer than eight. If he makes the All-Star team, he may have only five free days. Since he's usually on the road or leaving for a road trip during half of the off days, the family may end up with only two or three scattered free days for a whole summer.

True, he may have the rest of the year to vacation, but children have summers off and would enjoy a whole day then with their dad. Friends were surprised that we hadn't been to the beaches around New Jersey, but we never had any time to go.

Also, we could never share the traditional family get-together days, like the Fourth of July or Labor Day, because our husbands had doubleheaders. Our lifestyle was definitely different from that of our neighbors.

I really missed the time off when we were in Seattle. There were so many beautiful areas to visit that extra day-trips would have been a real treat.

B.B.

Ridgewood, New Jersey

DEAR NANCY,   May 5, 1966

This year has started out beautifully. Laurie Colette was born April 25, during a home stand. Jim went to the park, then I called his mom and asked her to take me to the hospital. Mom was rather anxious when I finished vacuuming before we left.

She called Jim, and he arrived at the hospital in time to be with me when my water broke in the maternity waiting room. He started yelling for help and was very excited, thinking that the baby would drop right then. I was more concerned with not getting my robe all wet (ever practical me). Like Michael, Laurie was born less than two hours after checking into the hospital. Boy, have I been lucky! However, waiting at home until the pains are three minutes apart is no picnic.

It's too bad Laurie's not a very cute baby; she looks more like your description of Becky. She has a lot of dark hair and looks old—sort of a face only a mother would love. But I'm thrilled! (She even had her birth announced on the scoreboard at Yankee Stadium.)

Michael is reading at two and a half. We've taught him by using the Glenn Doman method, and he loves it. Now that I'm busy with the baby, I don't have as much time as I'd like to to work on Michael's reading, but I do try to give him a lot of attention. Some days I'm just pooped and wonder how mothers with twins or—heaven forbid!—triplets do it.

This past year was a good lesson in dealing with the traditional baseball line, "What have you done for us lately?" After two super years, Jim had arm trouble. It never was bad enough for him to go on the disabled list, just a dull pain all year.

He went to different doctors and tried different things—double warm-ups, cortisone shots, etc.—but nothing worked. He finished with a 4–15, 4.83 ERA record. Rather discouraging, to say the least.

Jim's arm seems to be better now. It doesn't have that old snap yet, but we're hopeful. He has to prove himself after last year, and he hasn't had that many chances to pitch. He's been given mostly mop-ups and nonimportant starts, like pitching at West Point. Thank goodness we've had the baby, so if he's traded, it won't be so bad.

Somehow I don't think Jim will be traded this year. A couple of years ago Jim and I went with friends to a psychic, who, they said, was terrific. The psychic said that I would have a boy (I was pregnant with Michael), then eventually a girl and another boy.

This doesn't sound like much to go on, but he also knew I was the oldest of four children with two sisters and a brother and that my one sister was very young, either seven or eleven. (She was seven.) He knew that Jim was the oldest of three boys, etc. He was really fantastic, and I went back and asked him questions. He said that Jim would be traded in 1968. Hope he's right, and we don't have to worry for three more years.

Boy, it's a good thing that we didn't count on World Series money last year. One of the players bought a house, counting on a Series share. He's up a creek now.

How are things in the Marshall clan? Haven't heard from you lately. Drop me a line.

Best,
BOBBIE

East Lansing, Michigan
October 19, 1966

DEAR BOBBIE,

Mike's "last year" in baseball didn't turn out to be his last one, after all. I wonder how many wives have heard "This is going to be my last year" only to have to pack up the car and head for spring training one more time.

When Paul Owens became the new Phillies farm director, he asked

Mike to return again, but as a shortstop, not a pitcher. He said everything had changed now that he was in charge. Sure.

We drove to Dunedin, Florida, for spring training and were fortunate enough to find an apartment. We just happened to ride by and notice an elderly lady pounding a FOR RENT sign into her front lawn. I doubted that she'd want small children, but she even dug a crib out of her attic for Becky. It was only a two-room apartment, so Deborah slept in her playpen in the kitchen, and we put Becky in the hallway. It wasn't bad, except on rainy days.

Day after day Mike sat on the bench or, at best, played in backup games. Obviously, things had not changed at all. Finally, near the end of spring training, the Phillies traded Mike to the Detroit Tigers. Mike described the trade as "Mike Marshall for one broken Al Kaline bat." Actually, the Phillies received $5,000, or at least that's what they said. I believe Mike.

At the end of spring training, the Tigers assigned Mike to their AA ball club in Montgomery, Alabama. At first, he "sat the bench." Then, since others didn't do so hot, Mike began to play, first at third base, then finally at shortstop.

The manager of the Montgomery Rebels was Wayne "Blackie" Blackburn. Mike asked Blackie if he could play shortstop for thirty days and then pitch for thirty days. At the end of the time set for pitching, Blackie was to suggest which position, if either, he thought Mike should pursue. On the day that Blackie had agreed to let him start pitching, Mike was leading the team in hitting. Despite the fact that it meant giving up his leading hitter, Blackie stuck to his agreement. Most managers would have kept their top hitter in the line-up. Winning teams mean winning managers, which means promotion, which means more money. It was not in Blackie's best interest to stick to the bargain. He displayed integrity, rare in baseball, and kept his word. At the end of the season, Mike had 19 saves, had appeared in 51 games (nearly two-thirds of the remaining games), had an earned run average of 2.33, and had won 11 and lost 7. Not too shabby, if I do say so myself.

His pitching so much put a strain on my arms, too. After every home game he pitched in, he had me rub his arm for what seemed like hours. I've heard that if you do arm exercises it will improve your bustline. I'm living proof that is not true.

His switch to pitching also put a strain on my nervous system. I reacted to Mike's change to pitching by developing a rash on my wrist. By the time the summer was over, I had a sore the size of a fifty-cent piece. I finally went to a dermatologist and paid him to tell me what I already knew—it was nerves. When Mike would come into a game in relief, my stomach tied itself into about ten different knots.

Speaking of the dermatologist reminds me of a couple of other not-so-pleasant things last summer. The doctor was a very intelligent, educated man, who actually said that colored people can't be educated because their brains aren't as big as white folks'. Adrian, Michigan, the town I grew up in, had only a handful of black families. The only black people I've known are the guys on the ball clubs, and they certainly don't seem one bit different from any white people I know.

I also had to take one of the girls to the doctor's office at the end of our street and was totally shocked to see two doors leading into his office, one marked: COLORED ENTRANCE. It didn't make me feel any better to have the receptionist tell me that it wasn't used anymore. What a culture shock it was for me to see such discrimination. I understood the March on Selma much better.

I think all of the moving around, our poverty level, and being with the girls by myself so much of the time has finally taken its toll. Up until this summer I had never even raised my voice to either of the girls. This summer not only did I holler, but I went crazy on at least one occasion.

Just before we left for Florida, I bought myself a new lipstick. At the risk of starting the violins playing, that was a major expenditure for me. One morning the girls woke up early, went out to the living room, sprinkled baby powder all over the furniture and floor, and wrote all over the vinyl couch with my new lipstick. I was so upset that I took Deborah's blanket that she has carried since she was a baby and tore it into about eight pieces, hollering at her the whole time I was doing it that I hoped this made her know what it felt like to have someone ruin something that was important to her. I cringe just telling you this. I was ungodly immature and cruel.

That night I hugged her and cried while I told her how sorry I was. She sat at my feet while I very carefully sewed her "sunk" back together.

I'm going to school this term, but I'm finding it harder and harder to do. In the first place, I'm not too thrilled with the social work department at Michigan State. I'm afraid that by the time I get to put my education to any outside use, everything I've learned will be so outdated that my degree will be of no value at all. It's also hard taking care of the girls all day long, going to school at night, and trying to study when the kids are down for their naps. I'm not sure I want to work this hard for what might turn out to be a useless degree. On the plus side, it does get me out of the house and I am keeping my brain active. I think I need more in life than Captain Kangaroo and soap operas.

I'm really happy that you got your little girl. Believe me, they are a delight. Do you think Jim will play again next year?

NANCY

Ridgewood, New Jersey

DEAR NANCY,   December 22, 1966

I was happy to hear that Mike decided to stay with baseball another year and did so well. If he stays with pitching, you may have your nervous rash for a long time, believe me. I know. How exciting to be in the Tiger system. Weren't you a Tiger fan as a kid? Allegan isn't nearly as close to Detroit as Adrian is, but everyone there was a Tiger fan. I used to listen to every game and cried when they traded George Kell.

Jim will definitely try to pitch next year. He loves baseball too much to let a couple of off-years stop him. He finished up 3 and 8, but his ERA of 2.7 was good, and with a little luck the record would have been okay, too.

There are some interesting new people with the team. Dooley Womack, one of the all-time great baseball names, had played with Jim in Greensboro. Fritz and Marilyn Peterson are from the Midwest. Fritz is a typically romantic athlete. He gave Marilyn her engagement ring at a hockey game. And if that didn't set the mood enough, he placed the ring in a piece of fried chicken that his mother had fixed. I'm glad Marilyn didn't swallow it.

The other addition I like is Joe Pepitone's new wife, Diane. Not only is she helping Joe get himself together, but she wore slacks to the ball park. Hurrah! I've been wanting to for ages but never had the nerve. Now with the trail blazed, I can follow. I live in pants around the house but always felt it necessary to keep up appearances at the stadium. You do feel on display there. It's not like watching games at Western Michigan.

Right after I wrote to you in April, Johnny Keane was fired and replaced with Ralph Houk. I guess it didn't affect Jim's pitching that much, but, boy, it shows how transitory things can be in baseball. After winning the pennant in 1964, Keane was hired away from the Cards. But after the first-place Yanks dropped to sixth place in 1965, Keane was fired the following May. I'm sorry things didn't end up better for him.

Thanks to a newspaper strike this year, I was able to catch up some on the scrapbook. With two little ones to care for (and one big one),

41

I'm getting way behind on the scrapbooks and fan mail. I do the fan mail first because I remember what it was like when I wrote to ballplayers and movie stars as a kid.

I can relate to your feelings when you saw the COLORED ENTRANCE sign in Montgomery. And I understand why they had sit-ins in Greensboro, North Carolina. When I went there in 1960 to be with Jim, a colored man stepped into the gutter when I passed him on the sidewalk. I stopped, rather shocked, and then said, "Oh no, please, don't." He tipped his hat, smiled, and kept on going. I stood and watched him go with a sick feeling in the pit of my stomach.

We're looking to buy a larger house. Mike is upstairs by himself and we worry about him. We'd like three bedrooms on the same level and a dining room. Jim has been making money in the off-season speaking and playing basketball with a local all-star baseball group that included Eddie Kranepool and Jeff Torborg, so we feel we can swing it financially.

If we have a dining room, it will be easier to have Jim's family over. Usually the entertaining falls to Jim's mom, and she's great at it but we'd like to have everyone over, too. I'm really lucky to have inherited such a terrific family. We have a lot of fun during the holidays and other get-togethers. Hope your holidays are fun, too.

Best,
BOBBIE

DEAR NANCY,

Syracuse, New York
July 30, 1967

What a hectic year this has been! We all went to spring training and stayed on the beach in Ft. Lauderdale, which was terrific. Laurie was a big hit; they called her the toothless wonder. At eleven months, she's running around but still doesn't have any teeth. Must admit she's adorable, looks like a tiny Shirley Temple. A complete change from her baby days.

Since the Yankees have fallen out of first place and into the cellar, we no longer have the free cars. It certainly is true that everybody loves a winner, or you could say the world has a lot of first runners. Doesn't society realize that there are very few winners? What's wrong with just being good—or trying? We rented a "heap" to save money. The car was so beat-up that the other players were embarrassed to have it in the parking lot. I thought it was a great idea; maybe keeping up appearances isn't so important to me anymore.

In April we moved a couple of towns away to Wyckoff, New Jersey.

We bought a four-bedroom split on a prime lot. The street is a cul-de-sac with a dairy farm at the end. We actually wake to hear the cows mooing. And it's an easy commute to New York City.

Now that we have the extra room, we've started the paperwork for adopting an "unadoptable" child (an older child or a racially mixed child). This is something I've always wanted to do, and Jim is willing to give it a try. We've applied to Welcome House in Doylestown, Pennsylvania. We were supposed to go to an adoption meeting but missed it because Jim got sent down to AAA, Syracuse, New York, on twenty-four-hour recall. Must admit I've never heard of anyone being called back up in twenty-four hours. But we're hoping Jim does well and we won't be here long.

Being in the minors is quite a different experience. Here the wives can take their children to the park and let them play in the aisles, which is a nice change. At Yankee Stadium they would be trampled. Since I still go to most of the games, it's nice not to leave Laurie with a sitter. Mike is very good at the stadium, so I usually take him along. Here, I can also take some needlework and not feel like a traitor because I'm not paying 100 percent attention to the game. During Jim's games I do pay 100 percent.

There is a camaraderie here, and we often have team picnics or all go to an Italian restaurant after the game. I even took the kids on a road trip to Buffalo. Jim likes their catcher, a kid named Johnny Bench.

The children and I also went to Michigan by train for my grandparents' golden anniversary. What a lovely time we had during the visit. My grandparents could model for your typical grandparent portrait. In fact, my grandmother was once asked to be Mrs. Santa in a department store!

It was really special to share this time with them. It also makes me wish I could see them more than once a year. Let me hear from you soon.

Best,
BOBBIE

Needlework was one of the common interests that drew Nancy and me together: We used to scout around for the cheapest places to buy yarn and yard goods, and we shared patterns.

We both took some handiwork with us almost everywhere. Even watching the kids at a playground or a pool, we'd have a dress to hem or sleeve to knit. Wonder if others compared us to Madame La Farge?

Knitting does help soothe the soul. I strongly suspect this was one of the reasons we would click away. Also the old adage, "Idle hands are the devil's plaything," was probably an unconscious thought. Other benefits included having something you yourself created and, particularly in Nancy's case, saving money.

B.B.

DEAR BOBBIE,

East Lansing, Michigan
September 17, 1967

It's been an exciting if somewhat trying season. After spending spring training in Lakeland with Mike, we packed the girls in the car and drove eighteen hours nonstop from Lakeland, Florida, to Toledo, Ohio. We've found it's a lot easier to travel at night, when the girls usually sleep the whole way.

We found a cute house to rent in Toledo, and it seems I had just unpacked when the Tigers called Mike up to Detroit on May 31. For a while Mike commuted the sixty miles to Detroit, but eventually we rented a house in Westland, a suburb of Detroit. It meant packing and moving when I was eight months pregnant (I've got to find out soon what's causing this!), but it had to be done.

For most of the season Mike was the number-one relief pitcher, but as soon as he had a couple of bad games, Mayo Smith, the Tiger manager, abruptly stopped using him. That's what he did with all the relief pitchers this year. Guess he goes with the hot-hand theory. When Mike does get into a game now, he has trouble throwing strikes. It's hard to stay sharp sitting on the bench.

Kerry Jo was born in Adrian at five in the morning on July 14. My dad dropped me at the hospital around midnight; Mike was on a road trip to Washington, D.C. I had planned to have my doctor induce labor the next day. I wanted to have the baby while Mike was gone so that he could be in town for a few days after I got out of the hospital. While it was lonely being in labor with no one with me (I made my dad go home to bed), I felt I needed Mike more after the baby was born.

Even in labor for Kerry, it wasn't possible to escape being Mike Marshall's wife. At two in the morning one of the nurses opened the door of my room and asked if Mike had pitched that night. I looked at her and, not so kindly, said, "Excuse me. I think you have mistaken me for someone who gives a shit." Labor pains do not bring out the best in me.

44

When I found out I was pregnant with Kerry, I was about as depressed as I could be (again). It wasn't that I didn't want another baby, it's just that for once in my life I wanted to plan it. All these years Mike has been in charge of birth control. I now have three children under four years old. Can't say much for his proficiency! I was really looking forward to jumping in the sack and saying, "Okay, this is not just for pleasure, this is a determined, deliberate act to try to conceive." I may never get the chance to do that now. I'd like more kids, but I don't see how we can move around as we have been and continue to add to our family. It's nearly impossible as it is, particularly having them by myself as much as I do. And even in the winter Mike is too busy with school to be the active father I'd like him to be. I'm afraid my dad spoiled me. He used to come home from work and spend the rest of the night with me. We played ball together, rode bikes, ice-skated, and shared mowing the lawn. I'm not sure Mike would do that kind of thing even if he had the time. Doubt I'll ever find out; I'm convinced he is a confirmed workaholic.

It was shortly after I was back in Detroit after Kerry's birth that the riots broke out. Tiger Stadium is right in the heart of the riot area, so Mike had to weave his way very carefully through the back streets the night the riots started.

We had a strange experience during the riots. After Kerry was born, I had an allergic reaction to who knows what. The by-product was humongous hives all over my body. In order to keep from itching, I had to lie very still with ice packs on my stomach. The team physician was a dermatologist whose office was in the Henry Ford Hospital. Getting there was a real experience. The city of Detroit had banned all travel except for emergency vehicles. I don't know how we managed to get through, but we drove down the busiest expressway in Detroit and didn't pass anything but an occasional police car with shotguns sticking out the windows. It was scary as hell. When we finally got to the sixteenth floor of the hospital, we could look out the window of the doctor's office and see all the fires burning out of control on Twelfth Street.

I'm convinced that having the Tigers in the pennant race has helped calm the situation in Detroit. It has given the city something to cheer about, something for which all the people can pull together. Instead of just being a form of entertainment, baseball actually may have had some redeeming social value this summer, at least in Detroit.

The riots had a very bad psychological result for me, though. Because of them, the league transferred the Tiger's home games with the Orioles to Baltimore. After all, folks, the white people still have to be entertained! The result was that I ended up alone in Detroit with the girls. I don't know if it was postnatal depression or what, but I thought I was going Looney Tunes. I'd be feeding the baby and the other two would take off down the street in the opposite directions. I just couldn't figure out how to be in three places at one time. One day I got so upset I locked myself in the bathroom, sat down on the floor with my back leaning against the door, and bawled. I'm only twenty-five years old, but, man, do I feel old! And tired.

I had a taste of feeling out of place in the big leagues, much as you did in the beginning. Mike hasn't made much money, and we've had to stretch it so that he could go to school (as well as feed these kids I keep having), so there hasn't been any money for clothes. The girls get hand-me-downs from friends who have girls who are slightly older than ours. My sister-in-law gave me a bunch of maternity clothes, and the rest I made from the cheapest cotton material I could find. When I went to my first game in Detroit and saw Louise Kaline there in a beautiful lace dress, I felt very self-conscious. After Kerry was born, the wives gave Linda Dobson and me a baby shower. I was really touched when I opened my gift and found several frilly dresses for Kerry—my first *new* baby clothes. Even then I felt really odd. I didn't have a dress to wear, so I altered one of my maternity dresses. I kept comparing myself to Jean Northrup, who always looked as if she had just stepped off the cover of *Cosmopolitan*. I came away feeling more than a little drab and dowdy.

I'm probably going to regret it, but I've decided not to try to go back to school this fall. It was a terrible strain last year, and now with another baby, I just don't think I'm up to it.

Fondly,
NANCY

Every once in a while when I see a woman with several small children, I wonder how she manages. Then I recall that at one time I, too, had three kids under four years old. When Mike wasn't around to baby-sit while I went to the store, I had no choice but to take the whole crew. I'd get two grocery carts, put one kid in the seat of one of them, another kid in the basket of that cart, and another kid in the seat of the second cart. Then I'd push one and pull the other while putting groceries in the empty basket of the second cart.

Most of the time it never dawned on me that I was shopping under very adverse circumstances. Could be Irwin Shaw was right when he wrote in Rich Man, Poor Man *that "nature has provided women with a kind of lunacy for them to desire bringing children into the world." Or, at least, to take them all to the grocery store.*

N.M.

Wyckoff, New Jersey
DEAR NANCY,   December 19, 1967

Congratulations! I really like the name Kerry Jo. In fact, all your girls have pretty names. You must really be busy with three little ones. Guess I'll find out soon enough how to juggle three.

We've just about finished the adoption paperwork. We had to take pictures of the family—couldn't include a pet. Not that we have one, because with our schedule it would be difficult to say the least. These pictures are shown to the child, and it seems that one time a youngster expected his new family to include a Collie that had died. When there was no dog, the child was distraught.

We wanted to adopt a Vietnamese child, but they are almost impossible to get out of the country, especially boys. We want a healthy boy between the ages of Michael and Laurie. Our second choice was an American Indian child, but again boys are hard to find and they have a high TB rate.

The agency suggested a Korean American child, since they are so discriminated against that the mothers are more apt to give them up for adoption. We said fine. So they will let us know when they find a three-year-old boy.

Jim finished the year back with the Yankees. While in Syracuse, he was 2–8, with 3.36 ERA, and finished 1–0, 4.70 ERA with the Yanks. Not good, but he feels confident. It's terrific that Mike is in the majors now. I hope we are back there next year, too.

While we were in Syracuse, Laurie was bitten by a dog and had six stitches in her head. Jim was on a road trip, naturally. (I've heard it said they're never around when you need them.) I saw it happen; she just hugged the dog, and it turned on her. The kids said I picked the dog up and threw it. (It was a big dog.) To try to stop the bleeding —it was pouring—I applied direct pressure and wrapped a towel around her head. A neighbor drove me to a doctor, fortunately, because I didn't know my way around. Next time we move I will locate the hospital first thing!

It's hard to believe our fifth wedding anniversary will be in a few days. The years go so quickly . . . hope the next five are just as good.

Hope next year is good for you, too.

Best,
BOBBIE

DEAR NANCY,

Spring training was almost pure pleasure this year. The children and I really enjoyed Florida's offerings. Also, it was great not having a child in diapers. You can't buy Pampers in Florida. Wish I had a dollar for every ballplayer's car, crossing the state line, loaded with Pampers. The main satisfaction was that Jim had a good spring, and you know that helped take some of the pressure off.

In order to save money, Jim and I drove down to Ft. Lauderdale. Jim had to fly back with the team, but I came back in a caravan. One of our good friends, George Vecsey, a *Newsday* reporter, and his daughter joined in helping Mary, outfielder Bill Robinson's wife, her son, and me and my children drive back.

We got a real kick out of the reaction of the people in restaurants when we stopped to eat. George (one of my all-time favorite males) has a beard, and they must have thought he was a Mormon or something. He'd walk in with two women, one white, one black and pregnant, and four young children. Heads would turn. It was a good trip home; we even succumbed to the fifty million South of the Border signs and stopped to give the kids a treat—the amusement park.

Poor Mary, she's worried that Bill will be traded before the baby is born. Sound familiar? The team must cut one more player. I told her not to worry; that it will be Jim. Remember the psychic? He said 1968 would be the year Jim left the Yankees. I'm not sending out much laundry.

Boy, at twenty-eight I feel like an old pro. First telling Mary not to worry, then I did a Marv Albert show radio interview with a young Met wife, Nancy Seaver, to promote the Yankee-Met exhibition game. She was very pretty—young and enthusiastic about everything. Meanwhile, I've lived with the boos and bad years, and I cautioned her to hang in there if Tom doesn't do well. She said she hadn't heard any boos. Wouldn't it be nice to go through a baseball career without hearing boos?

It must be impossible because I remember being surprised at Bobby Richardson, Mr. Clean-cut, noncontroversial, top ballplayer being booed at the All-Star game in Cleveland. But Cleveland fans booed *all* the Yankees that game, even though they played on the same side.

I didn't mind appearing on the radio (having been a DJ on my college station), but I used to dread Yankee family day, when all the wives were interviewed on TV. There's something intimidating about having a big TV camera pointed at you and knowing you must perform. At least we had the children with us to help take off some of the pressure. You just had to hope one of the kids didn't pick his nose or say something bad.

So far Jim is 1–1. He just won his first game the other day. Hurrah! He feels fine, too. Just wish he'd have more chances to pitch. After a couple of bad seasons, it's tough to get good chances to pitch. Right now Jim's "whale shit" in the bullpen. Must admit I'm more than a little concerned about the pressure on Jim. Especially since I found a bottle in the linen closet covered with tape and asked Jim if he knew what it was. It turns out he had used DMSO on his arm. It's supposed to be some miracle drug, but it is still being tested and is not approved by the FDA.

I hate to think that winning ball games is so important to Jim that he would take such a risk. He said the minute he put it on his arm he had a metallic taste in his mouth. That sounds like powerful stuff to me. I only hope the testing doesn't turn up anything bad. Jim said Whitey Ford tried it, too. I just can't imagine trying anything like that. Maybe I'm not daring, but then maybe one risk-taker per family is enough.

> Hope you and your family are fine,
> BOBBIE

It can be bone-chilling to hear your husband booed. Little waves of nausea used to filter through my body. No one wants to hear people boo a loved one. You feel so helpless and uncomfortable. A wife can share the pressure and pain, but just like a war bride she has to serve by sitting and waiting.

I'm thankful that I missed the time Jim returned to New York with the Astros shortly after Ball Four *was released. His parents told me how uncomfortable they felt at the crowd's unmerciful reaction to Jim.*

I've always disliked boos anyway. People don't boo a dancer who slips or a violinist who hits a wrong note. Why not just cheer or give a standing ovation for something special?

Jim usually said that after a game started, he was unaware of the

crowd noise. Other players, like Reggie Jackson, seem very aware of the
fans and enjoy playing to them.

The whistles in Mexico were also disconcerting, but nothing is as bad
as the occasional vulgarity some fans yell. During some games I wanted
to reach over and cover my children's ears.

B.B.

Adrian, Michigan
DEAR BOBBIE,   September 15, 1968

Despite the fact that Mike had the lowest earned run average on
the Tigers in 1967, we were not back in Detroit this year. I'm not too
sure why, but I don't think it was because Mike forgot how to pitch
over the winter.

As usual Mike didn't report to spring training on time. It seemed
more important to complete his classes at Michigan State than
to stand around at Joker Marchant Stadium in Lakeland, Florida.
As you know, standing around consumes at least 75 percent of the
time spent in spring training. That did not sit well with the Tiger
brass.

Several of the players approached Mike in spring training about
becoming their union representative. He had unofficially represented
them on a couple of issues, so they knew he was very knowledgeable
about the Players Association.

I don't think any of these activities sat well with management. After
Mike got to camp he pitched only in reserve games, and not very often
at that. Then one of the Tiger coaches approached Mike and told him
he had better watch what he was doing because Mayo Smith didn't
want any smart-ass college kids on his team.

Mike was 15–9 as a starting pitcher for Toledo, the Tiger's AAA
club. He had an earned run average of 2.94 and was selected as the
right-handed pitcher of the year. The Tigers had told Mike that if he
did well, they would recall him. Apparently, being the best in the
league wasn't good enough for them. I don't believe the Tigers had
any intention of calling him back up to Detroit.

On the surface, it appears that Mayo Smith has robbed Mike of one
year of major league service, and since it appears that the Tigers will
win the pennant this year, he'll also lose a share of World Series
money. In reality Mayo probably did Mike a real favor by sending him
to Toledo. When the Tigers called him up last year, Mike had been
pitching only about three months. I think part of the success he had

at the beginning was because the hitters didn't know what he threw. He needed this year in the minors to develop his pitching skills.

During the off-season last year, Mike took classes in mechanical analysis and kinesiology. He learned how to take any movement, such as throwing, and analyze it in terms of how different muscles are used. Friends took high-speed film of Mike pitching, and then, using the information he had acquired from his classes, Mike analyzed his pitching motion. He also started working on a new pitch, a screwball. He tried to explain to me how he throws it. Said it has something to do with Bernoulli's principle. Huh? No wonder Mayo Smith didn't want him on the team!

All winter long Mike went over to the intramural building on campus and threw against a particular cement block on the wall. Day after day he threw hundreds of screwballs. Mike says it isn't too difficult to learn how to throw it, but it is nearly impossible to control.

Mike continued to work on the screwball in Toledo, something he wouldn't have been able to do had he been in Detroit. I felt sorry for Arlo Brunsberg, the Mudhens' catcher. In order to catch Mike, Arlo had to be a real contortionist behind the plate. Mike never knew where the screwball was going, so neither did Arlo. Arlo just sort of threw his body in front of the ball and hoped for the best. If he was lucky, Arlo would catch one out of ten. The rest he sort of smothered with his body. Maybe. He also spent a lot of time running to the backstop.

I have to say a kind word about Jack Tighe, the manager in Toledo. From June 6 to July 24 Mike didn't win a game. In one game Mike would pitch poorly; in the next he would pitch well but lose on an error; in another the team wouldn't score any runs; and then he would pitch poorly again. Most managers would have put him in the bullpen, you know, to protect themselves from criticism from both the press and the people they have to answer to, namely management. But Jack stuck with Mike. Another manager with integrity?

It was nice living just forty-five miles from my parents this summer. As usual we didn't live where the majority of the players stayed, so I frequently went to Adrian for the weekend. It was good for the girls to know they have grandparents. Since Kerry was sleeping in her playpen in a walk-in closet, I'm sure she was glad to get out of there.

We've decided to take the winter off from school and go to Mayagüez, Puerto Rico, for winter ball. In the meantime Deborah is starting kindergarten here in Adrian, and we are living with my parents until we leave. I'm really looking forward to having a break from our winter routine. Mike is nearly finished with his master's degree now. He's worked very hard on both his academic and his athletic career, so I think he deserves a rest, too. Sure won't miss Michigan weather.

NANCY

Throughout his career in the major leagues Mike was always active in the Players Association. I suspect that, aside from Marvin Miller, the executive director of the union, Mike probably influenced the growth of the association more than anyone else. He took strong stances and refused to allow the association to become anything but a strong organization.

His positions were occasionally hard for even the players to understand and were always offensive to the owners. For years he was truly the thorn in their side.

All too often it seemed Mike set himself up as the tough guy and made himself the scapegoat for outside criticism. One time that I recall most vividly was when the players and owners were negotiating over the free agency issue.

For years the owners held that their contracts bound the players to them for life. There was a statement in the contract that said the clubs had the option of renewing the contract for one year. The owners interpreted that as meaning year after year ad infinitum.

In 1976 the courts applied the "plain meaning" rule and said it means just what it says—one year. That meant that at the end of everyone's option year, he could play for any team he desired.

The owners panicked. They envisioned a mass exodus from teams particularly notorious for their low salaries. So when the basic agreement between the players and the owners expired, the owners tried, through negotiations, to get the players to give up the right to free agency that the court had granted them.

One day when Mike was talking on the phone with Marvin, he told Mike of his dilemma. Marvin said what he really needed was a hammer. Mike said, "What kind of hammer?" Marvin said what he really needed was for one of the players to say he would sue the association if he negotiated away any right to free agency.

That's all Mike needed to hear. The next day all the newspapers carried the story of how Mike Marshall was threatening to sue the association. Dick Young, sports columnist for the New York Daily News at the time, wrote that Mike was threatening the players' pension fund. He said it was time that all the players stopped being intimidated *by one little Mike Marshall. Evidently Dick never learned that you can't believe everything you read in the newspapers!*

It was a real treat to see how seriously people took the threat. Of course, the truth was that Mike had no intention of suing. It was simply a negotiating ploy. However, those kinds of press releases didn't help Mike's reputation.

N.M.

Wyckoff, New Jersey
October 1968

DEAR NANCY,

The psychic was right. The year 1968 was the year Jim left the Yankees; in fact he wound up in Seattle, about as far away from New York as you can go and still stay in the continental United States. Seattle is such a lovely area, and it will always have a special niche in my heart because I'll think of the wonderful summer we spent there and of Kyong Jo's arrival.

We really lucked out that Kyong Jo's plane stopped in Seattle because originally we would have met him in New York City. When we were sold to Seattle, I thought I'd have to fly back to New York to meet him and then return. I was not looking forward to a five-hour-plus flight each way. (We gave Laurie a pill to relax her on the way out; it had the opposite effect. She was running up and down the aisles. Never again!)

Jim and I took a crash course in Korean so that we could talk to Kyong Jo a little. We learned to say things like, "Do you have to go to the bathroom?" "Are you hungry?" and "We're going to take good care of you."

He arrived on August 28, a day after his fourth birthday. It was very exciting seeing the children come off the plane, then to see the tag KYONG JO FOR BOUTON, which he kept turning to face the right way. His big brown eyes showed panic and he crouched down, but Jim took his hand and said, "Let's go" and took him to the bathroom. Then I gave him a teddy bear, and we went to the car. Mike and Laurie were left at home, so we wouldn't overwhelm him immediately.

Jim had to leave on a road trip right after we got him, which meant I had full responsibility twenty-four hours a day during this rough transition period. He sobbed a lot the first week and didn't want to sleep in the bed, so we put his mattress on the floor. I kept reading Dr. Seuss to him, since he liked to hear the words. Also, I took him to all the parks and playgrounds in the Seattle area.

He had one really cute habit that I hated to see disappear. He would brush off the bottom of his shoes before coming into the house; this lasted all of two weeks.

The first week, I fixed rice and Oriental vegetables and fish for dinner, but Kyong Jo hardly touched the food. One day in a rush we stopped at MacDonald's, and, boy, did he make up for lost time! Once he almost ate a banana, skin and all.

Shortly after Jim came back from the road trip, we left by train for Michigan to see my family before returning home. Poor Kyong Jo had an abscess on his gum, and they stopped the train at a little town in Montana so that a doctor could treat him. (Can you believe that the doctor wouldn't take any money?)

In Michigan, we stayed at my mother's, and the kids had a great time. There were a lot of toys around, and Kyong Jo could be seen riding a tricycle while pulling a wagon with a big tractor or other toy inside. When he had to go to the bathroom or to eat, he would try to hide the toys to save them for himself. (He once put the bike and wagon under the picnic table.) It took him a while to learn that there would be something available for him to play with and that he didn't have to resort to hiding things.

When we got home, we took him right to a dentist, who pulled a tooth, then had to do root-canal work, fillings, six caps, etc., to try to save his second teeth. The dentist had never seen anything like it and said that the poor kid must have been in pain for a long time. Kyong Jo was so brave that it really tore at my heart, but I think he understood that we were helping him.

Kyong Jo has been going to nursery school with Michael, and he is learning English rapidly. His first English words were Mike, Dad, Laurie, Batman, and Mom. When we go for a drive, he keeps tapping Jim on the shoulder and saying, "Dad, truck! Dad, plane!" We also play word games with the *Richard Scarry's Best Word Book Ever.* Kyong Jo, find a car; Laurie, find a lollipop; Michael, find a giraffe.

I'm breathing a sigh of relief that things are working out beautifully. Michael has taken Kyong Jo under his wing and translates his needs to others. Laurie just wants to hug and kiss him, but he doesn't like too much open affection. I would have felt guilty if Kyong Jo didn't fit in so well. Jim was terrific to go along with this adoption idea of mine. I had a gut feeling again and just knew it would work.

Jim pitched pretty well, considering that he's trying the knuckleball. (I encouraged him to try it.) He threw the knuckler when he was younger but didn't use it in the major leagues. He used to have such a good fastball and curve that he didn't need a knuckleball. Now that he's older and the fastball has slowed, it's good to have an old pitch to resurrect. It's especially good because it's easy on the arm.

He experimented with his fingernails—took gelatin to strengthen them and tried to file them like a saw. Heaven help him if he gets a hangnail.

I'm looking forward to spring training in Arizona next year. (Marry a ballplayer and see the world!) I'm not sure how we'll get there. We may fly and have someone drive our car. I'd rather drive, but Jim doesn't want to travel that far with three kids.

It should be interesting being on a first-year expansion club. I just hope Jim has a good spring training and makes the big club. We made some nice friends in Seattle, and I want to see more of the Great Northwest. Most important of all, I want Jim to be happy, and I know that the Yankees selling him to Seattle AAA didn't exactly make him jump for joy. As you know, after a taste of the majors, the minors can be very minor.

With luck the knuckleball will knuckle, the fastball will zip, and there will be joy in Mudville, or wherever next year—for both of us.

Enjoy Puerto Rico and keep in touch,
BOBBIE

	Mayagüez, Puerto Rico
DEAR BOBBIE,	December 15, 1968

Let me tell you right now, Mayagüez is not the tourist mecca of the Caribbean! I shouldn't be sarcastic. After all, we are living in a penthouse. Sounds luxurious, doesn't it? It's on the roof of a three-story building; we do have a magnificent view of the ocean; and the place is spacious and clean. However, they haven't heard of elevators here, so we have to trudge up three flights of stairs. And there are no screens on the windows, so every night at dusk microscopic bugs invade the apartment and bite us, thus causing a lot of miserable itching. And there isn't much furniture. No television, and the only radio programs are in Spanish. However, so far we have overcome all of that and have had a very unusual time enjoying our interlude from school.

There are actually two penthouses. Another player, Mike Derrick, his wife, Jackie, and their two children have the other one. The first thing we did was rent a car together and enroll Deborah and their son, Mike, in school. The closest English-speaking school is twenty miles from Mayagüez, so rather than put Deborah in kindergarten, we enrolled her as a first-grader. Had we put her in kindergarten, we would have just returned home from taking her to school in time to turn around and go back and pick her up.

The typical baseball schedule down here is to play one game at home and the next on the road. Lately, it has rained like mad on the day the guys are gone, and because of poor sewers near the park, the rain floods the field and makes it too muddy to play the games at home the next day. That has worked out great because it has been absolutely beautiful on the home dates, so the Derricks and the Marshalls, all nine of us, pile into our car and head for one of the many beaches. That is, if the car is operating. We've had about five flats and ten dead batteries.

As I said, we don't have a television, so at night we rely on the children in the neighborhood to provide us with our recreation. They stand alongside the road that runs between our building and the ocean. One of them holds an old hubcap in his hand. As a car drives by, he throws the hubcap out into the middle of the road, and all of the kids yell at the driver of the car to stop. Sometimes the driver keeps on going; others stop and back up toward the kids. Whenever a driver stops, the kids run out into the street, pick up the hubcap, and run like mad. Sometimes the driver gets out, circles his car, discovers he still has all of his hubcaps, and drives on. That kind of driver isn't any fun at all. The fun begins when someone automatically assumes that the kids are running away with his hubcap and starts chasing after them.

One night, one of the kids ran up the stairs of our building hoping to get up on the roof. He didn't realize there are doors at the top of the stairs that we keep locked. Since the kids give us so many hours of laughs, we now open the door and let them inside. We are the neighborhood refuge.

There's some latticework that goes up the middle of our building. You won't believe this, but last night I woke up and, noticing that Mike wasn't in bed, I went looking for him. Get this: Mike was climbing the latticework! He was three storys off the ground when I spotted him. And here I've been worrying that one of the girls would climb on the wall around the roof and fall to the street. Guess I was concerned about the wrong child. I know lots of players have been introduced to "greenies," and it may be that Mike's tried them, too. But I know how health-conscious he is and how much he knows about the athlete's body, so I suspect anything like that would be a very temporary experiment for him. But, you know, I worry.

Playing baseball in Mayagüez is definitely an entirely different experience from playing in the States. Mike's old friend, Wayne Blackburn, is the manager, but this is certainly not Montgomery, Alabama. First of all, during the game the playing field is ringed with security guards. They never turn their backs to the stands. After the game, it isn't unusual to have rocks fly through the team bus window. Puerto

Rican fans have a unique way of displaying their disgust if they don't like the way you played. They stone you.

We should know soon whether Mike has been drafted. As long as Mayo Smith is managing in Detroit, there is no future for Mike in the Tiger organization, so who knows what will happen if he's passed over in the draft.

I am trying to capitalize on three years of high school Spanish. When Jackie and I go into town, I ask the natives to make me use their language. So far, the only thing I've mastered is the profanity.

Keep in touch!

NANCY

The Seattle Pilots was one of the four major league expansion teams in 1969. The American League also had the Kansas City Royals, while the National League added the Montreal Expos and San Diego Padres. This was the year that the New York Mets (an expansion club in 1962) won the World Series.

Expansion teams are allowed to draft from the other clubs after they have protected their top fifteen players. Needless to say, the new clubs do not have a chance to be contenders.

For its short existence, the club had obtained pitchers Gary Bell and Gene Brabender; hitters like Steve Hovely and Don Mitchner; and a base stealer, Tommy Harper. (One of their better choices, Lou Piniella, was unfortunately traded and became Rookie of the Year for the Royals.)

These were some of the players at Sicks Stadium, an AAA park that was never improved enough to be a major league stadium. Its redeeming feature was the view of Mt. Rainier over the center-field wall.

Unfortunately, the Pilots finished with a 64 win, 98 loss record and went bankrupt at the end of the season. The roster players and the team were then sold to Milwaukee and became the Brewers.

For more information about life with an expansion team, I highly recommend Ball Four.

B.B.

Wyckoff, New Jersey
February 25, 1969

DEAR NANCY,

It's terrific that Seattle has drafted Mike. You'll love the Great Northwest. I hope we also have a good spring training in Arizona.

After all the westerns I read as a kid, I can't wait to see the wide-open spaces. Jim has family in Tucson and Flagstaff, so we may have some sidetrips.

After I last dropped you a line, Jim went to Mexico to lobby for the American Committee on South Africa, trying to convince the Olympic people to exclude South Africa because of the apartheid policy in their athletic contests. This was shortly after we came home from Michigan. He wasn't gone that long, but I had my hands full. Kyong Jo didn't understand why Jim was gone. No way I could have joined Jim—drat!

Kyong Jo is still doing beautifully. He loved Christmas, ripped open packages in record time, and, proving how Americanized he's become, was very unhappy when they contained clothing. We had celebrated his birthday with Michael's in October, so he wouldn't feel left out in the gift department. He's a big hit in the neighborhood. Everyone is always giving him cookies to be rewarded by that bright smile. And things are still amiable among the children—Michael and Laurie are reacting well to a new sibling.

We discovered that there was a Korean family living nearby and took the kids to meet them. Kyong Jo refused to speak Korean. Pretended he didn't understand. It's interesting that he wants to be an American right away.

The most interesting thing that's happened during the winter is that Jim is going to do a book. A writer friend of ours, Lenny Shecter, approached him with the idea of a diary-type book. Jim has been thinking about doing a book for some time, so why not now? He's not going to tell many people about the book, so caution Mike to keep it under his hat.

Jim has written some articles before, and I've tried to encourage him to do more. He did some good things for a creative writing class he took recently at Fairleigh Dickinson University. He never finished at Western Michigan. He needs about one and a half more years and promised his dad he'd finish. (We also picked up a few credits when we took an art class together last fall.)

Jim and I both know that when a ballplayer is cut from a team, it's important to have another means of support. After all, other men of the same age are well established in a life-long career. An athlete has to start all over and is way behind the pack—unless he's been planning ahead. It's sad to read that someone who was once a top ballplayer is now driving a bus or working as a janitor.

When Jim leaves baseball, and that will come soon enough, it surely would be nice to have a degree to fall back on. I'm sure Mike would agree.

Hope you enjoyed the holidays.

See you soon,
BOBBIE

For a long time I was uncomfortable that Jim didn't have a college degree. He had promised his father that he would finish, so I had banked on this pledge. Later, when he did well as a sportscaster, my worries receded. He seemed to be doing just fine without taking the time to finish school.

For many ballplayers it's trauma time when they are released. Ex-Yankees Dale Long and Bill Kunkel tried to hang on in ball by becoming umpires. Bill was able to stick with this grind. Dale had to quit because it was too hard on his family.

Even before Ball Four, *we always knew Jim would never be a coach or be invited to join the front office. He had a reputation as a troublemaker or free spirit, definitely not a company man. Now he's not even invited back to Old-Timers Day.*

B.B.

Mike was a starting pitcher with the Seattle Pilots at the beginning of the 1969 season and was pitching well. One of his better games was a two-hitter against the Washington Senators—a feat that drew considerable praise from Ted Williams, the Washington manager.

However, when the team was in Cleveland, Ohio, four young men attacked Mike near the hotel where the team was staying. He wasn't seriously hurt, but the injuries he received severely hampered his ability to pitch. Because he dislocated his shoulder, after three or four innings he would stiffen up, and the jammed fingers on his pitching hand made it hard to throw a breaking ball. Before he could recover, he had lost eight games and won only three.

His pitching record wasn't the only problem, however. He had continual conflicts with Joe Schultz, the Seattle manager, and Sal Maglie, the pitching coach. No one understood the mechanics of Mike's screwball; therefore, they didn't like the pitch and even went so far as to forbid him to throw it.

Bobbie's husband, Jim, had some marvelous stories about Mike and the Seattle coaching staff in his book Ball Four. *Jim made what I'm sure is an accurate observation that Mike's intelligence was a threat to everyone. (I would have asked Jim to use quotes from his book, but under the circumstances, I wasn't willing to take the risk!)*

The Seattle club made so many personnel changes that spring that no one knew who was on the team from day to day. Ultimately, they optioned Mike to the Triple-A ball club in Vancouver, but he refused to go there. Mike told the general manager of the Pilots that the only team he would report to was the Toledo Mudhens. The Mudhen manager, Jack Tighe, liked Mike and quickly agreed to have Mike join the team—and that is how we happened to be back in Toledo.

N.M.

PART 2

HARD KNOCKS
1969–78

That certainly was a short season we had together.

Since my grandmother is in the hospital, we are living in her apartment, which is just behind my parents' house. Mike is making the forty-five-mile drive to Toledo and back each day. He's being used as a starting pitcher by Jack Tighe, so I go only when he is pitching. I'm rather enjoying being in my hometown again. A lot of my old girl friends are still in town. It sure makes the road trips more tolerable when you have something to do besides sit alone and watch the four walls of an apartment all day.

I thought it was ironic when I unpacked our things and came upon an article that was in one of the Seattle papers. It quoted Mike as saying:

> Whenever a man can be bought and sold and sent, something is wrong with the system. If he complains, he's fined and discredited. If he won't go, he won't find a job anywhere else in baseball.
>
> Because he's nothing, man. Just a piece of meat in a uniform.
>
> What union would stand for that? Supposedly, we're the preposterous fat cats killing the sport. Sure, we're the top 500 of the profession, with a four- or five-year membership in a very elite club.
>
> But we have no security, no seniority, and they could send us to Toledo tomorrow.

And here we are.

I think Deborah has the most to complain about this year. She started school in Adrian, then went to first grade in Puerto Rico, then back to kindergarten in East Lansing, then on to kindergarten in

Tempe, Arizona, and finished in Seattle. Five changes in her first year of school. Good thing she's bright and outgoing.

I think both Mike and I were relieved not to be with Seattle anymore. You and Jim both know how miserable the coaching staff made it for Mike. The only thing I miss is the good times Mary Gosger and Joyce Comer and I had this summer. Too bad you didn't live with us. The three of us would get the kids to sleep, open our doors, and sit out in the hallway and talk. Actually, we talked and drank a lot. This was the first summer Mike agreed to live with other players. Since he rarely leaves the apartment anyway, I don't think it bothered him much, and it made a world of difference to me!

Mary and Jim have been trying to have another baby. The scheduling this summer really made it rough on them. Jim had just been on a two-week road trip when he was sent to Vancouver, so Mary was alone for quite a stretch. In an effort to keep her spirits up, Joyce and I put a condom on a broom handle, leaned it against Mary's door, and knocked. When Mary opened the door, the broom handle fell in her face. After she stopped laughing she admitted that the handle actually looked good to her.

Mike is relieved to be pitching for Jack Tighe again. Jack just hands Mike the ball and lets him pitch. Mike seems to have recovered from the injuries he received when he was mugged in Cleveland; he can throw all his pitches. It's too bad he couldn't have gone on a disabled list for a while out in Seattle. Could be they offered to put him on one, for all I know. Mike is the kind of person who would prefer to pitch around an ailment rather than give in to it. I think, however, that the Pilots didn't want any part of a healthy Mike Marshall either.

As usual, we will be heading back to Michigan State once the season is over. I can't say I'm too enthusiastic about it. It means another winter of trying to get three kids to sleep in one bedroom, carrying on most of the daytime activities in basically one room, trying to keep the kids quiet so that Mike can study, and, most of all, it means not going anywhere at all. At least during the season I get out to the games and get to talk to some people once in a while. Since Mike decided to go on for his doctorate (a decision that makes sense if he's going to continue to play ball because where could he get a teaching job for just half of the year?), I find my state of mind deteriorates as the day to return to Michigan State approaches. I would like to go back to school, not necessarily for a specific degree but just to keep my mind active. But Mike barely has time to get his things done, let alone come home and take care of the kids while I go to school. Then, I remember what happened a couple of years ago. Kerry was only about six months old; it was one of those bitter-cold January days. Mike had arranged his schedule to come home in the afternoon for a couple of hours so that I could have the car to go to the grocery store. When I left, Deborah and Becky were outside playing in the snow. When I came back, Deborah met me at the door and said, "Mother, when you drove down the road, Becky went stomp, stomp, stomp down the road after you."

I looked at Mike. He was sitting at his desk in exactly the same position as when I left. I've often wondered if he got up at all during the whole time I was gone. I said to him, "Where's Becky?"

He answered, "I don't know."

I asked, "Have you even looked for her?"

"How am I supposed to know where she is?" Mike snapped at me.

It turned out that Deborah hadn't said a word to Mike about what Becky had done. But, then, Mike hadn't bothered to ask her where Becky was either. Becky was only three at the time. I couldn't believe that Mike hadn't questioned Deborah or at least gone outside and called for Becky. It turned out that she had followed me down the street, crossed one of the divided streets that runs through campus, and was sitting on the boulevard when the police came by and picked her up. She had been at the police station the entire time I was gone —about two hours. As it happens, the father of one of the girl's playmates is a police officer at MSU. Shortly after I called his house to see if Becky had gone in there, he called home and asked his wife if there was a little curly-headed girl named Becky who came to their house to play.

It took me about ten minutes to find her. Mike was furious because he was late for his appointment. Somehow it was my fault because I let the kids go into people's apartments to play. Since he didn't know where these people lived, he didn't know where to look for her.

At any rate, every time I think about going back to school I recall that day and decide that I'll postpone my education until all the kids are back in school. After all, I don't want Mike to be late for any more appointments.

All of a sudden I realize I've slipped into a very sarcastic tone of voice. That's what happens when I think about heading back to the ghetto. Hope the end product is worth it.

NANCY

Since the girls were used to moving frequently from the day they were born, they never considered it a hardship. They approached moving very nonchalantly. Had we been in one place for several years and then suddenly started our gypsy lifestyle, I'm sure it would have been much more difficult for them.

They attended schools in Tempe, Arizona; Seattle, Washington; Adrian, Michigan; Mayagüez, Puerto Rico; Oklahoma City, Oklahoma; Montreal, Quebec; and Los Angeles, California. As a result, I think they all have an incredible ability to adapt. They are so used to meeting new people that they have no problems now in strange situations, and they are equally as comfortable talking to adults as they are to their peers.

One of my favorite moving stories took place in Lakeland, Florida, at the close of spring training in 1967. When we had packed the car, we would fill up the wells behind the front seat so that they were level with the back seat. That way two kids could have room to lie down and sleep. In those days, kids wore white high-top shoes. Those buggers had hard soles, and if you ever got kicked by one of them, it could smart. So we always made the girls take them off the minute they got into the car.

We were just about packed and ready to head north. I looked over to the car and saw Deborah, who was three at the time, standing next to it. She was dangling her high tops in between her thumb and index finger as she said, "Mom, I ready to go now."

N.M.

Wyckoff, New Jersey
December 19, 1969

Dear Nancy,

You're right. It was a short season in Seattle, but since the Pilots have traded Mike to Houston this winter, we'll all be together with the Astros next spring. I didn't think I'd like living there and wasn't too happy when Jim was traded, but I discovered that the Houston area has a lot of nice places, especially Galveston. I hope we both have a chance to enjoy them next year.

This past year was so hectic I get the shakes looking at a suitcase. First, Jim was sent down to AAA Vancouver on twenty-four-hour recall. Fortunately, he was called back to Seattle before the kids and I had moved (although we did lose a deposit on a rental in Canada). Then you moved and left us your bike. Then Gary and Nan Bell moved and left us some lamps. Then we moved and left the bike and lamps to Steve Hovely. Not to mention the revolving door of other players coming up for a cup of coffee.

Getting to know Nan Bell was fun. Just watching her put on her false eyelashes was fascinating. She tried to let some of her glamour

66

rub off on me but gave up when I wore sneakers to a ball game. (You can take the girl out of the country. . . .) I later heard that several wives were upset. I wonder if it would have bothered anyone if Jim had had fifteen wins.

Do you know that I actually read about Jim's trade in the paper? The kids and I went to see a movie and Jim tried to call but missed us. When we came home, I picked up the paper and saw Jim's picture and read about the trade. I was happy for Jim and immediately started packing. I loaded the car to the gills and hired someone who would drive the car from Seattle to Chicago. Later, when we flew up from Houston, they met us at the airport and I dropped them off and drove on to Allegan.

I meant to drop you a line from Houston, but it was too hectic. We stayed in the Astroworld Hotel (they gave us a deal). You would have laughed at what we did. We rented a small refrigerator and ate as many meals as possible in the room. We became rather creative disguising groceries. It was Beverly Hillbilly style, but at least I shook the crumbs from the bedspreads in the bathtub. It was easier than in the spring when I hid Easter eggs in a motel room.

To me, the Astrodome is more like a theater than an athletic arena. I feel as if there should be polite applause rather than shouting and clapping. In fact, the applause isn't spontaneous. The fans respond when the scoreboard signals CHARGE! The scoreboard is unique. I found myself watching other people watching the scoreboard. Because it shows cartoons, the kids loved it.

Roger Angell, who writes for *The New Yorker,* calls the Astrodome "the cool bubble." He compares the scoreboard with a giant TV set with no "off" switch. He also admitted that by the middle innings he was giving the game only half of his attention; along with everyone else, he kept lifting his eyes to that "immense, waiting presence above the players." I find myself rereading his work; it's so beautifully written.

The kids and I were in Houston for only ten days. When Jim went on a long road trip, we left for Michigan, so I could be home for my brother's wedding. We were there for quite a while, so Michael started kindergarten. It was nice being home, but it was rotten not seeing Jim for three weeks and not being able to pick up many of the games on the radio. I used to really strain to hear some of them. Jim called almost everyday to keep in touch.

Being married to a relief pitcher is tough. The only thing worse is a relief pitcher who throws a difficult-to-control knuckleball. Just thinking about next year makes me nervous. At least, with a starting pitcher, you only have to chew your nails every three or four days.

I try sending positive vibrations and close my eyes and concentrate when Jim is pitching—it can't hurt.

This fall we attended the Peace Moratorium in Central Park. We took the children and marched in the parade. Laurie pooped out, so we had to carry her. Later, she said she really liked the song we sang. Jim said, yes, isn't that a nice song: it's called "Give Peace a Chance." Laurie said, no, she liked the other one: "One, Two, Three, Four, We Don't Like This Fucking War." Jim was one of the speakers. It was a very stirring day, and I hope Washington starts to listen.

Probably the two most important things that have happened this year are, first, that Kyong Jo changed his name to David. He complained that other children couldn't say his name correctly, so we asked if he'd like to change it. He said, yes; we suggested David, knowing that his best friend's brother was named David also; he said, yeah. He marched outside and said, "Hey, everybody, I'm David."

The other occasion was that Jim had a vasectomy. I had been having some minor problems with the pill and we were talking about what to do; Jim started thinking about a vasectomy. The more he talked, the more he liked the idea. He discussed it with the doctor and decided to have it done. We had to sign a form, and I took him to the doctor's office and waited while they operated. It was supposed to take only thirty minutes, and after forty-five minutes I started to worry.

It turns out that they could find only one vas. Jim was a bit sore from the probing but was up and around and working the next day. I was more hesitant about this operation than Jim. I agree we can adopt if we want more children. (David has proved to us that you can love an adopted child as your own.) It's just that if anything happened to me, Jim might remarry and his new wife might want children. After all, Jim's only thirty years old and his grandfather raised a second family. I guess I shouldn't feel guilty now for something that I hope will never happen.

Jim has really been busy working on the book. I miss him taping at night. Now it's editing time. What a job! Jim and Len are working practically nonstop. I'm also enjoying contributing my two cents and learning a lot of things I didn't know. Jim is sending a manuscript to Mike for advice on editing, so you'll get to read it soon. Some things will probably not go down too well with some of the baseball establishment, but it's lively reading. Hope you enjoy it as much as I do.

Be in touch,
BOBBIE

It was most unusual for an athlete to become politically involved in the sixties and seventies. When Jim signed a petition supporting the American Committee on South Africa in its quest to exclude South Africa from the Olympics, he thought that a large percentage of other baseball players would sign. Wrong. Only a handful signed, and they were non-white.

By supporting liberal politics, he went against the grain of most of those in the sports establishment. One reason he was in demand to appear at rallies, fund raisers, etc., was because he was one of the only "jocks" involved. Occasionally, someone like Phil Jackson, the basketball player, would join, but he had a reputation as a maverick also.

The first protesters against the Vietnam War were thought of as mainly hippies and radicals. Early dissenters also included the first congressman to express disapproval, Allard Lowenstein, and baby book author Dr. Benjamin Spock. I remember defending the doctor at a party where my usual placid nature couldn't take listening to someone degrading him. However, true to character, after making my point, I didn't continue on this subject because it was obviously making others uncomfortable.

Jim used to tell me about his "arguments" in the clubhouse. I'm sure that Jim never let the discussion drop for the sake of harmony. However, I do remember a column written much later quoting Steve Hamilton as saying Jim was ahead of his time. (This article also dealt with his strong support of Marvin Miller, the head of the baseball players' union.)

I haven't seen any dramatic changes since then in athletes taking political stands. Greatly influenced by others, basketball's Bill Walton or baseball's Bill Lee might make a little noise and Muhammad Ali stood his ground, but this is rare indeed. Occasionally, ex-athletes will enter the political arena (Bill Bradley, Jack Kemp); still very few current players are politically vocal.

B.B.

Oklahoma City, Oklahoma

DEAR BOBBIE,   May 22, 1970

I've put off writing you thinking that any day now the Astros will call Mike up. How many times before have I written that sentence?

I know I told you in person, but I want to thank both you and Jim for finding our apartment in Cocoa Beach. Then to arrive and find sheets already on the beds and food in the refrigerator was beyond belief. I'm used to having to drive around town for hours looking for a place to live.

There have been some hard lessons to learn in Oklahoma City. Number one: Don't leave your car windows open. The first and only time I did resulted in a solid layer of gritty sand throughout the car. Once again I had to impose on a neighbor and borrow her vacuum cleaner.

You know, that is something that is really starting to get to me— the borrowing. Because we bring with us only whatever we can fit into the trunk of the car, it seems I'm continually asking favors of people I hardly know. It's a bit embarrassing after a while.

Lesson number two: Take tornado alerts seriously. This one I learned the hard way. I had put off getting a phone installed (again thinking we'd be in Houston soon) but finally decided to go ahead and get one. I worry about being alone in a strange city with the girls. I decided the expense of having the phone installed was worth the comfort of knowing I could call the police or an ambulance in case of an emergency. (Sometimes my frugality borders on the absurd.)

Mike was on the road when I finally got the phone, so I tried to call him to give him our number. Although the game had been over for a couple of hours, he wasn't in the room. I wasn't too happy about being on the telephone, since it was storming outside. I was hit by lightning (indirectly) when I was a kid, so I've got this above-average fear of storms, and I don't like to talk on the phone during a storm. After trying for the third time to reach him, I left a rather sarcastic message with Mike's roommate. I told him the telephone number, said I didn't really care if he remembered it or not, and said for Mike not to call because I was tired and was going to go to sleep.

In the middle of the night I woke up and noticed that the bedroom curtains were sticking straight out the window. I thought about getting the girls up and taking them to a safer place but decided I was overreacting. There had been tornado warnings every day for the last two weeks and nothing had happened, so why wake up the children? Once you've managed to get three small children to sleep in one room, you don't like to tamper with your good luck! I ignored the wind and the fact that we had no electricity and just closed the window and went back to bed.

When I got up the next morning, I had quite a shock. A tornado had indeed gone through (no doubt that's why my curtains were sucked out the window) and leveled several buildings just a block away from our apartment. In fact, the unit right next to ours had damage to one wall.

The first thing I did was call my parents. I knew they would hear the report on the morning news and be concerned. However, I was still so irritated with Mike that I didn't call him. I haven't figured out why I was so angry, but I think it was because he never goes out with me that late, and also I'm tired of wanting to talk to him and not having him there. I keep telling myself that it's part of the lifestyle, but I'm growing weary.

Have you heard anything about the possibility of Mike getting called up? Couldn't Jim discreetly break one of the pitchers' legs?

NANCY

Houston, Texas
DEAR NANCY,   June 1, 1970

We're really happy that Mike was called up and that you'll be joining us in Houston soon. I'm looking forward to showing you around. (Found a good place for discount yarn.) My kids are also anxious to see the girls.

I'm glad you'll be staying at the same apartments with us. In the past, like most of the other players, Jim preferred to rent a house and not stay at apartments. It made it harder for me when he was gone because I had to travel to visit the other wives. You couldn't have someone just pop over at night if you were lonely or heard a spooky noise. I think Jim prefers some privacy or a break from the other players. I'd much rather stay in an apartment complex with other wives. Although none of the other players are staying here, some are nearby. One of the great added attractions here is the baby-sitting service—let's take advantage of it!

Enclosed are directions to Storybook apartments. Appropriate name, don't you think?

See you soon,
BOBBIE

Oklahoma City, Oklahoma
DEAR BOBBIE,   June 4, 1970

I don't know why I'm packing everything up to come to Houston. I know perfectly well we won't be there very long. Did Jim tell you about the first couple of days Mike had as an Astro? First of all, when Mike got to Houston, manager Harry Walker called him into his office and read a list of rules that Mike was to follow. No swimming, no golf, no tennis, no this, no that. Mike said the list went on and on. When

Harry finally stopped, Mike asked, "How many pieces of ass can I have each week?" (Harry was sitting there thinking of an answer when Mike walked out of the office.)

One of the things Harry told him he would have to do is use the Exer-Genie.® Mike has a very strong background in physiology and kinesiology, and he doesn't have much use for the machine, so he refused to use it. Then they said he had to run a five-minute mile. Well, Mike jogs every day but not for speed. One of the coaches took Mike to Colt Stadium in a golf cart. Supposedly he was going to time Mike as he ran the mile. The guy started his stopwatch, and Mike just kept sitting in the golf cart. After about two minutes, Mike said the coach turned to him and said, "You aren't going to run, are you?" Major league coaches catch on quick.

The general manager called Mike into his office the next day. Leaning on the top of his desk and balancing the top of his body on his knuckles, the G.M. glared down at Mike and said, "Mike, either you do as we say and follow our rules, or you're gone."

Mike claims he stood up and walked to the door. Just as he put his hand on the doorknob, the G.M. said, "Where are you going?"

Mike replied, "To pack my bag."

Eventually, I guess they had a more reasonable discussion, but I think it is clear that Mike isn't going to get along any better with Harry than he did with Joe Schultz.

I've got this awful feeling that I'm going to get settled in Houston just long enough to pack everything up and head out again.

See you in a few days. Thanks for the directions.

NANCY

Mike lasted seventeen days with the Astros. The entire family was in Houston for about two weeks when the powers that be demoted Mike to Oklahoma City. Mike refused to report (this was getting to be a habit) and asked to be sent to a team that was near our home in Michigan. At the time, he thought the Montreal Expo AAA farm team was in Buffalo, New York, but it turned out that the team had been moved to Winnipeg, Canada. To make matters worse, when the parent club, the Montreal Expos, wasn't playing at home, the Winnipeg team played their games in Montreal. That meant that even when the Winnipeg team was playing "home" games, they weren't really at home. Where the hell was a man's family supposed to stay?

Mike had decided that he would quit baseball if he hadn't been called up to the major league team within two weeks. Bearing that in mind, the girls and I went back to Adrian and perched with my parents once again.

N.M.

When we were together in Texas, one night Nancy and I popped some corn and put our kids in the back of my wagon and headed for the drive-in on dollar night. We planned to all watch Butch Cassidy and the Sundance Kid, *then the kids would sleep while Nancy and I watched the second show,* The Prime of Miss Jean Brodie. *Unfortunately, the kids were still bouncing around and making so much noise that we left early. (This was probably Nancy's night out for the month.)*

After this evening out, we talked about the difficulties of raising children. Nancy said, "One on one my kids are all great, but when I have them together for a while, I sometimes don't think I'll make it through the day." We didn't discuss this problem in connection with our husbands being gone for extended periods causing added responsibilities for us, but rather as any young mother worries about doing the best job she can in difficult circumstances. Even though we were good friends, it was many years before we would talk openly about our other problems.

Recently, I told Nancy that in writing this book, she is coming off like Butch and Sundance rolled into one and I'm just Emma.

B.B.

Houston, Texas
July 1970

DEAR NANCY,

What lousy timing! While you were in Houston had to be the most hectic time ever for me. We hardly had time to say hello before the Astros let Mike go. I'm glad we at least had time to relax and enjoy each other's company in Cocoa Beach during spring training.

Remember that strip joint we went to in Florida? Our husbands really take us to some classy places. When the one gal took that humongous snake out of the basket, I thought we'd trample each other trying to get as far away as possible. I'm not sure if going to that place is a reflection on the entertainment available in Cocoa Beach or on our willingness to go anywhere—as long as it's out.

Jim was quite low when the commissioner called him in for a meeting about *Ball Four* on June 1, and I had my hands full trying to keep his spirits up. He had called me from New York extremely upset because there had been an article that quoted Joe Pepitone calling Jim the "horniest bleep in baseball." He warned me there would probably be more uncomplimentary articles. I told him not to worry—I understood, and he *was* rather horny.

His prediction of more to come was quickly fulfilled. Another article called him a social leper. Thank goodness the kids don't really read yet. That one hurt. Wonder what my family feels? Fortunately, the Astro wives have not avoided me, so I haven't had to feel like a leper. I knew that was a possibility, but this is a pretty enlightened group, or maybe they're just courteous.

By the time you and Mike arrived, he was feeling pretty good because of all the terrific reviews, articles, and fan mail.

The mail has been overwhelmingly pro-Jim and from people who loved the book. At least 90 percent positive. I'm going off my gourd trying to keep the mail sorted, let alone answered. The scrapbook is almost up to date—terrific, considering I'm on my second *Ball Four* scrapbook already. Even with all the good press, I'm still afraid Jim may get punched sometime by some unhappy player or fan.

The children still aren't quite sure what's going on. Finding your living room full of TV cameras and lights and reporters gives you a clue that something is up. The children in Michael's kindergarten saw his picture in *Look,* so he was a miniceleb and enjoyed the feeling. I worry about how Michael always wants to pose for pictures. The other two I have to corral, but Michael is always ready to smile. (He probably knows his best side.)

We were out by the pool the other day, and Michael said to Jim, "Dad, go tell those people who you are." Just wish that he wasn't so outgoing, or, to use a baseball term, a *showboat.* It's hard explaining things to him because he sees the reaction of other people and knows his dad is doing something special. Wish I knew the best way of handling this problem. I've seen too many spoiled, cocky kids of celebrities or people with money and don't want mine to remotely resemble them.

I know things are also hectic for you now. But drop me a line when you find a chance.

Fondly,
BOBBIE

It was so long ago that Ball Four *was published and so many controversial sports books have been written since then that hardly anyone realizes what a bombshell it was in 1970.*
Since Jim liked Mike and treated him rather positively (and hon-

74

estly, too), I liked it. Other wives who didn't want to think about the times when their husbands were on the road, let alone read a story that confirmed their worst suspicions, were not as thrilled. And lots of fans didn't like having their heroes exposed as real people who didn't always behave maturely.

In retrospect, Ball Four *gave its readers a very small peek into the locker room, and because it did so with humor, the impact wasn't really all that harsh. If it was published today, just thirteen years later,* Ball Four *would still be funny and well worth reading, but there would be none of the controversy that accompanied it back then.*

N.M.

Jim really didn't have the breaks to survive as a pitcher in 1970. He was doing fairly well (2–2) when he hurt himself sliding into home plate against Chicago. It's no wonder he was hurt—what did he know about sliding into home? This was the first year that he could even get on base, thanks to Houston manager Harry Walker's batting tips. (Jim was batting .353.)

About the time he was feeling better, excerpts of the book came out in Look *magazine, and the reaction was overwhelming. Fans either loved it or hated it, and Jim was so busy with interviews and all the attention that he couldn't concentrate on pitching. Unfortunately, when you are a knuckleball pitcher, concentration is vital. Jim could no longer throw smoke, and as his concentration waned, he did progressively poorer. This caused the Astros to send him to AAA Oklahoma City. Hub Kittle (a great name), the manager, tried to talk Jim out of quitting. In 1982 I was happy to see that Hub was pitching coach of the world champion Cardinals.*

B.B.

DEAR BOBBIE,
East Lansing, Michigan
October 25, 1970

I have just one question I would like you to answer. Where the hell is that glamorous life I hear about that the wives of major league ballplayers lead?

Do you realize how many moves the kids and I made this year? Starting back in March, we packed up everything in our married housing apartment and moved the winter things to my grandmother's attic. Then we drove from Michigan to Cocoa Beach.

At the end of spring training, Mike and I drove nonstop to Dallas. He got on a plane and flew back to Orlando to rejoin the team, and I drove on to Oklahoma City with the girls. Of course, the team never knew he had even left town. Their stupid rule that the players all have to travel to Oklahoma City en masse sure makes it hard on the wives and children. I can't imagine driving by myself with three kids from Florida to Oklahoma City. Continuing, we were in Oklahoma City for five weeks. Then I packed everything up by myself and drove to Houston. How long did we stay there? Seventeen days? Once again, I was grateful that Jim helped me pack up the car. I'll never forget the lady who managed the furniture rental place telling me I *couldn't* return the furniture after just two weeks.

As you know, Mike flew back from Montreal and met me at the Houston airport, then we drove back to Michigan. I stayed with my parents for about a week while Mike was in Syracuse. Then he came into Toledo for a three-game series. Toledo is only about forty miles from my folks' house, so Mike stayed with us and drove back and forth. From there, the girls and I went on the next road trip with Mike. We all drove to Columbus, Ohio, and stayed in Mike's hotel room, then on to Louisville, Kentucky, for another three days. Mike drove us back to Columbus, where he left for Winnipeg. I drove back to Adrian with the girls and eventually moved into married housing again at Michigan State. Later in August, after Mike was called up to the Expos, the girls and I drove with friends to Cincinnati to meet Mike and then flew back to Montreal with the team. We stayed there for two weeks and then flew back to East Lansing. And, thank God, we haven't gone anywhere since.

The winter promises to be another dreary one. I'm so sick of trying to get all three girls to sleep in one small room. Actually, the worst part of living in married housing is the sickness. There's always some kid in the unit that has something wrong, and it just gets passed around from kid to kid. If one of the local doctors had any sense at all, he would open up a practice right in the middle of Spartan Village. In one year he'd be a very wealthy man.

If Mike follows his usual pattern, it will be another winter of trying to play catch-up. Somehow it doesn't seem right to complain that your husband works too hard. Still, I think there must be more to life than going to school all day, grabbing a quick supper, and burying yourself in the books until it's time to go to bed. Well, I nearly forgot, he does take time out to play touch football. Tell me, Bobbie, do people really go out on weekends?

After rereading this, I think I should have waited until a

more positive mood is upon me. But, then, you might never hear from me.

Keep in touch.

NANCY

After the wives' stadium waiting room, the outside walls I remember most are airport waiting rooms. What a loyal bunch we were, dressing up and driving in caravans to the airport at two in the morning.

Fighting Sunday night traffic back into the city and being stuck on the George Washington bridge was my nightmare. I hated feeling the bridge sway while waiting forever to get across.

Often I'd call and hear the flight was on time, then spend hours waiting. This was my biggest visiting time with other wives. When we lived in New Jersey full-time, I had family and local friends and didn't socialize as much with other wives, so waiting room time was my visiting time. Trying to visit with young children can be hectic.

In the minor leagues, the waiting room was your car—parked outside the stadium until the team bus arrived. Unfortunately, these stadiums were usually not in the best part of town. I made good use of our station wagon by putting the kids in sleeping bags in the back. I'd usually take something to knit or read while waiting, but never got much done as I'd look up every time a set of headlights came near, hoping my vigil was over. (The estimated-time-of-arrival for team buses is more erratic than for any airline.)

Occasionally, Jim would car-pool and I wouldn't have to wake the children to pick him up. In Seattle we car-pooled at night all the time because it was difficult lugging three sleepy children to the airport.

Sometimes we'd meet the team bus at the stadium, but most of the time the majority of wives would trudge out of town to the airport to be able to greet their husbands the minute they arrived in town. Meanwhile, as the players landed, they were reminding one another to "act horny."

B.B.

DEAR NANCY,

Wyckoff, New Jersey
December 1970

Hang in there. I know how you feel. We have seen so little of Jim lately it's worse than the baseball schedule. This summer I was read-

77

ing some of Abigail Adams's letters, and I really identified with her. It seems we "hold the fort" while our husbands do the impressive, glamorous things. I admire Abigail but don't think I could put up with the tough years that she had. Being married to a celebrity is fun, but it takes its toll in other ways, lack of time husbands spend with the family for one.

You probably read tht Jim was sent down to AAA Oklahoma City at the end of July. The children and I stayed in Houston until Jim decided what to do. Knowing how much Jim loves playing baseball, I realize it was a tough decision for him to quit and try something else. I let him know that whatever he decided was fine with me. He knows I'll go to Alaska with him if that's what he wants.

Jim had been offered the local ABC sportscasting job in July, but he turned it down to continue playing ball. After being sent down and not doing well, he had second thoughts and decided to give the TV job a shot.

When he announced he was quitting baseball on August 10, I had some mixed feelings. The new opportunities were exciting, but I was afraid that he might regret leaving pitching behind. As soon as we arrived in New Jersey, he was calling to play for some local teams, but he was only eligible to pitch in one tournament. It didn't surprise me one bit that he wanted to continue playing ball.

Being married to a sportscaster has been exciting, but I thought baseball hours were bad! These hours are ridiculous! (Plus no spring training.) Maybe he'll be able to let up soon, since he has adapted really well to the tube. He does the eleven o'clock news and leaves home around noon, sometimes one or two, but always before the kids are out of school. He doesn't return till after midnight. That means that the only meals he has with the kids are the occasional ones when he drags himself up for breakfast and then goes back to bed. Weekends just seem to disappear.

He still calls me after practically every show to ask my opinion. I guess I'm his unofficial reviewer. He's really done well since about the third show and has continued to improve. Sometimes he messes up, but overall he is doing very well, and the station is pleased.

He works with a lot of good people, both on and off the camera. Roger Grimsby, the anchorman, is my favorite. He is so quick and can convey so much with a slight gesture. Melba Tolivar is tops, too, besides being a lovely person.

Occasionally, I go with Jim to cover an event. I'm happy that he asks my advice on some stories, and I try to keep up on all the different sporting news to be helpful to him.

Jim still plugs the book, and sometimes I join him. I also went when he was interviewed by Dick Cavett and Merv Griffin. (I still can't believe *Ball Four* is a best-seller—seems like a dream.)

Jim also did some modeling for *Esquire* and *Penthouse*. For *Penthouse,* he modeled raincoats with a very pretty young woman. In one especially cozy shot, he is fondling her hair. I was a bit miffed and told him that he didn't have to get so intimate. He said he was only following directions; I reminded him that Eichmann had already used that excuse.

Jim and Len are writing a sequel to *Ball Four.* I'm organizing all the clippings, letters, etc., and it's quite a job. This book will be called, humorously, *I'm Glad You Didn't Take It Personally* and will be dedicated to Commissioner Bowie Kuhn and sportswriter Dick Young for their help in promoting *Ball Four.*

Jim has also been politically active. He helped stump for Allard Lowenstein this fall. Unfortunately, Al lost when his district was redrawn, but it was interesting meeting him and getting involved in a campaign. One fund-raiser was especially impressive. We met Mel Brooks, Anne Bancroft, and George Segal, then spent some time with Buck Henry and Peter and Paul, minus Mary. Must admit I've enjoyed talking to these people. One of the nice extras of being a celebrity's wife.

One of the qualities I like best about Al and his wife, Jennie, is that they are so unpretentious. She dresses even more casually than I do and seems very calm and low-key. I felt very comfortable, even in the confusion of their home with people walking in and out, meetings, kids, well-wishers, college student volunteers, etc. Jim really admires Al and what he is doing and trying to do—me, too. Hope next time he wins.

Keep in touch,
BOBBIE

I was involved and excited with Ball Four *from the beginning. Being an avid reader from way back, I especially enjoyed baseball books. However, with a few exceptions, such as* The Glory of Their Times *and* The Long Season *and some interesting fiction, all the baseball books were stories out of the same mold. So I was all for having a different type of book.*

Some nights when Jim was tired and wanted to skip taping, I would encourage him to do it before he'd forget things. We'd talk about the scenes and happenings and other players so that he could add new thoughts.

Later, after reading the original draft that Lenny Shecter had arranged and edited from these tapes, I was still excited. I hated seeing some funny stories being discarded when the final editing was done but thought that, all in all, it was great.

To me the sexual stories that were included in the book involved other players. In my mind, Jim was still innocent even though he included some stories about himself that I hadn't heard—such as his striptease at a party. But these stories had happened before we were married, so I didn't worry. Also, he had confided in me stories that couldn't be in the book.

Telling about the players' "beaver shooting" (or girl watching brought to a high art) didn't bother me at all. After all, I'm not really a prude—a bit old-fashioned, maybe, but not uptight. Since you could easily look out your hotel window into another where a teammate was putting on a show with the "local talent," this seemed like a fraternity prank and was not upsetting. So I blissfully did not search for hidden messages in the book and just enjoyed the fun of having a best-selling book dedicated to me.

B.B.

Wyckoff, New Jersey
May 8, 1971

DEAR NANCY,

Believe it or not, we are going to Europe in a couple of weeks. I finally talked Jim into it. It was touch-and-go, but he's going to do a piece on cricket and Lords Field in London to help pay for the trip. If I can keep coming up with new story ideas for places I want to visit, I'll be set for life.

We took the children to Antigua (Jim's idea) during Easter vacation. It was lovely and relaxing, except that while Laurie was jumping on the bed, she slipped and split her forehead open. We had to get her stitched up, and—wouldn't you know—there wasn't a surgeon on the island. Finally, a G.P. did the job, but poor Laurie couldn't swim the rest of the trip. This bothered her more than the cut. She's only five and has had her head stitched up twice!

Just before we went to Antigua, we had the good fortune to have dinner at McGeorge Bundy's apartment. A friend of Jim's, Howard Dressner, works at the Ford Foundation with Mr. Bundy and wanted to have Jim play the board game Bottlecap Baseball with him. The Bundys have often visited Antigua, and Mrs. Bundy told me about interesting things to see and do there.

The other dinner guest was John-John Kennedy, and I couldn't take my eyes off him. I kept remembering the little boy saluting. Now he's a polite young man whose pants are a little short. John lives in the same building and often visits the Bundys. He played the game with Jim, and I think Jim, for once in his life, almost tried not to win. (He was having the same memories that I did.) It was a pleasant evening.

Another pleasant evening we had was a baseball awards banquet we went to in Washington, D.C., in January.

Jim was funny this night, publicly thanking Bowie Kuhn for selling the book. Martha Mitchell was there. Ted Williams didn't show, darn it. We chatted with Jimmy Breslin and Johnny Bench. I sat next to Denny McLain, (baseball's other bad boy) and a charming Baltimore Oriole executive. Must admit at first I hadn't liked not being seated next to Jim, but I really did enjoy myself. Denny struck me as very naïve and very enthusiastic. He's playing the organ locally and is looking forward to this year. Did you know McLain when he was winning all those games with Detroit? It's funny because the first story Jim covered as a reporter was about McLain being suspended for carrying a gun and breaking probation. Poor Denny, I'm afraid he's going to continue to have problems.

It's funny that the book has opened so many new doors; we are still being interviewed. One article said I was a perfect complement to Jim's personality (that I liked), but it also quoted Jim as saying, "Bobbie was very understanding regarding the contents of the book; she is truly a wife with a liberal viewpoint." I'm not so sure I like that quote. Sounds as if I'm giving everything my blanket approval. I may be liberal, but it's more politically than morally. In many ways, I'm rather old-fashioned. I don't approve of ballplayers fooling around on the road, or anywhere else for that matter.

We stayed at the Shoreham in D.C., and Jim showed me the beaver-shooting possibilities he mentioned in *Ball Four*. That I can laugh about, but Baseball Annies are no laughing matter. I guess we all have doubts sometimes, but I can quickly push mine to the back of my brain. Maybe because I feel comfortable and happy in our marriage.

It's nice that Jim isn't on the road so much now. He still lectures at colleges and covered spring training without me, but overall he's home, so it's terrific. Maybe total timewise he's at home less, but at least I know I won't be sleeping alone so often.

Since Jim's been working so hard and wants to really relax on weekends, we bought a little cabin on a lake in western New Jersey. It borders the Kittatinny Mountains and is near the Appalachian

Trail. We run there every time we have a chance. The kids love it because they can fish or swim; we have a canoe and rowboat. I love it because it's country—beautiful and serene. It's four-plus acres, and that's fitting, since *Ball Four* helped pay for it. (Also Nest Egg Investments—a company that Jim set up to buy houses, fix them up, and rent them. We've been doing this for some time, ever since we noticed the problems ballplayers had in finding places to rent. I enjoy redecorating these houses. It gives me a chance to experiment with colors and designs, although I try to pick decorating schemes that most people will enjoy. I'm getting very handy with spackle and a paintbrush.)

Soon Jim will be pitching in the Metropolitan League (*no* road trips); that will cut into our Mecca Lake time. But every minute at the lake is the best of all possible worlds.

A year ago I could never have imagined how much things can change. It's a good thing that some things are constant, like good friends and family.

Hope you have a super year.

Fondly,
BOBBIE

Jim has always been a great competitor. He told me that when he was a kid, an outfielder made a bad play and Jim ran from the pitcher's mound to punch him.

This tenacity no doubt helped him become a big league athlete; however, he could carry the desire to win to extremes. We used to kid that he needed to wear a cup to play hearts.

One time I got mad at the advantage Jim was taking of the kids (they were quite young) while playing Monopoly, and I turned the board over. This was not like me at all.

Early in our marriage we would often do jigsaw puzzles. Even this became a win situation for Jim. He would leave for a road trip and take a piece or two with him so that he could have the satisfaction of putting in the last piece. For a while it would drive me nuts looking for the missing pieces, but eventually I learned his tricks. I would only try to beat him at categories or initials and only for a short period; needing to win is not one of my priorities. I like just friendly competition. Jim, on the other hand, would psyche himself up for a Ping-Pong game. He never lost—only time ran out. So they didn't call him the Bulldog for nothing.

B.B.

DEAR BOBBIE,

This letter is likely to go on and on; so much has happened this past season.

Mike started the season with the Montreal Expos with 6 quick saves, and then, from May 15 until the All-Star break, he couldn't do anything right. The press ripped him apart, and the fans were unmerciful.

I think part of the negative reaction toward Mike stemmed from the fact that he replaced Claude Raymond, a French-Canadian, as the number-one relief pitcher. Last year Claude saved twenty-three games. This year he hardly pitched at all. When Mike started to do poorly, the cries were loud and strong for the return of Claude.

One of the French sportswriters, J. P. Sarault, actually wrote that the reason Mike was doing so poorly was because he stayed out all night and was drunk all the time. This came from a man who got so drunk that he drove his car through the garage wall and into his family's playroom. Talk about the pot calling the kettle black! Of course, what J.P. didn't know was that Mike stopped drinking three years ago. When Mike woke up in his hotel room one morning and couldn't remember where he was, he decided that that was enough of that. I think he has convinced himself that he could be an alcoholic. If J.P. really knew Mike, he would realize that what Mike likes to do best would put him in bed early each night . . . not necessarily asleep but at least in the room.

By the time the All-Star break rolled around, Mike was 1–5 with an earned run average near 7.00. At every possible chance some of the writers ate Mike up and spit him out. One day I actually got into a fight with a man who was sitting behind me in the stands. You know me, old weak-kneed Nancy. Well, this guy came out with one too many "Fuck you, Mike Marshall"s. I turned and told him I would not tolerate him talking about Mike in front of my girls like that. You know what he said to me? "I paid for my ticket and I'll do or say anything I want."

For the life of me I can't see what makes anyone think that paying $3.50 to see a ball game gives him the right to be abusive. They wouldn't tolerate behavior like that at a ballet, yet fans at a baseball game can act like total assholes and get away with it.

I stopped taking the girls to the games after that. I couldn't explain to them why people were saying such awful things about their dad, and it would upset them so that eventually at least one of them would end up in tears. It just wasn't worth it.

There were a couple of bright spots in all of this. Ian MacDonald, who wrote for the *Gazette*, did an article around All-Star break in which he wrote, "The broken bat singles, dropped flyballs and seeing-eye grounders will become outs. Batters will continue swinging wildly at the dancing screwball. And Deborah, Rebekah, and Kerry Jo will be able to go and watch their daddy play ball again."

There was one family in Montreal that sent Mike the following telegram:

WE ARE WITH YOU THROUGH THE DIFFICULT TIMES.
STAY WITH IT. BETTER DAYS ARE AHEAD.

They were right. A couple of key events took place. First of all, Jim Gosger picked up that Mike was giving away his pitches. Every time Mike got ready to throw the screwball he squeezed his glove together. Mike stopped that in a hurry.

The second thing that occurred was that John Boccabella started catching Mike. During the All-Star break workout, Gene Mauch, the Expo manager, told Mike that he didn't like the selection of pitches that Mike had been throwing, and if things didn't improve, he was going to start calling Mike's pitches for him again.

Mike asked Gene: "What do you mean, 'start calling them again'?"

Gene answered: "Ever since the game that you pitched against Atlanta, on May 20, I haven't called any of your pitches. You did such a great job that night that from then on I decided to let you call your own game."

When Mike came home from the workout, he told me about his conversation with Gene. Mike was furious. First of all, I should explain how Gene calls the pitches from the bench. Gene's uniform number is 4. Whenever Gene wanted a pitcher to throw a particular pitch, he would signal the catcher. By extending four fingers and putting them up against his chest, the catcher would relay the message to the pitcher that Gene was calling the pitch. And, let me assure you, no one ever shook off Gene Mauch.

All during that bad streak Mike would come home and complain about the pitches Gene was having him throw. Now we discovered that Gene hadn't been calling them at all. John Bateman was flashing the four fingers up on his chest, when it was really he who was calling the pitch. Mike thought they were Mauch's calls, but they had been Bateman's instead.

Shortly after the second half of the season started, whenever Mike went in to pitch Gene started putting John Boccabella in to catch. At the end of the season, Mike broke down the innings when Bateman was his catcher and those that Boccabella caught. John Bateman caught him for seventy-five innings, and during that time Mike's earned run average was 5.04. John Boccabella caught him in just about the same number of innings, but Mike's earned run average was 2.18, and if it hadn't been for four runs that scored in one inning against St. Louis, it would have been 1.16.

Mike ended up with a 5–8 win/loss record and had 23 saves this year. A lot of the credit has to go to Gene Mauch. He showed some faith in Mike, understood how to help Mike pitch effectively, and wasn't intimidated by the criticism of the press and the fans.

Mike isn't too sure he'll be able to pitch anymore. What hardly anyone knew all season was that Mike's back was in terrible condition. Most of the time, Mike couldn't raise his right leg twelve inches off the floor. He used to squat to pick up the resin bag. Gene had suggested that Mike see a doctor in Philadelphia, who recently helped Bobby Wine with his back problems.

On a personal note, I have gone on a campaign to buy a house in East Lansing. We have lived in married housing since 1963. Mike seems reluctant to take on the financial responsibility of a house, but I figure that if schoolteachers who are making a lot less than he is can afford it, so can we. Besides, houses in East Lansing sell very easily. If something happens, we could always get out from under the mortgage. We've been married for almost nine years now, and the only furniture we have is a set of bunk beds, a television, and a rocking chair that my grandmother gave me. I think it's about time we start living a little more normal lifestyle, at least as normal as we can within this crazy profession. Mike seems to feel I'm being very demanding, but I'm willing to risk coming off like the town shrew. I've had enough of this confined living.

Hope you have a good winter.

NANCY

Wyckoff, New Jersey
December 1971

DEAR NANCY,

We certainly enjoyed seeing you in August, but the rest of our trip was a disaster. Renting a Winnebago® may be good when your kids are older and it doesn't rain everyday, but it wasn't good for us this year. We thought we'd really see the great outdoors. Hah! Parking five feet away from another trailer on a concrete slab is not my idea of getting back to nature. Well, we tried.

The rest of the summer was super. Jim played ball with the Ridgewood Barons, a local semipro team. He did well, and we enjoyed everything about the season. Two friends that Jim had known came to games, and I had a chance to become close to them also. Nancy Smith is especially nice and extremely knowledgeable about sports, a real fan though she's in a different field—publishing. The other new friend is Larry Ritter, a professor of finance at NYU, who wrote the classic *The Glory of Their Times.* He is a mensch (Yiddish, for "terrific guy.") Becoming friends with these two people has really enriched my summer.

Playing in a semipro league is quite a change from major or even minor league ball. Washing Jim's uniform is more than I bargained for, and I've given up trying to keep his hat clean. (It still comes off when he pitches—his old trademark.)

The kids' favorite field is one where the Good Humor man comes for every game. My favorite fields are the ones with bathrooms nearby. During a good game, it's annoying to have to drive a kid to a gas station. Not only do you miss the game, but usually you lose your parking space!

I'm glad Jim was able to pitch this summer. True, it cuts into the time we were able to get away to the lake, but I've always felt that Jim needed this competition. He thrives on it. During the winter, he works out, but it's not the same as head-on competition. Unfortunately, he doesn't limit his competition to just the ball field.

We recently went to a nice restaurant for a holiday dinner with Jim's family. I don't remember what started it, but Jim wouldn't stop arguing, and finally his mother left the table in tears. I kicked him under the table, but he really is a "bulldog." Later, he yelled at me for kicking him. It ruined everyone's meal, but he didn't care, as long as he got his point across.

This happens every now and then. Usually people don't argue with him, or they do it in a kidding way (like me). Maybe I should have said, "Jim, shut up, your ego is spoiling the evening," instead of kicking him under the table. But then he would have been mad that I wasn't supporting him. Oh, well, I guess if he weren't so tenacious he wouldn't be so good at what he does either. Must admit that it would be nice if he were a little more sensitive.

Maybe I'm just becoming a little too sensitive. I worry that all this adulation (first from baseball fans, now from TV followers) is going to his head a little too much. Not that he's overconceited, but he sometimes plays the role without even realizing it. It's gotten so that when we go to a restaurant, I don't bother to sit down at the table they lead us to, because Jim always picks a different one and we have to move.

There are other minor things that bother me, too, but I guess he wouldn't be human if he didn't play the star sometimes. I try to kid him a lot about keeping his feet on the ground.

How's Mike's back? Do try and visit soon,

BOBBIE

East Lansing, Michigan
March 15, 1972

DEAR BOBBIE,

Please note the new and *permanent* address. We moved into our house in December. It's a three-bedroom ranch, not too big, just a little over a thousand square feet of living space, but Mike has already started to tear the place apart to make it more livable. The basement has some real possibilities. Unfortunately, in order to assume the mortgage, we had to put every dime we had into the down payment. My parents have lent us enough money to get by on until Mike's first paycheck comes in next season.

We really did some bargain-hunting to furnish this place. Found an eighteen-year-old *pink* refrigerator, which I promptly painted green. We bought an old married-housing-apartment-size stove from the Michigan State salvage yard. I found a washing machine that a couple was willing to sell for fifteen dollars. Actually, I think they would have given it to us just to get it out of their basement. We furnished the living room from a rummage sale, and my parents gave me my bedroom furniture. It looks a lot like the Salvation Army, but I'll take it over married housing! The really great part about the house is its location, five blocks from the university and within walking distance of all of the schools.

One of the reasons I wanted to move into a house was so that we could have another baby. I read every article written on what to do to increase the odds of having a boy. I took my temperature each day to try to establish when I ovulated. When Mike and I discussed another baby, he decided we just couldn't manage all the moving we have to do with any more children. Since I won't have any after I'm thirty, unless we stop moving soon, our family is at its peak.

I thought Mike wanted more children, so I was quite taken aback by his decision. I'm very satisfied with three. Maybe Mike senses that and let that influence him.

As I wrote you in October, Mike went, as planned, to a back specialist in Philadelphia. The doctor injected pumice and glycerin into Mike's lower back in about six different places. Mike said the needle was about four inches long. *Yuk.* Supposedly, this procedure builds up scar tissue and holds the vertebrae of the lower back to-

87

gether better. Anyway, Mike is optimistic. If anyone had seen him when he came back from seeing the doctor, they would have wondered if Mike would ever walk again, let alone pitch. He had to crawl around on his hands and knees for days after getting the shots.

We're having quite a serious medical problem with Kerry Jo, although it's not nearly as bad as we originally feared. In early February I noticed that she seemed to have an extraordinary number of bruises on her legs. I was just about ready to call the doctor when I remembered that she had fallen off a kitchen chair. I figured she must have scraped her shins on the way down.

However, about a week later I noticed that she had bruises on her back. I called the doctor right away, and although he was not in the office, the nurse made arrangements to have some lab tests done that day. Around five o'clock that night we admitted her into Sparrow Hospital. At the time, she was admitted as a leukemia patient. After several days of testing, including a bone-marrow test, the pediatrician who was consulting with my doctor decided that she didn't have leukemia but had idiopathic thrombocytopenic purpura instead.

For some reason unknown to anyone, her bone marrow had stopped producing platelets. Since platelets are a crucial part of the clotting mechanism, she had the potential of bleeding to death, particularly if she fell and hit her head. A normal platelet count is between two and four hundred thousand. Kerry's was down to eight thousand. She might as well have had none at all.

They put her on a massive dose of cortisone, and by the time she left the hospital two weeks later, her count was over a million. Since that time, they gradually reduced the dosage. After a couple of weeks, her platelet count fell to two thousand. Just a few days before, it had been just fine.

When Dr. Zick called me to tell me about the latest lab results, he first asked me where Kerry was. I told him she was outside. He very quietly but firmly said to get her. I put the phone down and called her inside. When I got back to the phone, he asked me where she was. When I told him she was up in the tree in the backyard, I think the man nearly had a heart attack. When he told me she was down to a critical count again, I couldn't help but envision her up in that tree. My God, if she had fallen!

I discovered during Kerry's illness that the mind does very strange things when a person's under stress. I spent at least eight hours a day with Kerry every day she was in the hospital. I got through all kinds of blood tests, survived the suspense of not knowing whether she had leukemia. I was a rock through all of that. Then one night I asked Mike to go to the hospital so that I could stay home and wash

Deborah and Becky's hair. When I was combing out Becky's mane, I discovered that she had head lice! After getting through all the really tough stuff, I sat down on the bathroom floor and cried.

Now that the doctor has ruled out leukemia, he is suspicious that it may be lupus. I just refuse to believe that. Usually there will be a spontaneous remission if it's I.T.P. The cortisone is merely an artificial stimulant to get the bone marrow to produce platelets. Eventually, it should start to do so on its own.

Being in the children's ward for over two weeks was a sobering experience for me. Kerry became good friends with a girl named April. During the second week that Kerry was there, one of the nurses called me at home at midnight. When you have a kid in the hospital and a nurse calls at that time of the night, your heart sinks to your ankles in a real hurry. She called to tell me April had died and to ask me to be at the hospital before Kerry woke up. The first thing Kerry did everyday was go to April's room.

It's almost impossible to explain death to a four-year-old. A couple of weeks after April died, her grandfather brought one of her stuffed animals to Kerry. Up until that time, she had really been troubled about where April was. She had terrible nightmares about it. But having something of April's seemed to resolve whatever conflict she was having about her death.

I'm anxious to get to spring training. It's been a rough winter. Kerry will still have to have blood tests every three days, but Mike has a good physician lined up in Florida, so we're going ahead with our plans to join him for a couple of weeks.

NANCY

That eighteen-year-old pink refrigerator that I painted green eventually turned into a twenty-six-year-old refrigerator that I later painted gold. For the last year that we lived in East Lansing, the freezer section didn't work. When I suggested buying a new refrigerator, Mike in turn suggested I use the standup freezer in the basement. And I did. Every time I needed an ice cube I plunged down the stairs.

In retrospect, I wonder why I even asked to buy a new fridge. I was working full-time by then, but even if I wasn't, should I have had to ask permission? No woman should assume that kind of submissiveness just because her name isn't on the paycheck. But I did, and voluntarily.

It wasn't that we couldn't afford it. Mike was making more than one hundred thousand dollars a year by then. I'm sure if I had just bought the stupid refrigerator Mike would have at most been disgusted for a day and then forgotten all about it. But I didn't. Instead, I let the resentment build up like the frost in the freezer. Dumb.

N.M.

Wyckoff, New Jersey
April 8, 1972

DEAR NANCY,

Thank goodness Kerry doesn't have leukemia. I don't know anything about I.T.P., but it sounds as if they have it under control, and I hope this is something she can outgrow. Not a very easy time for you. Hang in there!

It doesn't seem possible that Kerry is four. It also doesn't seem possible that Laurie will be six in a few weeks, or that I'll be thirty-three this summer.

We spent some time with our friend Nancy Smith this February in Barbados and Tobago. We hated to leave, but we wanted to join Jim covering spring training. He also did a TV piece covering Disney World, and we got the special tour, including behind the scenes. The kids were thrilled—me, too.

The extra nice thing was that friends of ours, Steve and Anita Jacobson (he's a sportswriter for *Newsday*), were there at the same time. It was especially good being with them because Steve had a close call over New Year's when he had a cerebral hemorrhage. We had planned to throw a party together in the city. Thank God we were able to toast Steve's recovery.

During this party, there was a serious but funny discussion about buying the New Haven baseball team and running it with the fans in mind. For example, maybe we'd let a fan manage an inning, coach first base, or have cheerleaders—or anything different, to have more fun.

Many of the guests were sportswriters (Geroge Vecsey, Vic Ziegal, Lenny Shecter), and we all thought it would be fun to do the publicity and be innovative like Bill Veeck.

Jim, of course, would pitch. In fact, this is what started the whole idea. We all had so much fun talking that Larry Ritter actually made a presentation and bid on the team for the group. But there was already a deal to sell the team to a town in Canada.

It's just as well that Jim isn't pitching in New Haven because he decided to run for a delegate's spot at the McGovern convention this spring. Since the convention is county-wide, Jim's name should help him win a spot. It's exciting and a whole new field for him to "conquer."

90

Jim's been interested in politics for sometime. We've marched in the peace marches, campaigned for Al Lowenstein, and supported Gene McCarthy. Jim even once campaigned with Bobby Kennedy. (They were both supporting bottle-cap baseball's Howard Dressner.)

Jim has lent his name to zero population groups and talked about his vasectomy and Dave's adoption. Now he wants to take things one step further. He had toyed with the idea of running for Congress, but since the Democrats already had someone picked out, Jim supported him. I think the party people like Jim but don't feel that he's paid his dues. Also, Jim is a bit controversial, and that probably doesn't sit well. I also remind him that he doesn't have any tact and would have to work on acquiring some.

On the domestic side, we're looking to move. For many reasons, including wanting less time spent on the road for Jim. We also want a town that's integrated. Dave is the only non-white child in his school. In fact, after he started school, I received a call asking me why we hadn't informed the school that Dave was racially mixed. This floored me. We really are fond of our neighbors and this area in many ways, but we feel we need to introduce our children to other social situations.

I'm glad to hear you found a house. How did you manage to live out of a suitcase all those years? My hat's off to you. Now enjoy. Have a healthy year.

Fondly,
BOBBIE

DEAR BOBBIE,

Montreal, Quebec
July 22, 1972

As of yesterday, I passed the big three-zero milestone. Mike waited until just after midnight to call and wish me a happy birthday. I had fallen asleep on the living room couch, so I was right next to the phone. He said, "I just wanted to know how it feels to be thirty years old." (He's six months younger than I am and always likes it when I'm a year older than he. . . .) Despite just waking up, I was not at a loss for words. I held the phone at arm's length and said very loudly, "Hey, my husband wants to know how I feel now that I'm thirty." Mike declared me a true smartass.

It's been another one of those seasons! When the players voted to go on strike in spring training, we headed back to Michigan. It was a time of real indecision for everyone. Should you stay in Florida? Go to the city where you expected to play? Mike felt it was important that the players return home so that the owners would not get the impression that they weren't serious about striking.

He realized that although it appeared that the major issue was to get the owners to increase the pension plan to catch up with the cost of living that had eaten into the plan by 17 percent during the previous four years, there was a much more important issue at stake—namely, the survival of the Players Association. If the Major League Baseball Players Association ever expected to have any credibility with the owners, it was important that during the strike the players not collapse. Once they decided to strike, they had to be willing to make whatever sacrifices were necessary to give Marvin Miller the strength to negotiate for a united organization.

Since Jim was no doubt involved in covering the strike, I'm sure you're aware that several "name" players were anything but supportive of Marvin. Oddly enough, they are always the ones who have made their money. Probably they think they are going to get jobs with management after their playing days are over, and they don't want to make them angry. I think some of the name players spoke out against the strike because they are still part of the old school of thought. They trust the owners to take care of them after their playing days are over and don't want to risk their future in baseball.

The most infuriating aspect of the strike was sitting in our living room in East Lansing and watching our local sportscaster conduct "man-on-the-street" interviews with men who work in the local General Motors automotive plant. Each had his opinion about why the players were wrong to strike. They had insightful statements, such as, "If I made the money they make, I wouldn't need a pension plan" or "Let the players have to work for a living, and maybe they'll appreciate what they get."

These people had absolutely no idea what it is like to make your money playing baseball, and yet they had all the answers. I wondered at the time how those men would react if they were on strike and a baseball player went on television and said, "Anyone can screw a bolt onto a car. I don't see why they should get more money for doing such menial labor."

Mike has been in baseball for eleven years, two of those in the major leagues. We have three children to raise and educate and a new home with a mortgage. Mike's salary for the past eleven years averages out to $6,968.43. What was the man saying about the kind of money baseball players make?

All outsiders see is the glamour, the applause, the publicity in the papers. They don't know about minor leagues and incredible living expenses. (Playing in Montreal means we have provincial taxes, Canadian taxes, U.S. tax, and Michigan tax!) Granted, there are some fat cats, but there are a lot more scrawny alley cats.

The Montreal wives held their second annual fashion show between games of a doubleheader. Last year, all we got for our efforts was the opportunity to dish out a lot of money for baby-sitters and the chance to buy the clothes we wore at a discount. This year we formed a wives club and requested in return for our time and effort that the ball club donate $1,000 to St. Jude's Hospital. We figured that both the store putting on the show and the ball club would get a lot of good publicity out of it, and they could write off the contribution as a business expense. It was just another publicity gimmick to get people to the park. As Roger Savard, the director of publicity, said to me recently, "The name of the game is 'asses in seats.' "

During the fashion show, each wife made her grand entrance riding on the top of the back seat of a convertible. We circled the field until we reached either first or third base. One of those wives who had to ride around the field like a homecoming queen was Karen Bailey, Bob's wife. Karen is one of my closest friends. She is a deeply religious woman and a devoted wife and mother. As Karen passed the left-field bleachers, the fans in the stands bombarded her with a chorus of boos and threw beer at her. I, too, had been greeted with this kind of insane behavior in 1971, but not to the extent that Karen experienced it. Bob had been receiving the same kind of harassment in the French papers as Mike had received in 1971. And the fans were directing their vindictiveness at Bob that summer.

Time and time again, I've heard people say that since the fans pay their way into the ball games, they have the right to do whatever they want. Including ridiculing a player's wife? Anyone who thinks it's acceptable to boo a good woman like Karen has the intelligence of a kumquat.

The players elected Mike as their new player representative. I don't know how I feel about that. The player rep job is a thankless one. Of course, Mike will do one hell of a job because he's the kind of person who throughout his career has fought the absurdities in the system. I'm afraid it will mean a shortened major league career. Player reps have an acute history of being traded, released, etc. The only way it has affected me so far is that while the rest of the team was taking trips to the Laurentians during the All-Star break, Mike had to attend the player rep meeting. I didn't mourn his absence all that much, though, because we would have stayed home anyway.

My good friend Mary Gosger came back for a visit the other day. She and I and Cathy Woods went out the other night to a place called the Wine Cellar. Mary and I like to kid Cathy because she is the only black wife in the club. When we picked her up, we made her sit in the back seat, then when we were walking into the restaurant, we made her walk three feet behind us. I don't know when I have laughed as hard as I did that night. It suddenly dawned on me the other day that I'm getting so I heave a sigh of relief when Mike goes on the road. It means a week of being able to get together with a couple of my best friends and have a few laughs.

I really identified with your feelings when Jim upset the dinner with his folks. We don't go out very often, but it seems that every time we do go into town, Mike gets into some kind of an altercation. The people in Montreal drive like total assholes, no doubt about it, but it's part of their culture. They drive a lot like people do in Europe, fast and without much consideration for anyone else on the road. I've gotten to the point where I always drive with the window down so that I can flip someone the finger very quickly. Still, when I go out for an evening, I don't particularly enjoy it when Mike decides he has to teach one of the local drivers a lesson and puts the bumper of our car against that of the guy in front of us and pushes him through the intersection. Then, he gets out of the car and defies the guy to hit him. (Mike says he would never get into a fight with anyone, at least not hit him first, but he takes great delight in having someone take a swing at him and then overpowering the guy by just pushing him down on the ground. No one in his right mind should tangle with Mike; he's incredibly strong in his upper body from all the weight lifting he's done.) It isn't a matter of being right or wrong. Most of the time Mike is justified in being angry. It's the timing. The latest incident happened when friends of ours, Phil and Sue Ericson, came to visit. I just sat in the back seat of the car and held my head while Sue kept telling me not to let it upset me. I didn't care how justified Mike was. As far as I was concerned, he spoiled one of the very few nights that I was able to get out of the house.

I'm anxious to get back to East Lansing and see what our backyard looks like when everything is green. The Ericsons are living in our house for the summer. Phil is finishing his Ph.D. in communications, and they will go back to New York this fall.

I don't think I've ever mentioned Sue before. When we were living in married housing, I used to do my laundry late at night to avoid the rush. (It was also a lot easier than carrying three kids, plus laundry baskets, which is what I had to do if I washed during the day.) Sue and I were the only fools in the Laundromat at one in the morning, so naturally we chatted while waiting for the diapers to dry.

Sue has been my salvation for the past couple of winters. She loves to bake, knit, sew, and drink tea—so we have a lot of things in common. I'll miss her.

It was Sue who pointed out to me what I now refer to as the October Phenomenon. I wonder if you experience it with Jim. It's the one month out of the year that Mike and I do nothing but fight. All season long all Mike does is sleep, eat, and go to the ball park. He is never around to decide what time the kids go to bed, if they can spend the night at someone's house, if they can go swimming. But let October roll around, and all of a sudden he's in charge. No one can make a move without asking permission first. I have to check with him on what the kids can eat, where they can go, how long they can stay.

Used to be, I would let that upset me. Not anymore. Now I let him take charge for a while because I know perfectly well that in no time at all he will be busy with school again and won't care what the rest of the family is doing with their time. I've tried to figure out why he does that. I wonder if he feels guilty about being gone so much during the summer and tries to make up for that, or if all of a sudden being home all the time makes him realize that he's really been out of the mainstream of the family for months and feels compelled to get back into things. I'm all for that, but I think it could be done a little more smoothly. I'd also like him to stay there full-time. Someday, instead of playing the game in October, I'd like to tell him to go shit in his hat. Maybe I should just join parents without partners instead.

The best news of all, though, is that Kerry seems to have completely returned to normal. And the doctors assure me that her chances of getting the same thing again are no greater than any other child's. Actually, I think there are some changes in her, now that I think about it. Before she started taking the prednisone, she was a scrawny little kid who always had a smile on her face. The medicine puffed her up like a balloon and made her quite temperamental. She's been off the medication for three months now, but she still has the ten pounds that she gained while she was in the hospital, and I don't think her disposition is quite the same either. Who cares if she is a little ornery now; at least she is alive and healthy.

Take care,
NANCY

Normally I never went on a road trip with Mike, but each summer we were in Montreal I went to New York. And I always got together with Bobbie, and sometimes with Jim too.

One summer, Jim, Bobbie, Bobbie's sister and her husband, and I went to the Four Seasons for lunch. When we arrived at the restaurant, the maitre d' told Jim that in order to eat there he had to wear a tie. Frankly, I think that's a stupid rule. I've seen a lot of men wearing ties who look shabby. But Jim knew about the rule before he went there and chose to ignore it, and in addition made a bit of a scene. He told the maitre d' that fat people offended him and he didn't think the restaurant should allow them to eat there.

I felt as if I were out on the town in Montreal with Mike Marshall. When I watched Bobbie react, I thought I was looking in a mirror. She did her best to somehow get Jim to realize this was a rare occasion that shouldn't be spoiled, and she tried to do it in such a way that Jim would think she was backing him up. The typical tactic was to say something like "It's a dumb rule, Jim, but we don't need to let it spoil our lunch."

Jim ended up putting on a tie provided by the restaurant. It didn't come close to matching his shirt and looked ridiculous. If I had felt that strongly about a regulation I thought was pointless, I would have gone somewhere else to eat.

N.M.

My sister and brother-in-law may have forgotten about Jim's tie problem, but they still talk about the sexy crocheted outfit Nancy wore. On the other hand, I remember the tie.

This visit was about a year before the time Nancy stayed with us when she came to interview for a job as a TV sports commentator. It still annoys me that when females are hired for T.V. sports the main qualification seems to be looks, not any knowledge of sports. To me it's an affront to have a beauty queen as the female representative on a sports show. There are many women who really know sports and would be good at the job. At least someone had the good sense to interview Nancy. I think she could have qualified on both counts.

B.B.

Englewood, New Jersey

DEAR NANCY,   December 20, 1972

It's hard to know where to start, I've so much to fill you in on. When I wrote you last, Jim was going to run as a McGovern delegate. Well, he did, and he won. Not only did he win, but he was the assistant chairperson from New Jersey. Even though I watched TV the whole week, I saw him only once. I would like to have gone to Florida with him, but he figured it would be too hectic. So I didn't argue.

Before he went to the convention, ABC told him that they had an equal-time problem and that he couldn't be on the air. We hadn't figured on this, and it hurt financially. But Jim took advantage of the time off to stump politically and try out for the Pittsfield, Massachusetts, AA team.

He did well in Pittsfield, and we enjoyed the trip. However, we figure that some pressure was put on the team to nix Jim. The local reporters even agreed that he deserved a spot on the roster. Jim was a little discouraged, except that he has his fingers in so many pies that the disappointment quickly passed.

At the end of the summer, we moved to Englewood, New Jersey. We had met a terrific woman, Alice Twombly, at the New Jersey convention; she introduced us to Englewood. It is only a few minutes from New York City and has a United Nations mixture of people; it is a very progressive town.

What really convinced us that Englewood was the right town was a sign we saw after a peace rally. (We had marched with black balloons in the cold rain, then heard Jim and others, including Dr. Spock, talk.) When we were returning to our car, we passed a drenched high-school band that had marched in the parade also. The band had an Englewood High School banner. An omen.

We knew we'd done the right thing when we asked Dave how he liked the the new school. He said, "Great! In Wyckoff everyone was the same, but here everyone is different."

The house is charming, and we've done a lot of redecorating. Jim doesn't want to do the physical work himself, so he has hired someone. I feel we're overspending and want to do the work slowly and do more myself; this has caused a few arguments. Jim points out that his time is more valuable than mine. Jeeze, I hate to argue. This has been our first continual series of arguments ever. At one point Jim really upset me by saying he didn't want me to buy even an ashtray without his approval. Sometimes I wish he'd be like most husbands and leave the house to me.

Shortly after we moved in, we had a big fund-raiser for McGovern. We had the Alan Aldas, Marvin Kitmans, and Geraldo Rivera as special guests. Also several local political figures. We've known the Kitmans for several years, and the Aldas are friends of theirs. Geraldo works with Jim at ABC.

I was a little concerned about this party, since the house is still being fixed and we hardly have any furniture in half the rooms. (The house has twenty rooms; it only hurts when I clean.) The party was fine. Alice and the other helpers from Englewood were very happy with the results.

The next big fund-raiser was a big get-together at Madison Square Garden for McGovern. Simon & Garfunkel, Nichols and May, Peter, Paul, and Mary, and Dionne Warwick performed. This was some event. The "ushers" included Warren Beatty, Paul Newman, Jack Nicholson, Dustin Hoffman, Jon Voight, Ryan O'Neal, Goldie Hawn, and Jim. We were invited to a penthouse party afterward and even talked to these celebrities. (I walked around with a smile for weeks.) It really was such an up occasion for everyone there.

But the best event was when Senator McGovern came to ABC on a night that I was there watching Jim. After he was on the air, the senator came over to me and thanked me for not begrudging Jim the time he had spent campaigning. That such a busy man would even care or think about thanking me showed how sensitive he is and made me wish I had a million votes.

Unfortunately, I didn't, and we were crushed when he lost. Englewood did support him; this fact confirmed our thoughts about the town. But it was a sad night for all of us workers. (I had done some canvassing until Jim told me not to volunteer anymore because his schedule was hectic and he wanted me home when he was home. This seemed a bit chauvinistic, but I understood his feelings and it's nice to feel needed.) Lowenstein also lost; politically, I'm worried for our future.

I'm glad your baseball future looks bright. Hope Mike has another good year.

Best,
BOBBIE

Englewood, New Jersey
DEAR NANCY,   May 1973

Guess what Jim is up to now! He's filming a movie, *The Long Goodbye,* with Elliott Gould. How did this happen, you might ask. During the McGovern campaign, we met Elliott; he is a big sports fan. He called our house one day, and I answered and almost fell over when he identified himself.

After we had dinner together a couple of months later, Elliott called Jim and suggested he do a bit part in his new movie. Robert Altman is the director and liked the idea. Jim met Altman, and it was settled.

The kids and I went to L.A. for some of the filming. We stayed at

Malibu, where they filmed at Altman's beach house. The feelings I had about the California façade were reconfirmed. Every ad in the paper is for contact lenses, losing weight, etc. (anything to make yourself more attractive). The only other ads are for abortions. L.A. is too much for a country girl like me.

Altman let Jim do most of his own dialogue, just so it fit with the plot. I kidded that he was typecast (a wife murderer). Jim asked me for help deciding on a line for his good-bye to Elliott. So my line— a flip "¡Vaya con Dios!"—is in the movie.

Later Jim filmed in Mexico, but we couldn't join him because we couldn't get a visa for David. Seems Mexico and Korea don't have an agreement. We'll have to make Dave a citizen soon to avoid this hassle again.

Talking about hassles, I'm glad that things have had a chance to cool down a little over the Peterson-Kekich story. When Fritz called to tell Jim what happened, Jim wasn't home. So Fritz told me he had "traded" his wife Marilyn for Suzanne Kekich. I thought he was kidding. But as we all know now, it was true. It's hard to believe the publicity they've had. Other than the *Ball Four* reaction, I haven't seen anything like it. We've been in touch with both couples. I hope they all work things out okay. I know Fritz and Suzanne want to get married, but Marilyn and Mike are having doubts. I really don't know Suzanne, but I certainly am fond of the others and am rooting for them.

Being a sports figure certainly puts one in a goldfish bowl. Other couples "swap" wives, but, of course, it makes the front page when ballplayers want to change. It's funny how reporters protect players they see fooling around on the road, but then they blow something that can really hurt two families completely out of proportion. Even with all her emotional pain, it's good that Marilyn still has a sense of humor about the situation. She quipped that one thing that really annoyed her was that most articles made her a year older.

I would hate to have my personal life, complete with pictures, on the back page of the *Daily News.* Even though I say okay to most interviews, I like my privacy. Publicity is good for Jim, but if we had a problem, like a sick child or something, I'd hide.

We had enough publicity after *Ball Four* to last me a lifetime. Sitting on the front steps while my ice cream melted, because Jim was being interviewed on TV, wasn't my idea of a treat. And being asked all kinds of questions that you'd like to have time to weigh the answers to and can't isn't fun either.

I usually ask the reporter to send us a copy for the scrapbook, but sometimes I wish I hadn't. Sometimes it's hard to recognize what you've said when it's been changed to fit an article. Admittedly, most writers do an honest job and some are very good, but some turn their facts completely backward.

We really tried to cooperate on stories about adopting David. Welcome House did tell us that they had many responses from people who had read these articles, so we were pleased.

The only thing I like about family articles is when they take pictures of the children. It's always nice to have these; Laurie and Dave don't like to pose, but Michael and Jim are pros. I try to stay out of any pictures, but sometimes it's necessary to be in them. I usually wind up with my eyes closed and hate seeing my picture in the paper. Oh, well, it goes with the territory.

Looks as if Mike's on his way to another good year. Enjoy.

Best,
BOBBIE

Looking back I realize that the Kekich-Peterson story was treated as a cause célèbre. *It was hard to find a paper or magazine that didn't do a feature story on the two couples.*

Since the split, Fritz and Suzanne have married and have added two girls to their family. Fritz still stays in touch with the baseball scene as a player-coordinator for Baseball Chapel.

Mike married a nurse and is studying to be a doctor. He is still playing some ball in Mexico and has a bunch of old friends rooting for him.

Marilyn and I have remained close friends. I am extremely fond of her and her new husband, Peter. While this book was still in manuscript, I asked her to read it and give me her reaction. She confessed that it was painful for her to read because it was so honest and authentic. It brought back memories of the problems of being an athlete's wife that she had buried and preferred to keep buried.

B.B.

East Lansing, Michigan
DEAR BOBBIE,   December 20, 1973

We're going to have to start writing more frequently because I'm finding it hard to remember all the things that have gone on in a year.

Kerry started first grade this fall, which means the house is very empty all day long. Much as I enjoy the girls, I'm kind of glad to have some time to myself. I'm taking advantage of my freedom and getting out of the house a bit.

I'm also taking my sewing more seriously. I've always made a lot of our clothes, but I decided I wanted to do it right, so I started taking classes and now make almost all of our clothes. Since Mike's wardrobe was really in sad shape, I devoted a lot of time last winter to outfitting him. In addition to three leisure suits and half a dozen pairs of pants, I made a bunch of shirts. I cut out ten at a time, prepared all the parts so they would be ready to sew, and stacked them on the sewing table. Whenever I had ten minutes here and there, I'd stitch in a sleeve or a cuff. Eventually, I got them done in time for him to take them to spring training. I particularly enjoyed designing some of the shirts.

Considering Mike's inclination to come up with the most grotesque combinations of shirts and pants, I probably made a mistake not putting labels that are color-coded into each garment. Maybe I should have used geranimals, like they put in kids' clothing?

In early May, after spending one more hilarious night consuming too many Margaritas with Mary Gosger in Port Huron, I drove nonstop to Montreal with the girls. Opening night in Montreal was not a winner.

Mike had been in town for at least a month, and during that time he was supposed to find us an apartment. I had specifically requested that we not live in the apartments that we were renting when you visited us in 1971. While our apartment was clean, there was no place but an alley for the girls to play in. Since money was no longer such an issue with us, I felt we could find a more suitable place to live. However, Mike called me early in April and told me that he had been unable to find a place that would let us have a short-term lease, so he had gone back to the apartments on Pardo. I wasn't thrilled with the thought, but at least Ron and Cathy Woods were going to be there, and I was looking forward to many a good bridge game with them.

I arrived at the apartment at about seven o'clock in the evening. When Cathy and I went down to my apartment and walked in the door, we just looked at each other. The manager of the building was in the living room trying to clean out the place. I had never seen such incredible filth in my entire life. Four young men had lived in the apartment and had actually used the four corners of the living room as urinals. I recall saying to the manager, "Look, I don't mind helping you clean, but where is the furniture?"

She said, "We burned it."

I asked, "Where are my kids supposed to sleep tonight? There are no beds!"

She replied, "Mrs. Marshall, I wouldn't have let you sleep in those beds. We had to burn everything that was in this apartment."

By now it was eight o'clock. Cathy didn't have room for us to stay with her, so I went to my baby-sitter's house. The previous summer I had become friends with her parents, Sam and Mary Schiralli. Sam and Mary head a wonderful Italian family. Whatever is theirs is yours. While the kids amused themselves, I got on the phone and started calling around. Finally, Sandy Renko told me of town houses just a couple of miles down the road, where Joyce and John Boccabella were staying; she was sure they had short-term leases. As you know, that is really the key issue.

I called the rental office, and they said they did have a unit available. We could get in the next day. So, we ended up with a three-level town house right across from an elementary school. We rented just enough furniture to get by, and I bought some flowered sheets and used them as drapes. This place even let us have the cat.

Speaking of the cat . . . who but the Marshalls would have a pet cat that becomes carousing partners with the local skunk? True. Several times I watched the skunk walk Kimba to our back door and then trek off back to the woods.

The only bad part about not living on Pardo was that I didn't spend as much time with Cathy Woods as I would have liked. Occasionally, we went to a game together. We have exceeded our tolerance for watching baseball games or, at least, watching them sober. We got so that we fixed a jug of whiskey sours and took it to the game with us.

One night Cathy also took along her binoculars. I borrowed them, focused on her husband, Ron, who was playing in center field, and promptly observed that after every pitch he adjusted his cup. At one point I suggested that if several hitters got up in one inning, Ron might get off right out in center field. We got to laughing so hard about it that we attracted the attention of the people in front of us. One man turned around and said to me, "Are you married to one of the players?"

Cathy got even more hysterical when I said, "Yes, Ron Woods." Do you think we've lost that starry-eyed–cheerleader attitude we used to have about these heroes?

Last year one of the local department stores put on a fashion show at the ball park using players' wives as models. This year the Ladies Garment Workers' Union sponsored the fashion show. In addition to doing the show at Jarry Park, they flew twelve wives to Toronto and we did the show there also. A month later, six of us flew to Winnipeg and Vancouver to do two more shows. It was a real treat and the beginning of a new outlook on life for me, I think. It was the first time

I've been away by myself—without Mike or children. You know, there is life after wifedom and motherhood.

In Vancouver, two other wives, Gail Stinson and Patti Foli, and I rented bikes and rode around Stanley Park. That night, while the rest of the wives stayed in their hotel rooms, we walked through Chinatown and ate a late dinner at the Spaghetti Factory. It was all very innocent, but it's been a long time since I've felt so exhilarated. Having a bit of time to myself made coming back home to the family a real pleasure.

You know how wives always seem to take care of one another— well, I had a really comical experience with one of the non-English-speaking wives in the club. Since she enjoyed my girls, I invited her to come have dinner at the apartment when the guys were on the road. When I picked her up at her apartment, she wasn't quite ready, so I went in and waited for her. Her way of getting ready was to squirt some perfume under her armpits! After we got back to our place, Deborah came into the kitchen and said, "You're not going to believe what the woman is doing upstairs!" Seems she decided to take a shower and had washed out her underwear and hung them on the shower rod to dry. Must be we made her feel at home!

Mike had another fantastic year and, unfortunately, was voted the Most Valuable Player of the Year. That guaranteed another wave of controversy.

During the middle of the '72 season, O'Keefe Brewery announced that they were giving a new Cadillac Eldorado to the Expos' Most Valuable Player. All of the players were invited to the gala event. Since Mike hates parties of this sort, we were absent as usual.

The following day, Gene Mauch told Mike about the car; he also said that he had told someone from O'Keefe that he should take care of the income tax on the gift. That Eldorado was worth $10,000. For many of the players, the tax burden on that kind of gift would be overwhelming. Gene was concerned for those players whose salaries prohibited shelling out four or five thousand dollars in additional income tax. Gene asked Mike as player representative to make sure that O'Keefe arranged to pay the taxes.

Of course, at the end of the year, when Mike was chosen as the MVP of the Expos and was awarded the car, all his efforts to make sure that the taxes were paid suddenly seemed to be very self-serving. Somehow, the fact that the negotiations for the tax considerations were initiated long before anyone knew who would win the car was ignored.

This year O'Keefe decided to give $5,000 to the MVP. That would eliminate the tax problem that Mike had caused. (By now everyone saw it as Mike's doing.) In addition, they gave Player of the Month awards.

For the life of me, I can't see any good reason to have these awards. As Mike pointed out so many times, the idea of putting players in competition with one another can only cause problems and dissension.

During the season, Mike announced to his teammates that if he won the money, he would not accept it. He was hoping someone at O'Keefe's would have the smarts to at least give the money to charity in the name of the winner. Aside from eliminating the award entirely, that would have been the next best solution.

I really hoped Mike wouldn't win the stupid award. Much as I admire him for standing up for issues he believes in, I get to the point sometimes when I wish he could let a few things slide by uncontested. I knew for sure that this would not be one of those times; he felt too strongly about it.

Before flying back to Montreal in October to attend the awards dinner, Mike carefully penned a letter to O'Keefe in which he asked them to donate the money to St. Jude's Hospital, specifically for the purpose of doing research on sickle-cell anemia. Then, in his speech, he explained why he could not accept the award.

O'Keefe Brewery officials were furious, and club officials were embarrassed. Mike had spanked their hands in public. And once again Mike came off as the asshole. I told him he was the only person I knew who could look so bad for doing such a good thing. He has a real knack for that.

Since the baseball season doesn't end before school starts at Michigan State, I sometimes cover Mike's classes for him for a couple of weeks. Usually I just sit in and tape the lectures, but this fall I got involved a bit more than I would have liked. Mike was enrolled in a physiological psychology class. When I went to the first class, I asked the man who taught it if they would be doing anything offensive in the laboratory part. He assured me that they wouldn't be, so I followed the class downstairs to the lab. It didn't bother me when they anesthetized a rat, but when the assistant picked up a big pair of scissors and cut off its head, I nearly lost my lunch.

I'm beginning to think that buying this house was not a wise decision. I recall talking in 1971 with Jackie Hunt, the wife of the Expo second baseman, about the perils of moving from city to city. At the time, we were still living in married housing. (Translated, this means that all three girls were in one bedroom.) I could hardly wait to get out of there. Jackie lamented leaving her home each summer. Now that we have our own house, I understand how she felt. What

I used to see as a reprieve from the ghetto, I now see as time away from the place I'd much rather be—in my own bed or tending my own garden. Must be getting old.

Take care,
NANCY

While I enjoyed seeing and living in different parts of the country, all that rental decor was at best depressing: sturdy matching pieces with nothing homey about them. Of course, we rented the bare minimum and were just happy to be able to find anything.

Hauling our own furniture or buying would have been too impractical. Many of the younger players saved by buying a couple of lawn chairs and putting a mattress on the floor. We all used trunks as tables at one time or another.

My favorite story of ballplayers saving rent money occurred when Jim was in the Texas League. Some players pitched a tent down the sidelines inside the park. They hung a light bulb on a cord down the middle and furnished the tent with cots. Then they simply used the stadium's bathrooms and ate out. You could do that if you were single, but not if you had small children, though both Nancy and I put kids in closets to sleep at various times! Laurie also slept on her gym mat part of one summer. I know when Nancy and I packed, we took along only the bare minimum—one set of sheets for each bed, five plates, half-a-dozen towels, and only enough pots and pans to cook one meal. If something wouldn't fit in the car, it didn't go along.

I always felt sorry about leaving even the smallest of the children's toys behind, and taking a bike along was out of the question. Once Laurie asked me where her little blond doll was. I said, "Home." "Home," she responded, "which home?"

B.B.

DEAR NANCY,

Englewood, New Jersey
December 1973

The Long Goodbye was released out here and Jim had some favorable mentions. I hope it does well; I was impressed with Altman and all the work involved.

Just before the movie was released, Jim was fired from ABC. The station tried to say that his popularity had dropped, but what a crock! It was purely political. Some of the big muckey-mucks don't like Jim.

(He wouldn't promo some network stuff, etc.) Some of his co-workers protested and even marched with signs, but it was over their heads. I think ABC will be sorry.

We were lucky because CBS-TV signed him a short time later. CBS had been interested before, but Jim liked working at ABC and felt loyal to them.

Jim fit in nicely at CBS, but he's working those horrendous hours again. This will end after a while, but for now he's doing both the six and eleven o'clock news. *Ugh!*

Before he started working for CBS in October, Jim and I tore ourselves away from watching Watergate and took a vacation in Spain and Portugal. (My idea this time was to film a piece on bullfighting.)

Most of Jim's best TV pieces had him trying some unusual sport, like roller derby, rodeo, etc. I even call him the poor man's Plimpton. So we figured he could try fighting a small bull. Only the bull didn't look that small! I thought I would have heart failure watching, but Jim did fine—considering the crash course—and the piece turned out well.

We were lucky that some new friends stayed with the kids. We met Barbara and Randy Newmann when Jim did a story on Randy. He's a boxer, and she is working to put him through college while he boxes on the side. They have joined our Sunday dinners with Larry Ritter, Nancy Smith, and Bob and Alice Twombly. It's probably just as well in the long run that Jim left ABC. He wasn't getting along with one of his co-workers, and things were turning nasty. In fact, we suspect this guy of playing a dirty trick on us.

One day I had a call from a woman who acted very upset, told me that her daughter was seeing Jim, that she didn't approve of miscegenation, and that she wanted me to stop Jim from seeing her daughter.

I remembered the daughter's name and told Jim; he denied the accusation. He said the girl was beautiful and that she often dated Walt Frazier—why would she be interested in Jim? He thought someone was playing a trick, which had been my first reaction, too, but then we figured it had to be someone wanting to cause Jim some trouble. We narrowed it down and figured out that it probably was his ABC colleague.

I'm glad I mentioned it to Jim. Keeping it to myself would have bothered me, even though I didn't really believe it. Thank goodness we can communicate our feelings, and Jim made it very clear how much I mean to him and how lucky he is to have me.

Even though we have a strong marriage, it still bothers me when we go to parties and Jim is the center of attention, with the girls almost fighting to be next to him. I have often been so tempted to give some "sweet young thing" an elbow in the ribs when Jim and I are standing together and she pushes between us to bat her eyes at Jim. I think what makes me boil the most is that Jim makes no attempt to alleviate the situation. Somehow he conveniently forgets I'm next to him. Only if the woman is unattractive do I get an introduction.

In self-preservation, I'm starting to mingle more with other people. But at one party that we took Larry and Nancy to, Jim didn't talk to us all night—he was on his own high. Larry and Nancy don't like big parties anyway, and I thought it rather rotten that Jim, who took us, ignored us the rest of the evening. So Larry, Nancy, and I spent the evening having a three-way chat. I like meeting other people; it's just my shyness slows me down. Little by little, I'm coming out of my shell.

Do you know I sometimes find it a treat to go to a party and just be me. If I say my name and someone doesn't say, "Oh, Jim Bouton's wife," but just keeps chatting, it's terrific. Then if we get into discussing a current book or something we have both enjoyed, it really makes my night.

Someone once told me that he felt that Jim was like a king holding court. He certainly enjoys being the center of attention. I guess he's earned it, but it doesn't make it easy on a spouse.

After you've been asked a hundred times what it's like to be Jim Bouton's wife, you start to wonder about your place in the order of things. It's fun being invited to affairs where you meet other celebrities, but everything's so superficial. Give me my good old friends anytime.

Hey, good old friend, how about a visit?

Fondly,
BOBBIE

Englewood, New Jersey
DEAR NANCY,   February 1974

Pardon my rotten mood, but I wanted to tell someone how unfair things can be. The husband of our close friend Alice (she ran the McGovern campaign in Englewood) just left her with two small children (five and one). He wavered back and forth a few times and opted to leave home.

My heart really goes out to Alice. She is a bright (one of the brightest people I know), attractive, warm woman. She said they had been shaky for a while, but she never expected this.

Jim and I have been including Alice in our social life even more now. We had often had Bob and Alice Twombly, Barbara and Randy Neumann, Nancy Smith and Larry Ritter for dinner. We hit it off well as a group.

Alice and I are both ballet nuts, so we go when we can. I feel guilty going too often because of the expense, but since I'm saving money not having a cleaning lady, this is where it goes.

One night we took Alice to the Lion's Head Bar (we go there often), and who shows up but Bob and a girl friend. They even had the nerve to join our group. Alice played it beautifully. I would have left. I was churning inside: the whole scene upset me so. Maybe it's not good to have so much empathy. I really admire how she's handling it; I would be dying.

I want to have Marilyn Peterson and Alice meet. Maybe they can get together and help each other out. Marilyn seems to be doing well. She's dating steadily and is teaching school. When she needed legal advice, I introduced her to my neighbor, Jerry Levien, and he later told me he'd bet she will remarry soon.

I remember how hard it was for Marilyn to go out at first. Boy, I can't imagine how tough it must be. Marilyn is such an open, vulnerable person, and she hates being alone. Let's hope Jerry is right.

Things at the Bouton household are fine. We're getting back to normal, and I'm sewing and volunteering in the school library again.

Jim is happy at CBS. He's working with another good group. They televise from the newsroom, and it's interesting to watch. Usually I go into the city Friday night. Larry, Nancy, and I (now sometimes Alice) go to a show or something, then watch the news. Jim joins us for a late dinner.

I still watch all of Jim's shows, although I hardly ever give him ideas or make suggestions anymore. He really is good on camera and enjoys his job. It's amazing how many people recognize him when we walk down the street. Ten times as many as when he played ball. It's hard to believe he's been out of major league ball for four years.

We were hiking on the Appalachian Trail out by our lake house, and a young man going the other way said, "Hi, Jim." We laughed —can't get away from it. Not that Jim wants too.

We're lucky that Jim is covering spring training for CBS, and we're all going with him for the week. Hurrah! I miss spring training, but now it would be harder to plan, with the kids all in school and other things. I don't envy you; how do you work it out? My tutoring our kids for just one week will be a cinch.

How do you like L.A.? Quite a change from Michigan, right? From what little I've seen, it's not my kind of place. Knowing you, you'll do fine out where Gertrude Stein says, "There's no there, there."

Hi to Mike and the girls. Thanks for the ear.

Best,
BOBBIE

Los Angeles, California
June 15, 1974

DEAR BOBBIE,

I have a trivia question for you. Who was the pitcher who relieved Al Downing after he gave up the home run to Henry Aaron that broke Babe Ruth's record?

The start of the season has not been too great for Mike, at least as he measures his performances. Most people place heavy emphasis on just wins, losses, and saves. Mike also worries about the runs he lets in that go against the starting pitcher's record. In April, eleven of the fifteen men who were on base when Mike came into the game eventually scored. In May, it was eight of thirteen. Granted, sometimes they scored on fly balls or infield outs, but Mike is not pleased.

Part of the problem is that Mike's style of pitching requires an unusual defense. Gene Mauch knew exactly how to set up the defense for every hitter. When Mike was with the Expos, he and Gene, the Montreal manager, talked about it before every game. Mike hasn't developed that kind of relationship with Walt Alston, the L.A. manager, yet. You can't just walk onto a new club and start telling people where you want them to play.

Somehow I always envisioned Los Angeles as the ultimate place to play baseball. And in some ways it is. After living in some pretty scanty places in past summers, we now have a gorgeous apartment. It's just ten minutes from the airport, twenty minutes to the ball park, and, best of all, just fifteen minutes from the beach. And it actually has drapes at the windows. No more sheets for this kid! The weather is incredible. I've been playing tennis every day since the middle of April. It never rains. The ball park is without a doubt the most gorgeous yard I've ever seen. It's up on the top of a hill, and as you look out past the right-field fence, there is a hillside that is covered periodically with a lavender ground-flower. It's absolutely beautiful.

So where's the "but," you ask? I don't know if I can explain it. It's more a feeling I have. You hear about how people out here are so tolerant and "let you do your own thing." Well, I'm not sure if it's tolerance or indifference. It's a plastic society. Whenever you meet anyone, they ask two questions. One: Where are you from? Two: What's your sign?

After coming from the Expos, where all the guys were mediocre talents, marginal minor leaguers, or fading superstars, suddenly we're thrown in with a bunch of incredibly talented young men. Oddly enough, along with all that talent go some pretty healthy egos and some petty jealousies. Everyone seems to be so concerned that someone else is going to get just a little more money or a little better press. There sure isn't that "let's pull together and help each other out" feeling that there was in Montreal.

For example, earlier this year I took the girls down to San Diego when the team had a weekend series there. Mike wasn't thrilled about our coming down, but for once in my life I ignored him and did what I wanted to do. After the last game of the series, Mike drove home with us. The next morning he got a call from Al Campanis, the general manager. As best I can remember the conversation, Al said, "Mike, is it true that you were the only one that didn't ride the bus home from San Diego?"

Mike replied, "I don't know, Al. I wasn't on the bus."

Al said, "Well, everyone is supposed to ride the bus back to Los Angeles."

Mike said, "Once I take off that uniform, I think I'm free to go anywhere I want. I couldn't see any sense in my riding the bus, while my wife and family were trailing behind in the car. If I had looked out the bus window and seen my family get in an accident, I'd always think that if I had been with them, maybe it wouldn't have happened. If my family had been killed while I looked on, I wouldn't be able to live with myself."

Al answered, "I understand that, Mike, but it would be better than *all* of you getting killed."

Honest to God, Bobbie, he really did say that. I was listening in on the extension and heard it with my own ears.

The next day the team had a meeting to discuss this really big issue. Davey Lopes got up and called Mike a motherfucker, and who the fuck did Mike think he was that he didn't have to obey the rules like the rest of them! I mean, really! Here are a bunch of grown men screaming at another teammate because he rode home with his family! This is heavy-duty stuff compared to poverty, murder, political assassinations, etc.

Apparently, Davey must really resent Mike. They live just a couple of blocks from us, and his wife Lynn occasionally comes over to the house. One day when she was over, she got into a discussion about Mike's contract and the "special privileges" that he gets. When I got

110

her to be specific, she cited such things as (1) the team pays for Mike to have a single room, and (2) the team pays for Mike's rental car when he's on the road. I tried to make her see that there was no difference in taking $100,000 and having the team pay for the room and the car, from taking a contract worth $105,000 and paying for them yourself. The contract is all one total package, and whether you get your bucks in actual cash or incidentals is really irrelevant. I also pointed out that anyone on the team could have negotiated those things if they were important to them. But I'm sure she still sees them as signs of favoritism. And I'm sure she didn't come up with her concern all on her own. I suspect Davey sees Mike's contract as being full of special privileges. I think they both ought to worry about Davey's contract and forget who else gets what.

It sort of reminds me of Mary Gosger out in Seattle. Her young girls used to fight over how many M & Ms each one got in her dish, so Mary would count them out to make sure they got equal amounts. Then, not satisfied with the amount, the girls would fight over the colors. So Mary would make sure they each had the same number of each color. You expect this in young kids but somehow not in grown men.

On a personal note, I also had a really weird experience with one of the wives. When I was in San Diego, Dee Crawford, one of our outfielders' wives, asked for a ride to the ball park. On the way to the game, she said to me, "You know, Nancy, some of the wives aren't going to accept you."

I was sort of dismayed by this statement and asked, "What do you mean?"

She replied, "Well, you being married to Mike and all."

I questioned, "What about my being married to Mike?"

She answered, "Some of the wives are going to find it hard to accept a black woman being married to a white man."

Needless to say, I was in a state of shock. Mike and I have tried to figure out what would make her think that I'm black and I think we have it narrowed down. First of all I am sporting an Afro, and when I get tan, I can look black. This isn't the first time that someone has questioned my heritage. But I think it has more to do with the fact that Willie, Dee's husband, first met me in Montreal when I was with Ron and Cathy Woods, good friends of ours who happen to be black. Also, during the winter, it leaked out that Mike gave the $5,000 MVP money to St. Jude's Hospital and earmarked it for the study of sickle-cell anemia. According to Jo Wynn, another black wife I've become good friends with, Dee spends a good bit of time trying to prove that I am really passing for white. Now that I know that, I

111

spend a lot of my time making little slips of the tongue that serve to egg her on. Ahhhh, the games people play.

There are some good people out here, though. I've met a delightful woman, Edith Brownstone, whose husband manufactures furniture. She works very hard at juggling the schedule of her maid, gardener, window washer, and pool man so that she has most of the day left to play tennis! It is Edith who told me that she gave the following advice to her daughter. She said it is just as easy to fall in love with a rich man as with a poor one. Then she went one step further and said it's just as easy to fall in love with a rich man who likes to eat out. Edith says the one thing she makes best for dinner is reservations.

Edith doesn't think I indulge myself enough and has promised to turn me into a Jewish American Princess before the summer is over. Ye Gods, first I'm black, now I'm going Jewish!

Take care,
NANCY

East Lansing, Michigan
DEAR BOBBIE, September 5, 1974

Once again, I am back in Michigan minding the fort by myself. It seems so good to be back in my own home again. I can work in the yard, run over to the neighbors' for a drink at happy hour, have lunch with my friends. I enjoyed Los Angeles, but all the beaches and tours of Universal Studio can't compare to being in my own home with my friends and family.

Mike is having one of those unbelievable years. Before the season is over, I know he will have broken just about every record imaginable for a relief pitcher. And I wouldn't be surprised if he wins the Cy Young Award. As you probably know, he was chosen for the All-Star game in Pittsburgh. The Dodgers flew all of the wives out there, but Mike informed me he didn't want me to go. His explanation was that he had to attend the Players Association meeting all of one day, so there really wasn't any sense in my going along. He doesn't know it, but I was very hurt. It wasn't that I was all that keyed up about seeing the game, but I would have loved to have three days without the kids and have been with him by myself.

Cindy Garvey asked me if I was going, and I put on my flip act and said, "No, Pittsburgh is too far away to go just to see another baseball game."

Of course, I felt badly that after sharing all of the struggles to get there, Mike didn't want me to share this honor with him.

112

Mike acted very nonchalant about the whole thing, but I know he was more excited than he let on. You know what he did? He hired a White Tie Limousine to pick up all the players and their wives and drive them to the L.A. airport. He said, "All-Stars shouldn't have to ride the bus." This All-Star wife would have gladly hitchhiked if she'd had to.

Since I've been back in Michigan, I've discovered that not only did one of Mike's good friends from East Lansing fly in for the game, but there was a young lady from Pittsburgh who occupied my All-Star seat. I haven't said anything about that to Mike. You know, if I had an X ray taken of my back, I'm sure they would discover I have no spine.

I did watch the All-Star game, however. After the game, when the broadcaster was interviewing Steve Garvey, the man asked Steve, "How does it feel to be the most valuable player in the All-Star game?"

Steve replied, "This has got to be the most important thing that has happened to me in my life."

The friend who was watching the game with me turned and said, "What is the most important thing that has happened to you?"

Without hesitating, I answered, "My first orgasm."

Mike must be doing a better job of dressing himself. Tom Loomis, who writes for the *Toledo Blade,* interviewed him in Pittsburgh and wrote in his column that Mike had a suit on that had to cost over $200. It was one I made, and it may have cost $40. I've decided, however, not to sew for him anymore. Can't see busting my ass so that he can look good for someone else.

Remember the incident in San Diego when Mike didn't ride the team bus? I thought you might be amused to know that on the next trip back from San Diego, exactly thirteen players rode the bus back to L.A. And there was no team meeting! So much for that rule!

Take care,
NANCY

With the possible exceptions of the World Series and the All-Star game, players were not encouraged to take their wives on the road. In fact, in 1974 a player was fined $700 for having his wife join him in California. When the player protested, the club explained that taking wives on the road was bad because they behaved like tourists, dragging their husbands around on shopping sprees, sightseeing, and keeping them up late.

Of course, the real reason is that the traveling wife might accidently see some other player with a woman not his wife. Things haven't changed—a recent copy of The Waiting Room, *a newsletter for baseball wives published by Maryanne Simmons, mentions that you are expected to be "blind" on the road.*

One time I had the kids with me on a road trip, and they observed a player leaving the restaurant and going to his room with two women. Michael was old enough to be impressed and mentioned this later in front of the player's wife. Fortunately, he had mistaken the player for someone with similar features. In the words of Roseanne Roseannadanna, "I thought I'd die!"

In Ball Four, *Jim told about the "Baseball Annies," or groupies who were always available to bestow favors on visiting players. We heard that after the book came out, the percentage of wives traveling on road trips jumped appreciably.*

B.B.

East Lansing, Michigan
November 1974

DEAR BOBBIE,

I've been reading through some of your old letters and couldn't help but compare your reaction to the World Series in 1963 with mine. I'm beginning to wonder if there is something wrong with me, since I found the entire week to be a royal pain in the ass. The only good part of it was that I got a few days' vacation, and I do love San Francisco.

Of course, Mike couldn't get through the Series without getting involved in controversy a couple of times. You were aware that Charlie Finley came up with the "designated runner" in the form of an ex-Michigan State University sprinter named Herb Washington? Well, Herb could run like the wind, but he didn't know how to read a pitcher's pick-off move. Mike nailed him cold turkey at first base. After the game, all the reporters could talk about was the pick-off and kept bringing up the fact that while Herb was an undergraduate at M.S.U., he took a physical education class that Mike taught. Mike felt the tone of the questioning was aimed at making Herb look bad, and eventually he refused to talk about it anymore. That, of course, severely pissed off a good share of the media people.

Then, in the last game, with the score tied 1–1, Mike gave up a home run to Joe Rudi to lose the game. Just before Joe came up to bat, some fans in the bleachers began throwing things at Bill Buckner, the Dodger left fielder. The game was delayed several minutes.

114

When play resumed, Joe hit the first pitch over the left-field wall. Mike got ripped severely by the press because he hadn't warmed up during or after the time-out. They decided that was the reason Joe hit the home run. Of course, they ignored the fact that Mike retired the next three hitters handily. Guess that one pitch to Joe warmed him up! The reporters conveniently forgot that the Dodgers didn't score any runs.

I have trouble swallowing all the media hype regarding the Series and all of the postseason awards, including the Cy Young. It's a bunch of bullshit designed to keep baseball in the papers during the off-season. Mike had an unbelievable season. He pitched in thirteen consecutive games. Actually, he pitched on sixteen consecutive days, but he didn't pitch in the second game of a doubleheader, so the string of games was broken.

He pitched a record-setting 208 innings. He broke his own appearance record by pitching in 106 games. Still, neither Mike nor I got terribly excited when Jack Lang called to tell him he had won the Cy Young Award. First of all, baseball writers do the choosing, and somehow their opinion just doesn't seem to matter. Second, I think Mike deserved it a lot more for the years he had in Montreal. He achieved exceptional records with a team that had about half the talent of the Dodgers. I wonder if he would have won had he had this same year in Montreal. The Dodgers' publicity department has to be the best.

I suppose most people would have loved the attention Mike got from winning the award. He handled it a bit differently. He put on our answering service so that he didn't have to talk to hundreds of people. That's what we get for having a listed telephone number.

In your early letters, you kept wishing that Mike would make the major leagues. I'm beginning to wonder about that. In the minor leagues, there was a camaraderie not only among the players but also among their wives. In Montreal I found the warmth still there but not to the degree that I experienced it in the minors.

It seemed as if there was always some underlying conflict going on among the wives this year. Some of them seemed more concerned about who was getting the front row seats, who was getting their pictures taken, etc. Cindy Garvey was the brunt of a great deal of criticism about her capacity to always be in front of a camera. She has quite properly denied some wives' allegations that she sometimes has difficulty telling the truth. Frankly, I have trouble understanding why anyone gives a shit.

One of the wives, who won't put anything on her body unless it costs $200, made the remark that if some of us didn't start dressing better, we would lose our husbands. I made it a point to wear blue jeans and moccasins from that day on.

I almost forgot to tell you about the bomb scare in Pittsburgh during the division play-offs. After the second game in Pittsburgh, when the bus arrived at the airport, a policeman stopped it from pulling up to the Dodgers plane. He informed us that someone had called and said there was a bomb on the plane and to search the plane they were using dogs who were specifically trained to sniff out powder.

Several players became apprehensive when the policeman added that the dogs would also find any marijuana that was in the suitcases.

At the close of the season, the Dodgers had Fan Appreciation Day. All of the players were introduced; Mike was greeted with a chorus of boos. After the year he had, don't you find that unbelievable? I think the fans resent the fact that he won't sign autographs or let them have any part of his life other than what he gives them on the field. Mike just can't accept being idolized or being made out to be anything more than what he is—a man who plays baseball for a living.

Hope the winter goes well for you.

NANCY

Englewood, New Jersey
DEAR NANCY,   December 1974

Another hectic year gone by. After I last dropped you a line, we went to spring training with Jim. Everything was terrific; we stayed in St. Pete, and the kids loved fooling around with Met pitcher Tug McGraw, who played "tickle shark" with them.

The day we flew home I had cramps, but I figured that it was because I had skipped breakfast, which is rare for me. The pains bothered me on and off all day, and finally, about two in the morning, I decided to go to the hospital. Jim stayed with the kids and I drove myself.

Unfortunately, I don't have a doctor—only my gynecologist. I'm really lucky to be so healthy, but from now on, I'll try to find some doctor before going to the emergency room. It was not my night. Since the hospital was overcrowded, I was in the hall half the night. Because I try to grin and bear it, I got very little attention, whereas the drunk across the hall with a leg problem demanded attention almost every minute.

I really believe there is a way to control pain with one's mind, but I also realize that it was stupid not to request more help. The pains were worse than being in labor, and, as you know, that's no picnic!

To make a long story short, by the time they operated on me, my appendix had ruptured and I had to stay a while in the hospital. Thank goodness it happened at home, or I would have been stuck in Florida.

What bothered me most was Jim driving me home. Jim has a theory, when he drives, that the faster the car goes, the smaller it becomes. Thus, a space that looks too small can be traversed if you speed. We call him Johnny Dark. He picked me up in the Karmann-Ghia instead of the station wagon (getting in was painful), and proceeded to break the limit and hit every bump in the road until I groaned. It's true I'm not fragile, but sometimes it would be pleasant to be treated like a breakable object.

Barbara, and later Nancy and Alice, gave me a hand at home. Maybe I was still upset from the medication, because I rarely take pills, but when Jim started complimenting Barbara on how beautifully she ironed and how well she baked cookies, it teed me off. Never in twelve years has he said anything about my ironing (I am as good as anyone—big deal!), and rarely does he admire how I bake the same cookies, although he surely eats enough of them.

I appreciated Barbara's help, but I certainly didn't appreciate Jim's response. Maybe he was trying to express his gratitude, but maybe he should realize I could use a compliment now and then, too, even about everyday things.

Later in the year, I did get some thanks—for helping him market the Baseball Brain, a slide computer to help you see what a certain batter would do against a certain pitcher.

We marketed this in the New York area and would have done well, except that we ordered way above our handling capacity. I supervised neighborhood kids in packing and did the special scoring with help from Nancy Smith. We'll probably try it again on a smaller scale to help recoup our loss.

Jim didn't play as much baseball this year. He wasn't even the best pitcher on his team, and I think that bothered him. Dale Berra, Yogi's son, played for Jim's team. Dale is really a nice young man, and it was good to see his mother again. Playing for the Teaneck Blues is quite a contrast to the majors. Sometimes we have a jockstrap hanging to dry from the aerial of our car. Often Jim changes in the car while I drive so that he's not late for work or a game. Must admit cleaning the uniform is getting tougher. Jim's is always filthy from diving, sprawling, or whatever he tries to stop line drives.

Jim's also been doing guest spots on some TV shows, mostly "Whats My Line?" I went to watch a few and enjoyed the change of pace.

I've also started volunteering in the children's school, working in the library again. The Parent Teachers Organization also keeps me busy. The children are doing well in school, and we're pleased with their teachers.

But Michael did something recently that disturbed me. His fifth-grade class did their time-lines. Things like: 1963—I was born. 1967 —I went to nursery school. 1969—I learned to ride a two-wheel bike, etc. Unfortunately, Michael wrote: "1963—I was born. 1964—My dad won 18 games for the Yankees. 1968—My dad was traded to Seattle. 1970—My dad started work at ABC-TV," etc. I've been worried about his overidentification with Jim for a long time, but I don't know how to correct it. I hope that time and Michael's starting to take ballet lessons and dancing in the local *Nutcracker* will give him his own thing.

Boy, your Mike surely did his own thing this year. Tell him congratulations from us. I hope you have a good year, too, Nancy. I can understand your hurt in not going to the All-Star game. Try not to read more into the incident; it's not good to let things eat at you.

Hang in there.
BOBBIE

I'm sure that there are a lot of people who will read this and wonder why Bobbie stayed home from the World Series game in St. Louis and why I didn't insist on going to the All-Star game in Pittsburgh. That's a question I've asked myself and have yet to find a satisfactory answer to. For whatever reason, I just didn't have the gumption to assert myself back then. It takes a lot of self-confidence and security to rock the boat, particularly if tipping the boat over completely means raising and supporting a family by yourself.

A good friend of mine pointed out that I should remember what the times were like back then and also my middle-class upbringing. Although perhaps not as strongly as they did in our parents' generation, the men definitely still ruled the roost. When you're married to a man who is famous and very good at what he does and his name is on the paychecks, it's easy to fall into the habit of saying to yourself, "All I do is stay at home and take care of kids."

Although it's clear that we should have been on the plane, what we did, in fact, was stay at home and take care of those kids—just like good wives and mothers are supposed to do.

N.M.

DEAR NANCY,

This is going to be one of those get-it-off-my-chest letters. I have a feeling that you can empathize with me on this problem.

A couple of months ago we went to a dinner party at Rita Moreno's apartment. Peter Cook, the English comic, and Tony Walton, the designer, and their girl friends were also invited. We were having a nice visit until someone started discussing the Caribbean.

Jim then started talking about snorkeling and watching out for sharks, moray eels, etc. (He enjoys snorkeling and has never had any trouble.) Next, Jim described how a moray eel could take a big chunk out of a person so quickly that they wouldn't know what happened. He expanded on this theme, telling explicit stories about how blood in the water attracts sharks and what they might do. Peter's date was obviously not enjoying the turn of the conversation, and I was trying to poke Jim (sitting next to him on a couch doesn't give you the privacy of kicking him under the table) to signal him to cool it. Finally, I said, "Let's change the subject." But Jim ignored me and kept on telling gruesome stories until the poor girl left the room. Then Jim said, "Did I upset her?" Peter said that she'd be all right and went after her.

Why was "holding the floor" so important to Jim? Why was I embarrassed? Jim should have been, but he wasn't. It's easy for me to empathize, but why doesn't Jim know the meaning of the word anymore?

When we first started dating, I thought he was one of the most sensitive men I had ever met. In high school Jim was a bit of a loner and had barely made the baseball team. Because he had been an "underdog," he identified with others in the same boat—or used to.

Being a New York Yankee can instill pride in anyone, I guess. Not that he didn't have confidence to start with, but he never used to be so arrogant. It's hard for me to forget the vulnerable college student and replace him with the successful person I now know.

The change has been gradual. He used to be like a kid in a candy store. Being a major leaguer was a dream come true. Now being on TV has made his recognition-factor higher than ever. It's incredible the number of people who recognize him when we are out somewhere. Even people who are celebrities in their own right say hello. One day Philip Roth stopped us on the street to tell Jim how much he enjoyed *Ball Four.* I guess it's no wonder Jim enjoys being the center of attention.

The chance to have dinner with Rita and her husband came from

Jim's meeting her at different fund-raisers. I'm proud that Jim has given a great deal of time appearing at these, but it's certainly an ego-massager when Joanne Woodward invites you to a Planned Parenthood fund-raiser. I called him the token jock.

It's true that I've changed, too, but not as much. The East has rubbed off on me. When I go back home, everyone says I've changed (mostly accent and politics). I'm the flaming liberal from New York, the one who thought *The Graduate* was a great movie.

Certainly I have adapted to Eastern ways by bringing a gift when we're invited out, and now I don't think of the hugging and kissing greetings as phony. But even though I'm now thirty-six, I still have my casual drop-in-anytime Midwestern ways. A friend recently told me I had the only house in town where you can stop by day or night and always feel welcome. Sometimes I worry that I'm too casual and need to work on being more sophisticated. Fat chance.

Has Mike changed much since he's been in the public eye? More than you bargained for, I mean? I hope he hasn't. Living in glamorous L.A. could affect a person; after all, you're rubbing elbows with movie stars.

Hope you have a good year,
BOBBIE

Los Angeles, California
June 25, 1975

DEAR BOBBIE,

I know that you still miss baseball, but I have to tell you that I think you're nuts. I've gotten to the point that nothing is fun about the lifestyle. I really do envy you staying in your own home twelve months out of the year, getting to sleep in your own bed, having your friends close by. Looks as if this is going to be one of those Pitsville letters again.

The winter was, without a doubt, the worst I've spent in Michigan . . . and I don't mean the weather. Mike was gone all of the time. When he did manage to come home, he locked himself in his study and came out only to have dinner. I was so anxious to get out of there that I moved out at the beginning of the season, something I've not done in years.

Mike's mother drove out with me. I did all the driving while she entertained Deborah, Becky, and Kerry. We made a couple of stops at the Painted Desert and Petrified Forest. The girls are twelve, nine, and seven now, still not really old enough to appreciate all of the natural beauty they saw. After we arrived in L.A., Mike's mother said something that will endear her to me for life. I already had food in the cupboards and sheets on the bed and was down in the garage under our apartment unloading the Ford. As she stood by and watched me wrestle the spare tire out of the car-top carrier (I can pack the trunk of the car better if I put it up there), struggle to try to keep it from falling against the car, roll it back to the trunk, and heave it into the car, she said, "Now I know why Mike doesn't mind moving all the time." You got to love that woman.

Earlier this month I drove to San Diego (two hours by freeway) to join Diane Campbell and her two girls for a day at the zoo. (Dave played with Mike in Toledo and is now doing play by play on the radio broadcasts of the Padres.) I had heard this zoo is the best in the world, and I wanted to make sure the girls saw it before Mike was traded again (with his history, it's just a matter of time). When Mike came home from the road trip and found out that I had gone down there, he threw a fit, called me a few uncomplimentary names, and asked me how I could be so stupid. In the past, I probably would have said I was sorry (for what, I wouldn't always be so sure) and assumed that he was right. This time I couldn't do it. I asked him why he thought I was incapable of driving two hours to San Diego when just two months earlier I had managed to drive from Michigan to California all by myself. You know what his answer to me was? "That's different." Sure is. It's about twenty-two thousand miles farther! He then went on to say that drivers in California are nuts. (Oddly enough, the only time I've feared for my life is when I've been riding with Mike.) He said it was dangerous for me to have driven from here to San Diego. Does that strike you as logical? I have to assume that if it's dangerous for me to drive from here to there, it must be just as dangerous to be living in the middle of Los Angeles by myself half of the time, but I don't see him objecting to that. The area where we are living has the reputation for being one of the highest drug-pushing areas around. Yet the man is worried about my driving to San Diego?

I get a lot angrier when things like this San Diego business come up because I feel it's demeaning. You know, Mike leaves a large number of things that husbands normally take care of to me. We've been in our house since December 1971, and he has yet to put a single storm window up in the fall. Last year he did help me, though; he looked out his study window and thought I looked cold, so he brought me a sweat shirt.

I think that all of this nonsense involves a power struggle. There were a lot of years when I looked to Mike to make all my decisions. I wouldn't have thought of doing anything that he didn't like. I've learned to trust my own judgment, and I don't think he's adjusted to that. I can't pretend to be terribly incompetent when he's around when the rest of the time I'm taking care of the household quite handily, sometimes for months at a time. And I think I can decide whether to take the girls to San Diego or not.

My God. I just reread this and realized how angry I sound. Could be I sound that way because I am. I'm also frustrated and confused. There is a lot of stuff going on with Mike that I'm just not up to talking about. Things were so bad in May that I actually started to pack everything in the car and head back to Michigan. My dad gently talked me out of that. My frustration comes from not being able to talk with Mike. If he ever does listen, he doesn't believe or understand what I'm telling him. Seems he's always looking for the hidden message behind my words. For about a year now, whenever I've tried to talk to him about our problems, he ends the conversation before it even starts by saying, "If you don't like my lifestyle, get out."

Enough of this garbage.

Mike is having a rough season. He injured his rib while pitching against the Giants on April 20. He tried to come back too soon and reinjured it severely against the Pirates on May 8. (He also gave up 9 runs in the process. That ought to skyrocket the earned run average.) He started pitching again on June 6, but the rib still isn't right. Compared to most relief pitchers, he's still having a good season, but if you compare it to what he's accomplished the past three years, his record doesn't measure up. It's too bad that people around here have come to expect the exceptional. The boo-birds have been all over Mike. They don't seem willing to accept just "good."

I've decided to go back to school this fall. The girls are old enough not to need my constant attention. I'm tired of sewing and knitting. Besides, I don't think it ever hurts to be prepared to support yourself. Can't wait for the season to be over so that I can get my brain back to work.

NANCY

East Lansing, Michigan
DEAR BOBBIE,   September 11, 1975

Do you remember that small-town girl who for ten years stayed at home with her children, baked bread, and made wonderful creatures out of Play-Doh? If you know where she is, I wish you'd send her back.

Somehow my life has gotten out of control. By most people's standards, I'm not neglecting my kids, but by mine I sure am. Somehow

I'm always in a state of anger or defiance, and I know it's wearing on the girls.

For years I never went anywhere without Mike. When other wives were getting together and going out to dinner or a movie, I stayed home with my kids. Either I told myself we couldn't afford a baby-sitter (despite the fact that Mike has made $75,000 for the past few years) or I felt too guilty going out without Mike. Boy, has the pendulum swung the other way. The minute the guys go on the road, Jo Wynn and I hit the streets. First, we go to a predominantly black nightclub, where I pass for black. Then we hit one of the meat markets in Marina del Rey, and she tries to act white. Neither of us does a very good job, but we sure have a helluva lot of fun. It seems that every time we go out, I end up on the bandstand. Somehow it doesn't seem very matronly to think of me crawling around on the floor behind the disc jockey's desk. The last night I was in L.A. I tried to hide under the table when the lead singer sang, "I Want to Do Something Freaky to You," and dedicated the song to me.

One time this summer I got into something that was way out of my league. I went out one night with a couple of women I met last summer. We went to a private club down by the ocean. A man who had been talking to us asked if we would like to join him at a party that was being given after the rock awards. I knew I was getting in with a crowd of people that was used to moving a lot faster than I wanted to go, so I suggested they take me home.

We were sitting in the alley outside the club waiting for some people to join us when one of the guys came to the car and asked us if we wanted some coke. I declined, but everyone else took a hit. I sat there terribly concerned yet fascinated. I had never seen anyone sniff cocaine. I kept asking if they were all right, and they kept saying they were.

Then the guy came back a second time and offered them a second hit, and they took it. Well, I don't know what was in the second batch, but it sure wasn't cocaine. After about thirty seconds, the gal who was driving got the strangest look on her face, turned to me, and said, "Nancy, you drive this car!"

The drive home was not fun. First of all, at one point a police car appeared to be after us, so I had to do a bit of fancy driving to elude it. All I could think of was what wonderful headlines this would make for the sports page. When I finally got them back to the apartment, both my friends were out of touch with reality. I took my baby-sitter home, then rushed back to their apartment. For the next four hours I walked one of the girls the circle from the kitchen to the living room to the dining room and back to the kitchen. She was sure she was losing her mind and kept pleading with me not to leave her alone. By six that morning the drugs had finally worn off, and I left both of the girls sleeping.

It seems as if it has been a summer of unpleasantries. One night after a game Mike was walking out of the stadium with Deborah on one side and Kerry on the other. I was walking several paces behind, with Becky. As we headed for the car, a young man, who appeared a bit on the grubby side, said in a very whiny, sarcastic voice, "Can I have your autograph, Mike?"

It was obvious that the kid knew Mike didn't sign autographs. Mike didn't even acknowledge him. As I walked by him, he said in a much quieter voice but loud enough so that I heard it, "What an asshole."

I totally lost my cool. I put my face about six inches from him and started hollering at him as I backed him up against a wall. I said, "Who do you think you are calling my husband names in front of his children? I'm not going to listen to you talk that way in front of them." The young man got very wide-eyed. Mike came over and pulled me away by my elbow and very quietly said to him, "When I'm by myself you can say whatever you like to me, but not when I'm with my family. I don't want you upsetting them."

The kid kept saying over and over, "I'm sorry, Mrs. Marshall. I'm sorry." Why is it that people think celebrities are not people—people who have feelings?

As anxious as I was to get out of East Lansing in the spring, I found I was twice as anxious to get back. A gal who is in graduate school with Mike flew down to L.A. from Alaska and drove back to Michigan with the girls and me. We got up at three in the morning and started driving so that we could get to the Grand Canyon in time to spend the night. What a magnificent sight that was. I think even the girls were impressed.

Liz and I had both been operating on West Coast time for so long that neither of us was ready to quit driving and go to bed very early, so we really put in some long hauls. The drive was a piece of cake up until the last day. I ran into some terrible weather in Ohio, and, of course, that was when the girls decided they had run out of patience and started horsing around in the back seat.

I tried several times to get them to quiet down. I reasoned with them that the weather was making driving very hazardous and that I couldn't be distracted with their tomfoolery. I finally got so angry with them that I took one of the off ramps, dropped them at the top of it, and started down the road without them. They weren't impressed. Guess they knew I wouldn't really leave them. I should have done what Mary Gosger used to do with her kids. She kept a flyswatter handy so she could reach into the back seat and give them a smack while still keeping the car rolling down the road.

I followed through on my promise to myself and am going back to school. However, I've decided to major in communications not social work. In addition to going to school, I'm helping a friend out with a business she has started. Ginny wrote and published a book on sewing. She has asked me to do telephone sales from her home.

Since my summer with Mike didn't go a great deal smoother than all of last winter, I'm determined to get my ass out of the house. No one should voluntarily submit herself to the kind of rejection I've been getting from him for the past year. My being out of the house certainly won't cure the problem, but at least it will help me live through it with some measure of peace of mind.

What happened to the good old days?

NANCY

Mike's reluctance to sign autographs has been the topic of many an argument with friends and colleagues. While neither Mike nor I thought very much of "hero worshiping," we didn't think there was anything wrong with emulating someone who has provided good leadership. Usually, all one has to do is look around their own family to find a very qualified hero.

Unfortunately, too many people look elsewhere. And what they usually select are papier-mâché idols. It's important to realize that even "idols" are real people. After Mike won the Cy Young Award in 1974, a woman who had known us for years came up and asked me what it was like to live with Mike now that he was a celebrity. I tried to shrug it off as no big deal, but she wouldn't let me off that easy. Finally, after she bugged me about it for the third time, I said, "I know this is going to come as a real surprise to you, but Mike's shit stinks just like everyone else's."

I like the following quote from Dr. Wayne Dyer's Your Erroneous Zones.

All the great heroes of your life have taught you nothing. And they are no better than you, in any way. Politicians, actors, athletes, rock-stars, your boss, therapist, teacher, spouse or whoever, are just skilled at what they do—nothing more. And if you make

125

them your heroes and elevate them to positions above yourself,
then you are into that external bag of giving others the responsi-
bility for your good feelings.

N.M.

Englewood, New Jersey
November 1975

We have a new family member, Misty. She's a Belgian sheep dog.
She looks like a black German shepherd but with longer fur. This
summer Englewood had a rapist on the loose who murdered an
acquaintance of mine (Alice's best friend.) Since Jim is gone so much
and I hate being alone in our big house, we decided to get a watchdog.

Jim said he would train her if I took her to obedience classes. Only
problem was that the first thing the trainer said was whoever brings
the dog has to work with her. Wonderful. We did fine, came in second
in the test, even took home a trophy. The cat, Columbus, isn't so sure
he approves, but we have plenty of room for him to hide. We bought
Misty after we returned from Portland. Jim just couldn't stay away
from playing pro ball, so he played A ball with the Portland Mavericks for three weeks in August.

Jim flew out and pitched one game, then wanted to return, so we
all went with him. It was super being in the Great Northwest again.
The owner of the team is Bing Russell, an actor who used to be on
"Bonanza." Since he's an independent owner, he could sign Jim without a hassle from higher-ups.

The manager is a nut, and the players all try to be Pete Rose—in
other words, it's a terrific team peoplewise. The fans really turn out,
and no wonder—the Mavs put on a show! Even Bing's son, Kurt, also
an actor, plays when he's available. The whole scene is super.

The kids really enjoyed themselves, even David, who had to settle
for another birthday on the road. We had dinner at a Greek restaurant, and they put a candle in the baklava.

We were lent a car and were able to take some side trips. Nancy
Smith flew out and joined us in seeing Seal Rock, Agate Beach, and
the Oregon coast. Jim finished up very well and still has the itch to
play ball, a surprise to no one.

It reminds me of a line from Jim Brosnan's *The Long Season,* about
the last day of the season: "It is virtually impossible for a ballplayer
to convince himself that he will never play the game again. On the last
day of the season baseball, truly, is in his blood."

Michael is going to dance in the *Nutcracker* again. I am now on the board as well as the guild of the Classic Ballet Company of New Jersey. This is our big season coming up, and I'll be busy working on costumes, decorations, publicity, etc. Must admit I enjoy myself. Michael does very well and even at twelve has good stage presence. (Not surprising.) He certainly didn't inherit it from me. He also loves to sign autographs, unlike your Mike. Not only am I married to a star, but now I'm the mother of one, too. Some people have all the breaks.

Hope you "break a leg" this year and that you and your friends stay out of trouble. I'm still staying home knitting and feel guilty when I go to the ballet without Jim. But, at least, we usually go out on Friday and Larry Ritter's a terrific escort until Jim is off. I'm not very adventurous and find it hard to imagine you "painting the town." Maybe someday I'll have enough mettle to join you.

Fondly,
BOBBIE

East Lansing, Michigan
DEAR BOBBIE,   March 1976

This has not been a winter to cherish. Are you getting tired of these letters that piss and moan all the time? Believe me, I'm working on getting my life together, but I feel as if I have a giant thumb on top of me most of the time.

I'm sure you read that the man who runs the Men's Intramural Building at Michigan State got a criminal complaint taken out against Mike for using the baseball net in the sports arena. The net has been there for years; and Mike has always used it. In fact, he donates money to the athletic department to help maintain it. The university recently put Astroturf on the floor of the arena, and when they did that, they also put in two tennis courts. Unfortunately, they installed them in such a way that one of the courts is in conflict with the net.

Mike really tried in every way possible to resolve the problem, including giving them money to move the courts around. However, since Mike has had a running battle with the intramural director for years, his efforts didn't get him anywhere.

The people who play tennis are adamantly opposed to Mike's position, and there are confrontations with them continually. The problem is that Mike is in the middle of a catch-22. There is no way to reserve time to use the net. Mike tried reserving the tennis court, but the director put an end to that by saying that if he reserved it, he had to play tennis. We've gotten around that by having friends use the tennis court while Mike uses the baseball net. Mike Steinberg, a friend

127

of Mike's who works out in the net with him, and I have been standing in line for hours all winter waiting to reserve the court. Mike won't do it; he doesn't think he should have to. I think he's right. However, I'm having trouble understanding why he thinks it's okay for me to do it then. He must approve, though, because he drives me over there at seven in the morning so that I can get in line before anyone else gets there.

The entire situation got out of hand, and ultimately the director suspended Mike from the building—something he didn't have the power to do without a hearing. Of course, Mike ignored it, and he was charged with trespassing.

The funny part was that Fran Tarkenton was in town filming a spot on Mike for NBC's "Grandstand" show, which airs before the football game on Sundays. Since we knew the police were coming, the film crew wired Mike with a portable microphone.

My weird sense of humor got me in trouble with Mike one more time. When the police were searching him, I told them to look under his protective cup—that there was a lethal weapon hidden there. Mike didn't think that I showed the proper attitude. Personally, I thought my remark was apropos.

No doubt I shouldn't have been laughing, but the whole scene was so ridiculous that it was hard to take it seriously. The police even handcuffed Mike's arms behind his back and tried to sneak him out the back of the building. What the hell did they think Mike was going to do, take hostages?

When the police asked NBC's film crew to leave the building, Mike suggested to them that they go to the back of the building. As a result the film crew recorded Mike's arrest on film and NBC aired it the following Sunday on national television.

It's not unusual these days for Mike to be displeased with my attitude; I guess I can't really blame him. I'm not living up to his idea of what a good wife and mother should be, i.e., I'm not devoting all my time to the family. When I'm not in class, I'm usually at Ginny's house working with her. Since I'm not making any money, Mike doesn't understand why I'm doing it. Although part of my motivation is to escape from the house, I'm also excited to be able to help a woman who is trying to make a go of her own business.

In addition to working on her book, Ginny and I spend a lot of time hashing over ideas about the women's movement and where we fit into it. Personally, I feel as if I'm caught in the middle of two radically different philosophies. My old middle-class upbringing tells me I should be in the kitchen baking bread and should feel guilty because I'm not. The not-so-old part of me says I should be able to do it all

—work, develop a life outside of the family, and still throw a loaf in the oven now and then (or, better yet, let someone else in the family do it for me!).

Mike resents just about everything I'm doing these days, and probably he has justification. Because I'm really angry—at what I'm not real sure—I'm not carrying off this shift of attitude and position very smoothly. I should be able to make him realize why it's important to me to grow just as he has. Because I've given him so much latitude to just be whoever Mike Marshall wants, I resent the fact that he seems unwilling or incapable of giving it back. I may not be going about this just right, but I also think I should be allowed to fuck up now and then!

One of the nice things that has happened in my life is that I've come to really appreciate women. I've always thought we were a pretty boring group, but not so now. My next-door neighbor, June Mack, has been a real godsend to me. She is, without a doubt, one of the most competent, sensible women I've ever met. Among other things, she runs the electron microscope at Michigan State.

June has done more for me than I can ever thank her for. She badgered me into going back to school. She has made me realize that I have lots of time left to have a career outside of the house, and, most important, she has instilled in me a self-confidence that up until now was sorely lacking. And you know what the best part is? Despite disapproving of a lot of things I do, like swearing like a trooper and refusing to get up at five in the morning to go "birding" with her, she loves me anyway. Thanks to June I'm slipping out from under that thumb.

Since Deborah is in junior high now and has different teachers for all of her classes, we won't be joining Mike in Los Angeles until school is out. Every other year the girls have finished the school year in whatever city Mike was playing in, but we felt it would be unfair to ask Deborah to do that now. It means a three-month separation from Mike, but that just might be good for us.

NANCY

DEAR NANCY,

Englewood, New Jersey
April 21, 1976

Just had to drop you a line and let you know that the *Ball Four* sitcom idea is going to pilot. (CBS is going to film a show.) I'm not surprised, since I "pushed" the idea on Jim and had one of my "feelings" that it would sell.

Because Jim seemed to be getting bored at work, I suggested he work on *Ball Four* as a TV show. He was interested in the idea, and we talked to our friend, Marvin Kitman, a TV critic, about how to go about selling the idea. Then they got together with Vic Ziegel, a humorous sportswriter friend, and worked on a presentation.

Jim and I worked on the idea before he met with Marvin and Vic. We decided that the team should be based in Washington, D.C., and we talked about different characters, etc. We usually work at night in bed; it's cozy, and we are relaxed and laugh a lot. It's nice to be so close even after thirteen years of marriage.

I think Jim would rather be playing ball, but this may be the next best thing. But the hours he's put in on top of doing his regular news have been brutal. I'm glad I can work with him; it gives us time together. We also work together making stained-glass art. We took an adult ed class and Jim has really enjoyed working with his hands again. I help him with his big stuff and do little things on my own.

He's also taking acting lessons with Lee Strasberg. He started last year; in fact, we were invited to a New Year's Eve party at the Strasbergs' apartment.

What a treat to have a peek at the kind of party you read about in the newspaper columns. The Strasbergs were charming, the apartment just what you would expect; overlooking Central Park, baby grand piano, hundreds of eight-by-ten photos on the wall. (Nonchalantly, I tried to identify the people in the pictures.)

The talent at the party was quality all the way. Their total of Oscars, Tonys, and TV award nominations must have been in the double figures. We had a chance to talk to Janet Leigh, a favorite of mine since *Little Women,* and Jean Marsh, whom I had loved in *Upstairs, Downstairs.* It was easy to chat because I had read that they were both in town for Broadway shows, and both were friendly. At one point, Janet wanted to take her shoes off—a lady after my own heart.

Shelley Winters breezed around, and Ellen Burstyn looked girlish in a white cotton and lace gown. Faye Dunaway surprised me by being very casually dressed in a shapeless skirt and cardigan. You had to look close to see those beautiful features; you probably would have missed her on the street.

Of course, after this "top-drawer" party, I had to go home and mop the kitchen floor the next day. Life has a way of putting you back in perspective.

Jim's going to take a leave of absence from CBS news. It's too hard on him working two jobs. The kids rarely see him anymore. Thank goodness I can work "behind the scenes" with him because it's as if he were taking road trips again and I was once more relegated to handling the kids alone.

Laurie, who just turned ten, has gymnastics, and David plays hockey. Hockey is something else. They play and practice at ungodly hours, like 6:00 A.M. on Saturday or Sunday. Fortunately, I'm beginning to enjoy watching, and Dave plays well.

Now that the kids are older and each into his own thing, I'm glad that Jim isn't playing ball. It would be too hard moving them away from their activities, friends and school. It must be difficult for you and the girls.

It's also nice to be spared the hassle of cleaning out all your drawers and closets so that you can rent your house during the season. Our house is so full of stuff it would take me forever.

Tell Mike not to worry—there's no Mike Marshall character in the TV *Ball Four*. He wouldn't be believable.

Hope you have a good year and get rid of that giant thumb.

Fondly,
BOBBIE

DEAR BOBBIE,

Atlanta, Georgia
August 1976

Add another city to our list. Three days before the trading deadline (and just hours before the girls and I were to fly to Los Angeles), the Dodgers traded Mike to Atlanta. Usually, the girls and I take these sudden changes and moves in stride but not this one.

I had a few friends in for dinner that night, but by the time Mike called only my good friend Charlie Beach and his girl friend, Cheryl, remained. When Becky heard that Mike had been traded, she crawled up on Charlie's lap, wrapped her arms around his neck, and cried. She had tears rolling down her cheeks as she said, "Charlie, why doesn't anyone like my daddy?"

There is no doubt in my mind they traded him because he just didn't fit the Dodger image. All the controversy Mike is involved in at Michigan State isn't the kind of publicity the Dodgers like. Peter O'Malley asked Mike if he was going to be able to settle his dispute with M.S.U. with a handshake. When Mike said that wasn't possible, I'm sure that did it.

The players (Tom Lasorda's boys mainly) weren't helpful either. A reporter told Mike that Steve Garvey had admitted to him that he had gone to the Dodgers brass and asked, for the good of the team, that Mike be traded. I don't know how good it was for the team, but it sure was a relief for Mike to be out of there.

Mike's problems at Michigan State have escalated, and the situation is so involved it's almost impossible to figure out what's going on anymore.

I support Mike, sort of, at least. I do think he has been discriminated against. The problem is I'm really tired of always being in the middle of a storm. No matter what city Mike plays in, invariably the fans grow to dislike him very quickly. It's not that I care what a bunch of strangers think, but I'm to the point where I don't even think about going out in public with him.

And it's starting to invade the girls' life. Someone wrote "Fuck Mike Marshall" on the blackboard in the cafeteria where Becky and Kerry go to school. That really hurt them. Then we have to talk to them about how people make judgments about others based on what they read in the papers. Mike keeps telling me that I don't have to take his roller-coaster rides with him. How do I manage that?

When Mike was charged with trespassing last spring, the newspapers got the report wrong. They had Mike hitting baseballs at people. Mike wasn't even batting, and the guys who were hitting were inside the net enclosure that is designed for that purpose. And of course, that article went nationwide. Had it been any other student but Mike, it probably wouldn't have made the paper at all. Actually, Mike went to trial, defended himself, there was a hung jury (5–1 in his favor) and the district attorney eventually dropped the charges.

I have the feeling sports fans don't want to hear about Mike Marshall's battles. The front page has enough war news. I have such mixed feelings. I think people should fight for their rights and should battle for the principles they believe in. It just seems to me there are a lot more worthy causes than the right to use the baseball net in the intramural building. It doesn't seem worth risking his career in education over an issue hardly anyone but Mike cares about or understands. If he really wants to make changes at the university, he should run for a position on the board of trustees.

I have to be careful what I say to Mike these days. Any questioning I do results in the immediate accusation that I don't support him. Frankly, I'm running out of the patience and the energy it takes to do so. Do you think Martha Washington said something like, "Please, George, not another battle!"

One of the more memorable events this summer was the husband-wife game. It was raining before the game and there was some doubt that it would be played, but the weather cleared. All the gals were sitting in the dugout with their husbands, all but me that is. Mike was nowhere to be seen. Jim Wynn could see that I was getting hot and kept asking me if I wanted him to go look for Mike. I started out calmly by saying Mike would be out soon, but after the third time Jim asked, I rather testily replied, "Fuck him."

I sat alone in the dugout while the rest of the couples were introduced. Later, Mike apologized, and I know he genuinely felt bad. He was involved in an interview and didn't know the ceremony had started. The fact still remained; it never occurred to him to check on little ole insignificant me.

The good part of being in Atlanta is my reunion with JoAnn Wynn. She has a toughness about her, street-smarts, that I'm hoping will rub off on me just a bit. I'm tired of being hurt easily.

At the father-children game, Jim, JoAnn, and I were walking arm in arm around the field when a photographer started clicking away at us with his trusty Nikon. Jo doesn't care much for that sort of thing and said very loudly, "Okay, everyone smile and say 'pussy.'" The Marshalls now have a new word to make someone smile for the camera.

While Jo and I are still hitting the night spots occasionally, we're much more inclined to play a little tennis, drink a bit of wine, and listen to some good music at home. It really is much more my style. I think I may be getting back into control of my life.

Always,
NANCY

P.S. I've started a rather huge project this summer. After taking a creative writing class spring term, the teacher, Mike Steinberg, encouraged me to continue writing. Since so many people have approached Mike about doing a book about his career, I've decided to try it. Don't know if I have the skills, but I sure have a lot of knowledge.

I've enclosed one of the pieces I wrote for class. I woke up at three in the morning, typed it, and didn't change a word. Think it says something about my state of mind?

There was a pond. Not a small pond. Not a big pond. The pond was just right.

There was a lily pad. Not a small lily pad. Not a big lily pad. The lily pad was just right, too.

The lily pad belonged to a quiet, happy lady frog. She was at peace with herself and the world. Freda. Freda the frog. Freda's frog Fred used to sit on the pad with Freda and discuss algae. Fred doesn't discuss algae with Freda anymore. Fred jumps from lily pad to lily pad. Fred doesn't want to die before he experiences all the lily pads in the pond. Freda doesn't sit on the lily pad anymore either. It doesn't fit her body like it used to. Sad.

There was a day when the lily pad would wrap itself around Freda and mold itself to her shape. Freda sat in the sun, felt the gentle wind on the soft skin under her chin. The lily pad would rise and fall as the waves flowed under her. Even in thunderous storms the lily pad held together and supported Freda.

So.

Fred loved Freda. Strike that. Fred didn't know what love meant, but Fred liked Freda. Sort of. Hooray for Freda. Hooray for Fred. Fred wanted Freda to experience all the lily pads in the pond, so one day when Freda wasn't looking, he nudged her in the ass with a stick. Oh, for sure, the stick didn't have a sharp point. Fred didn't want to hurt Freda; he just wanted her to move her ass. What did Freda do? What would you do if someone stuck a stick up your ass? Freda jumped. Oh, not very far. In fact, she didn't make it off the lily pad. Trouble was, after she moved, the lily pad didn't feel comfortable anymore. The bumps were all in the wrong places.

Freda thought she would give her new resting place a try, however. Soon she found she liked the old spot best and inched her way back to the hollowed-out place in the lily pad that tenderly held her paunchy underside. Much better, right, Freda?

Wrong. Look out, Freda, here comes Fred with the stick again. Up your ass, Freda. So what if you didn't want to move! Fred's stick says move, lady. This time Freda jumped and landed in the water. Swim, Freda. Don't go under, Freda! Great! Freda made it to the next lily pad. "Fuck!" This lily pad was hard as a rock. No place for Freda.

"Back to the pad I call home," said Freda. Poor Freda. After she made it back to her pad, it no longer seemed the same. Freda had been gone too long. It didn't fit her anymore.

There is a pond. So what?

There is a lily pad. Who cares?

So long, Fred.

Tough shit, Freda.

DEAR BOBBIE,

East Lansing, Michigan
November 1976

I have to tell you that trying to write a book can be a lot of fun, but then you already know that. I flew to Minneapolis for the Twins' last home stand and spent six hours with Gene Mauch discussing Mike's days in Montreal. I have such love for that man—he is in my opinion the person responsible for Mike's success. Granted, Mike had the ability, but it took a special person to see that talent and understand what had to be done to capitalize on it. Gene actually got very emotional when he recollected the times he and Mike spent discussing baseball strategy.

Gene's nickname is the Little General, but my memories of him are not of a harsh disciplinarian. Before the father-son game in 1973, Deborah, my shy nine-year-old, went up to Gene and complained that it wasn't fair that the girls had to be cheerleaders instead of playing in the game. When the game started, Gene made sure the girls got to bat. I think the "general" is actually an old softy.

When I was riding from the Minneapolis airport to the hotel, three TWA pilots started talking to me. Eventually, they invited me to have dinner with them. I had dinner with Gene but had a drink with them later that night. They were dead-heading a plane to Nice the next day and invited me to go along. I was actually tempted, but then I thought about what would happen if someone in France discovered I was there without a passport. I also pictured what would happen if I called Mike and said, "Oh, by the way, I won't be home tomorrow. . . ." Now I regret not doing it. Wouldn't that be a great story to tell my grandchildren?

Writing has also made me very conscious of things around me. For instance, here are two events from the Chicago airport on the way home from Minneapolis. I noticed a large sign with an arrow on it standing in the corridor. The sign read: THIS WAY TO THE SNACK BAR. The funny part was that the arrow was pointing toward the door of the women's bathroom.

As I continued down the corridor, I noticed several men looked at me strangely. Then when I got to the gate, the ticket agent kept staring at me oddly. I had become rather self-conscious by this time, also slightly irritated. I said to the guy, "Is there something wrong with the way I'm dressed?"

He hemmed and hawed and finally sputtered, "Well, it's obvious that you're not wearing a bra."

Before I had time to think better of it, I snapped, "I doubt if you're wearing a jockstrap, but I'm not staring at your crotch."

This fall when I was in New York I sat in on a negotiating meeting at the Players Association. Actually, the new agreement had been signed, and this meeting was organized to work on the wording of the basic agreement.

Dick Moss, the lawyer for the Players Association, introduced me as Nancy Marshall, but he offered no explanation of who I was or why I was there. John Gaherin was representing the owners, but the National League President, Chub Feeney, and several lawyers were also there.

At one point, John became very animated and said, "If there weren't a lady present, I'd be using much stronger language right now."

I looked him in the eye and said, "Mr. Gaherin, I frankly don't give a fuck how you talk."

Gaherin's eyes got huge, Dick Moss broke out laughing, and Chub Feeney grinned and said, "That's my kind of girl!"

The next day Dick told me that John had called him and tried to find out who I was. Dick finally said to him, "Do you mean you really didn't recognize her? That was Jane Fonda." Dick swears Gaherin actually believed it for a while. Someday I'd like to be in the same room with Jane and see for myself if we look alike.

Fondly,
NANCY

When I first met Nancy, she was 5 feet 6 inches, 107 pounds, had short dark-brown hair, high cheekbones, blue eyes, and a wide smile. She also had a certain energetic tension about her. She could readily fit the description of the classic cheerleader.

Currently Nancy is 110 pounds and still has the energetic tenseness. (She calls herself hyper.) She also has been one of those lucky people whose looks improve with age. Even though her hair is streaked with gray (earned the hard way), it appears more like ash blond highlights, and it is easy to see why many people have compared her looks to Jane Fonda's.

B.B.

DEAR NANCY,

Englewood, New Jersey
December 1976

Where to start? How about Calgary, a terrific spot anytime. We went there this summer so Jim could pitch in a tournament. (My idea for seeing the Canadian Rockies.) It was totally terrific.

Jim pitched for the Calgary Jimmies for two weeks. This included some all-day tournaments, where families come in their pickups with a big picnic basket and spend the whole day watching different teams compete. The friendly country feeling in a place like Red Deer can be contagious. Aye? We had the use of a four-wheel-drive Rover and went up to Banff, Jasper, etc. Gorgeous.

Next, I don't know if you caught any of the "Ball Four" shows, since they weren't on long. The final show was October 27. We were all disappointed that it was canceled, but we felt good that it had even made it on the air. Out of 2,000 ideas, CBS commissions around 150 scripts and then about 25 pilots. Then, only three new series make it into the fall schedule, so to go that far was special.

The work involved was incredible. I read every script idea submitted and was very disappointed that even writers with good credentials turned in stuff that was common. Basically, the idea was good, but there wasn't enough time or talent to bring it off. Since I helped Jim write a preliminary draft for one show and worked on others, they were going to give me credit. But it would have involved joining the unions, so we decided it would have cost more than it was worth. Too bad we didn't get you to write for the show. I loved "Freda."

I won't miss trying to juggle tickets. (Almost as bad as World Series time.) I will miss attending the affiliate affairs. We went to L.A. for a big bash and had a chance to meet Carol Burnett, Jean Stapleton, and others whose talents I admire. Also, Alan Alda and Alan Wagner and his wife (he's a vice-president at CBS-TV) have been very kind.

Jim is really worn-out and let-down. He worked night and day and had a tremendous amount of pressure on him. Starring in your own TV series, especially for a novice actor, is a big load to carry.

Now Jim and Marvin are writing a book about the whole experience. The tentative title is *Down the Toilet,* a line the producer used all the time, which proved prophetic.

By the way, if you happen to browse in a bookstore, you might see *The Superwives.* Believe it or not, there's a chapter on me. If you read the whole book, you'll find my chapter turns out pretty well, but I was disappointed with a few of my "quotes." Surprisingly, my picture is even on the cover. That's rather a heavy ego trip.

Don't be surprised if next year we turn up playing ball somewhere. Jim is making a lot of inquiries. I've even suggested the Netherlands and Italy, as well as Japan.

It won't be easy if he decides to go back to pitching. But I want him to be happy and will support him 100 percent. It may be disruptive for the children and me—moving around again—but it may be a good experience, too. I'm going to think positively; I know what you'll say. But we've had six years of relative stability. I may be out of shape for

137

moving, but isn't it like riding a bicycle? Once you learn how, you never forget?

Best,
BOBBIE

DEAR BOBBIE,

I'm glad you liked "Freda." I still consider her my finest hour. You shouldn't have complimented me, though, because I'm now enclosing even more for you to read.

The material I'm sending you is part of my chapter that I have labeled "When I'm Not with the One I Love. . . ." I took your advice and read *The Superwives.* I didn't find anything like my material in it. Wonder why?

Most of the screwing around that occurs on the road is just recreational sex (a term coined by *your husband,* I might add!). They're bored and adored, so they get laid. I think just about everyone knows about that. What I don't think anyone has ever given much thought to is how the wives of professional athletes react to it.

I've lived through fourteen baseball seasons to date, and have had a lot of time to observe wives, and I see the same pattern repeat itself time and time again. There are three stages wives go through. Actually, some never make it through all three.

I call the first stage the "true believer" period. In this stage, each wife admits, "Yes, I know that there is a lot of fucking around that takes place on the road [although I'm sure they would put that more delicately than I], but my husband doesn't take part in it." If you ask twenty-five wives, twenty-three would probably claim their husbands are innocent. And who can blame them? Every woman, or man for that matter, likes to think that she or he is special. Who doesn't want to believe that they can fulfill every wish their marital partner desires? It's not very rewarding to have to admit to yourself that you may not be everything your husband wants. And it's even harder to admit that your husband may not be the man you thought he was.

It's hard to fathom how these women can remain in stage one, but many of them do for years and years. Most newly married wives belong in stage one. They still have rice in their hair. Women who have small children to take care of are usually too busy to even think about what their husbands are doing when they're away from them, so they usually fall into stage one. And you can bet that any woman

138

you see with a charm bracelet full of mementos of her husband's career is still in stage one.

Very frequently, the guys will put out a pretty good propaganda campaign to convince their wives they are faithful. One of their best techniques is to come back from a road trip and tell their wife about another ballplayer's indiscretions, and talk about how he thinks that guy is stupid and shallow for giving in to his sexual weakness. They make fun of the quality of woman that the other guys accept. They talk about how this *other* guy needs these sexual encounters to bolster a weak self-image, giving the impression, of course, that they never, never, never would consider behaving similarly.

Mike and I have this little inside saying that we use whenever we don't believe someone is being quite honest. I'm sure you've heard it. It's the story of the salesman who was trying to sell some land in Florida. He said, "You can have this land for an incredibly low price because it has a little water on it." Of course, later the buyer finds that piece of land with only a "little" water on it was really a swamp. Now whenever we don't quite buy something we say, "You got a piece of land you want to sell?"

Well, after a while it gets pretty hard to buy those "pieces of land" the guys want to sell. I call what comes next the "knock-on-the-head" stage. No one in this stage, two, will admit it to anyone else, but inside their heads they know it isn't everyone else's husband who is partaking of the extracurricular fun and games. It's theirs. And after that, they can no longer accept the lies. They find it impossible to trust this man they believed in wholeheartedly not so long ago. And that's the hard knock on the head.

In the early phases of stage two, there is also a lot of indecision. Somehow, this wife has to reconcile the image she used to have of her husband with some conflicting evidence. She doesn't want to be guilty of jumping to the wrong conclusion, so she tries to get verification for her suspicions. Actually, she really works particularly hard to prove the suspicions are wrong.

Stage two wives will blame someone other than their husbands for his actions. You were in Jeanne Parr's book *The Superwives*. Didn't you notice how several of the wives moaned and groaned about the groupies, the "Camp Annies"? Somehow it's these girls' fault that their husbands behave in such a lewd and lascivious manner. (I love those two words! Don't they just roll off your tongue?!) That strikes me as being about as ridiculous as cussing out the wastebasket because you stubbed your toe on it. These girls are only out for a good time. They take their ego trips by laying someone who is well known. I thought the anger was misdirected. These are grown men we're talking about, who are in complete control of their zippers. No one holds a gun to their heads and makes them open their flies.

You and I both know about the universal rule in baseball: We don't tell one another what we have heard or seen. But, if you are really clever, you can trick someone into telling you what you want to know. But you have to know how to listen real good. All you do is say to someone you suspect might have some inside information, "You know, I think my husband is fooling around, but I'm not sure. I know I could deal with it a lot better if I only knew the truth." If the other wife is certain that your husband is innocent of the charges, she will quickly come to his defense. If she doesn't know anything one way or the other, she'll reply something like, "I haven't heard anything." And if she is reasonably certain that he's guilty, she'll turn her eyes away and be as quiet as a mouse. That silence is as good as a verbal affirmation.

I've always found this code of silence to be very interesting. Any woman who has made it her business to inform another wife about her husband's indiscretion is not only scorned by the players (you'd expect them to be upset), but the wives don't treat her very gently either. Somehow, the fact that the guy is screwing around is ignored. You see, tattling is worse than free-fucking the world.

Sometimes a gradual awakening takes place to first-stage wives. Sometimes it happens all too abruptly. I know of all kinds of wives who have unpacked their husbands' suitcases or cleaned out the pockets of their sports coats and found a jagged piece of paper with a girl's name and telephone number scribbled on it. Wives have found entire address books full of girls' names, all of them written in their husband's handwriting. And he'll contend, "Those girls' numbers don't belong to me. I'm just keeping them for one of the other players." The fact that the other player may be thousands of miles away and on a different team for two years doesn't matter one bit. He'll say that the guy calls him up long distance if he wants to know a telephone number. When I was thinking about a title for my book, one that occurred to me was *It's Not My Telephone Number, Honey.* I felt that most wives would understand its significance immediately.

I don't think very many people like to be lied to. But sometimes people ask questions that are impossible to answer truthfully. For instance, suppose a wife asks her husband about that piece of paper with the girl's name and telephone number on it. What's he going to say? You can bet your sweet bippy he's not going to tell her, "Well, after the game, I was feeling bored, so I went down to the hotel bar. While I was there, this real knockout of a broad came over and started

140

talking to me. After a couple of drinks, I suggested we go to my room and watch some television, and after we got there, I screwed her until she was so weak she could hardly walk." Anytime someone thinks the ramifications from telling the truth will be negative, they'll lie. We learn that as very small children.

The problem is, of course, that once you've told one lie, the chances are you'll have to tell another to cover up the first. And conversations will be very strained if you're continually on guard for fear of inadvertently leaking your deception. And what is the wife apt to do? If she suspects that she hasn't gotten the truth, she'll likely ask some more "lie questions" until eventually she and her husband are involved in their own little Watergate.

And, you know, those lies start to eat at you like cancer. You begin to think things like, "If he lied about this, what else has he lied about?" And it doesn't take long before you doubt everything that is told to you, including "I love you."

Obviously, what we have here is the old chicken/egg problem. The women say that, if the men didn't bullshit them, they wouldn't ask those "lie questions," and the men contend that the women start the cycle.

Sometimes a wife gets her education in a more painful way than finding a phone number on a piece of paper. Once, when we were in the minor leagues, several of the wives decided they would drive to a nearby city and watch their husbands play in the game that night. And they left early enough in the day so they would be able to see them before the game. For one of the girls, it turned into a real surprise party because, when she got to her husband's hotel room, he was in bed with another woman. I've always been amazed that he didn't say, "This girl doesn't really belong to me. I'm only keeping her for one of the other guys."

Some of the women I've known have had an incredible ability to be "true believers." They've taken all kinds of bumps on the head and never even complained of a headache. I don't know if they consciously make the decision to ignore it, if it's a defense mechanism, or if they are just trusting and naïve.

It's my feeling that an awful lot of stage-one women walk an emotional tightrope. Sometimes it doesn't take much to make her lose her balance and fall over the edge into stage two. Sometimes the swamp salesman comes to call one too many times.

And when they do fall, they do one of two things. The really unfortunate ones stay trapped in stage two. They never recover from the shock and can't accept their husband's behavior. Their suspicions and jealousies make them miserable. Fortunately, I haven't seen too many women like this. Most either keep the faith or move on to stage three.

I've termed this the "realism" stage. Stage-three women recognize that their husbands' flings on the road are no reflection on them. They see it for what it is. Entertainment. However, they also throw their charm bracelets in a drawer.

The thing I like most about stage-three wives is their sense of humor. If you can ever get one of them to talk about the topic, the laughs are plentiful. They talk about the hazards of going on road trips with their husbands. Some of the things you come to expect are (1) your husband will always sleep by the telephone, even if it means sleeping on the side of the bed you usually occupy, (2) he'll put a "hold" on all calls, (3) and you'll get severely bruised by the rush for the phone if he by some freak chance forgets to take the side of the bed by the telephone.

A good friend of mine from Michigan asked me if Mike had ever tipped his hat to me from the dugout. I told her I didn't think so. She said, "Mine did. I thought it was such a nice thing to do. Then I looked behind me and four other women were waving at him, too."

I've never told Mike about the time I answered the phone and some sweet young thing asked to speak to him. I said to the girl, "I'm sorry, dear, but he has his legal pussy along on this trip. But he'll be back through here in September; why don't you give him a call then?"

One of my friends came up with what I think is the all-time great name for Camp Annies. I'd like to give her credit but I'm not sure she would appreciate it. She calls them "Come Garglers." Believe me, she got a lot of laughs when she came up with that one.

Of course, stage-three wives don't always smile. A good friend of mine went on a road trip with her husband, and while he was in the bathroom showering, she went to his briefcase to get a pen. Lo and behold, what did she find but her husband's address book. Not the one that contained the "legit" numbers but the "other" one.

She told me, "I was sitting on the edge of the bed paging through it. It was fascinating reading. Not only were there names, addresses, and telephone numbers, but there were descriptions beside each name. Stuff like 'good blow job.' I was still looking through his book when he came out of the bathroom. He was furious with me for having found it. He said to me, 'She who seeks shall find.' All he could talk about was what a terrible person I was for rifling through his briefcase."

"Well, what did you do?" I asked.

She replied, "I packed my suitcase and split."

"Why? You knew all along that whenever you weren't around he had someone on the side." (If I had been really clever, I would have said "on the back.")

"Well, I can accept his screwing around; that I understood," she said. "But I wasn't about to take that 'she who seeks shall find' shit."

And therein lies the problem for stage-three wives. The shit. You can't buy a bunch of swampland and try to build a sturdy house on it. The foundation just won't hold.

When Mike signed his contract with the Dodgers in 1975, there was a provision in it that they would try to get water beds for him in as many hotels as possible. Water beds were just getting popular at the time, and, of course, the rumor was that sex was even better on a water bed. Joe Falls, who wrote for the *Detroit Free Press* at the time, came down to East Lansing to interview Mike. When Mike left the room, Joe turned to me and asked how I felt about his having the water bed. Apparently, he thought I should be upset. How many times have you heard reporters ask wives how they feel about their husbands being on the road all alone. It's always amused me that it never occurs to anyone that while the guys are on the road, the wives are home by themselves. All alone. Just once I would like to have a reporter ask a ballplayer, "Do you worry about what your wife is doing while you're gone?"

If they don't, maybe they should. I'm thinking of heading a movement to stop taking the double standard standing up! I'm going to call the organization "Pussy Power." I'm convinced that's what rules the world. Most problems are caused by too much pussy, too little pussy, giving it to the wrong person, or giving it to the right person but for the wrong reason.

Better yet, let's legalize sex. After all, it is a biological function, just like the need to sleep and eat. Right? Well, do you hear anyone objecting to people eating in different restaurants now and then?

Well, what do you think? A friend of mine read this and suggested that I should be worried about the way my mind operates.

Fondly,
NANCY

Knoxville, Tennessee
DEAR NANCY,   May 1977

Enjoyed your stages chapter and can't wait to read the rest of your book. Thank goodness I've never found a little black book. Jim did

143

tell me about the time he opened his hotel room door and found a naked "Annie" in his bed with a rose in her teeth. He asked her to leave; I hope he walked out until she did. In fact, I hope your stages are only 75 percent true; otherwise, it's too depressing. Since I'm basically an optimist, I'll hope it never includes me.

Speaking of optimistic: After calling everyone in the baseball world, Jim was able to get a chance for a comeback with the White Sox, thanks to Bill Veeck. We had many long discussions on how this would affect the family and our lives and decided to go for it.

Jim and I agreed that we wouldn't let our separations be for more than a couple of weeks; I'd go visit him or vice versa. I even went to spring training twice, once with the children and once alone. We really enjoyed Sarasota; it's my favorite of our Florida spring training cities. It was also a treat meeting Bill Veeck. Believe it or not, he would sprawl in the grass to watch the games and stub cigarettes out on his wooden leg. My type of baseball executive!

Originally, we agreed that the children would finish school in Englewood, but Jim wanted us to join him earlier so we transferred them to school in Knoxville, the White Sox AA town. Dave stayed with our neighbors, the Leviens, till he finished his hockey tournament.

Jim was mad at me when he called and wanted us to come earlier although I pointed out the problems of moving early. He called me a "downer" (that hurt) but called later and asked me to come alone and we'd work things out. So I joined him, and we found an apartment and rented furniture, etc.

I farmed out my plants to four different people, cleaned out the closets and drawers in the hope that the realtors could rent the house, packed, and left. Nancy Smith was a true friend and drove down with us. We also brought the dog and cat.

We arrived to find dirty dishes in the sink, clothes on door knobs, bed unmade, etc. No wonder he missed me. I think he also missed my cooking. (We had been seeing a nutritionist and are eating healthy foods—no sugar, lots of vegetables.) Now I pack Jim lunches for the doubleheaders. Reminds me of his last year as a Yankee, when I did the same thing—anything to help give him an edge.

On Mother's Day, Jim apologized for my gifts—a mop, a broom, and a good-bye kiss. Welcome back to baseball! One cute thing. We lost three straight games to Jacksonville, and Laurie asked, "Do we have to play this team till we beat them?"

Transferring the kids wasn't too bad. The main problem was that every wife I listed for an emergency phone number at the school was released or called up to AAA. I had to change three times.

144

I feel so old; these wives are kids. But it's a good group, and for the first time we're in an apartment complex where a bunch of other players stay. We're staying here partly for economical reasons and partly because there weren't a lot of rentals to choose from. It's nice and low-key here; many of the wives are into crafts, and we all take our needlework to the ball park. Also, a lot of the girls and guys come to me for advice—on making a roast—or to borrow something. It's not so bad being a thirty-seven-year-old "housemother."

I guess I remembered pretty well what to take; so far, it seems that no major item was forgotten. I brought my sewing machine and have been making a lot of things for Laurie and me. Am also making a quilt for Jim and me, with a *B* embroidered in the middle.

Financially, we're hurting. The owner of the team was going to give us a loan, but he backed out at the last minute. We're going to sell our lake place. I hate to give it up, but it's necessary so that Jim can continue to play. I think now that Jim might wish we had saved some money and not bought everything we did or put so much into the house. But then again, maybe not—he is a live-for-the-moment man.

There was an interesting article on why players can't quit, by John Jansonne in *Newsday* last month. It quoted Dr. Bruce Ogilvie, a psychologist who studies athletics, "Very few areas of life have the ego stroking you get in sports—the charge of 65,000 people rewarding your effort with applause. There's nothing more addictive in the world than hand-clapping. . . . these men have enormous egos. Enormous egos. How do you step down comfortably from that pedestal?" Boy, does that hit home!

Jim was also quoted in the article, he said how the personal test has its lure. Also, mentions that for an athlete to retire, it's not retiring from a job. It's retiring from life.

Robin Roberts was also quoted and mentioned how hard it was to give up the thrill created by pressure: "It's so much a part of your life." The article was really well done. It reinforced my feelings on why it's important that I cooperate in every way to give Jim this chance.

Nobody ever said being married to an athlete was easy. You know what bothers me the most? The old knots in the pit of my stomach when he's in a jam. And since he isn't doing that well, I have a lot of knots.

Hope you have a knot-free year.

Best,
BOBBIE

DEAR NANCY,

What a hectic month! After Jim was released from Knoxville, he was able to hook up with Durango, a team in the Mexican League. I stayed till the kids finished school, then loaded up all our belongings and drove home to New Jersey. Two trunks fit on top of the wagon so the dog had some room in back.

The first day the dog threw up and the kids fought, but we stopped at the lovely Biltmore mansion and that helped compensate. In fact, the whole drive through the Smokies would have been lovely if I could have shut my ears.

The second day we stopped at Monticello, and the kids actually enjoyed themselves and were a bit better travelers. The last day it rained, but we stopped at Gettysburg anyway.

We arrived home, in the rain, around five-thirty Thursday. Jim called around six and said he missed us and wanted us to fly down to Mexico City Friday night. The team was going to be there for a few days, and we could be together. I said I couldn't make it that fast, so we agreed on Saturday morning.

So, in thirty-six hours, we were there. I'm still not sure how I unpacked, laundered, repacked, spent a half day at the Mexican consulate getting a visa for the cat, plus getting papers from our lawyer giving one parent permission to take the kids out of the country, Dave's naturalization papers, finding a place for the dog, taking care of financial matters, etc. You know how it is—somehow we do it.

It was worth it because Jim had a bouquet of forget-me-nots with a love note waiting in the hotel room. He also took the pillows, which were like rocks, out of the cases and stuffed them with underwear. He gave me the T-shirts, and he took the socks.

Unfortunately, what we really needed was cat litter. You can't buy it in Mexico City, so I had to scoop sand from the big metal ashtrays in the hotel halls. Sorting out the butts wasn't bad, but people spit in them, too!

After a few days in Mexico City sightseeing and watching ball games, we flew to Durango. It's a lovely town but not what one would call a tourist area. I don't mind not having a car or phone, but I sure miss having a Laundromat! We have a scrub board and a deal whereby the kids each wash two things per night. I do the rest, including Jim's baseball stuff. We keep a clothesline in the shower and front window (goes with the typical rental decor). You can get all over town by bus for about eight cents. These buses are something else. I think they ship down school buses that have been used by rowdy kids for twenty years. But you can't beat the price.

A special bus picks up the players and takes them to the park. Families can ride with the players, and that's fun. They don't have showers at the stadium, so the players ride back and forth in their uniforms and shower at home. The ride home is not Chanel No. 5.

This is really a great experience for the children. They have made friends, and they play games and get by with a little Spanish. We go shopping together, and it's a real learning experience. There are unrecognizable cuts of meat, but with our high school Spanish and a dictionary we do okay.

The athletes in Mexico are really idolized. The mob scene here is like Yankee Stadium minus the guards. The crowds at the game are so enthusiastic—yelling at every pitch and whistling if they're unhappy. It's exciting, probably similar to U.S. baseball in the early years.

It was strange seeing Jim in a green and gold uniform and white shoes. For his first game they had to paint his spikes, since he had only black ones. The team is the *Alacranes* (Scorpions). I think this is the scorpion capital of the world. A wife told me she killed one in her shower the other day. Thank goodness we're on the third floor.

Jim has been pitching well but is weak from a bad case of *tourista.* The kids and I have had it on and off but, knock on wood, not too bad. Laurie did get sick with a 104-degree fever when Jim was on the road. I took her to the hotel, where there is a movie company, filming *Dog Soldiers* with Michael Moriarty, Nick Nolte, and Tuesday Weld, and got help there in finding a doctor to see her.

We've also had the chance to watch some of the filming and meet the crew. I really think Moriarty is nice. We talked about his grandfather, who played for the Detroit Tigers (my team). He lent our Michael his jacket when he saw him shiver, and I watched him get a chair for an old man. Also enjoyed talking to Nolte about *North Dallas Forty.* He wants to film it. I think it will be tough but worth a try. Anthony Zerbe, a supporting actor you've seen many times, was especially nice in buying books for the kids when he went to Mexico City. We die for any reading material here. When anyone from the movie crew goes to the States, they get a list of stuff to bring back for everyone, things it's tough to live without, like Oreo cookies, Reese's peanut butter cups, and a current newspaper!

All in all I think it's a terrific experience for all of us. Jim is happy, except that he says the team eats at places he wouldn't stop in to go to the bathroom.

The whole pace of living is different here, and it's really a lovely area—surrounded by mountains and parks. It's especially pleasant on Sunday. First you hear the church bells; then it's the first game of a doubleheader, then across town to a bullfight, then the second baseball game, next eating out where you hear someone playing guitar, finally walking home under a million stars.

Since the only news we get is ancient, let me know how you are doing. Hope this gets to you. We laugh because the Mexican airmail stamp has a picture of a bicycle on it. Hi to Mike and the girls.

Best,

BOBBIE

We didn't have any pets until Jim retired from baseball in 1970. It would have been too difficult traveling with a dog or cat. Many landlords didn't want to take three children. If you talked them into allowing three kids and then tried to include a pet—forget it!

Appropriately, our cat was named Columbus, and he traveled everywhere with us. He really was a great cat. Once he was almost left behind in Portland when we were all packed and ready to leave for the plane —no pussycat. We searched everywhere, then canceled our flight and made reservations for the next day. Twenty minutes later, we found him checking out the neighborhood, rushed to the airport, and caught our original flight.

In Mexico you couldn't carry a cat on local flights. We put ours in a plastic carrier that looked like a record player, covered it with a pillow case, and had one of the kids carry it. Fortunately no one questioned us.

Jim started being allergic to Columbus, nicknamed Tiger, shortly before he made his comeback. Michael, who loved the cat as much as anyone, also started having the same reactions. At one point, I remember Jim saying it was either him or the cat. The kids were so upset that we just arranged to keep him out of our bedroom. By then we also had a dog, which didn't seem to bother Jim or Michael.

During the summer of 1978, I was afraid we'd have to give the cat away because Jim's asthma was worse than ever. Later, I was glad we still had the cat because I'm sure the stress Jim was under keeping his affair secret was the main cause for the breathing problems, not the cat.

We had Columbus for about ten years, and when he died of a virus in early 1982, it was a hard blow. Laurie's boyfriend promptly presented her with a tiger kitten. Princess is turning out to be as affectionate as Columbus, but she can never truly replace him.

B.B.

DEAR BOBBIE,

Another summer, another port of call. Arlington, Texas, is definitely not the place to be in the summertime. We rented a house from a man who coaches in the Ranger farm system. I thought I would miss not being in an apartment complex that had a pool but found out very quickly that it's too hot here even to go swimming. It's another summer of sitting around with not much to do.

Actually, this has been a two-stop summer. Mike started the season in Atlanta. For the first few weeks of the season, I was taking classes at Michigan State and commuting to Atlanta at the same time. As soon as my morning class on Thursday was over, I'd fly to Atlanta, stay until Sunday, and go back to Michigan. From Sunday night until Thursday morning, I got the household chores finished, took care of the girls, and did my homework for the entire week.

I know you've probably gotten bits and pieces in my recent letters to indicate that things are not going well with Mike and me. I haven't talked to anybody about our problems, including Mike. Oh, I tried a couple of times but never seemed to get anywhere, so eventually I just shut up and withdrew.

Early this year, Mike and I had reached a point where we were just coexisting. Finally, one morning Mike started talking to me about our problems. I've known for a long time that Mike has been seeing other women, and Mike has been equally aware that for the last couple of years I haven't been the epitome of the faithful wife. Mike wasn't nearly as good at ignoring it as I was. We spent three days leveling with each other about how we had been leading our lives and how we felt about our marriage. Mike said he could take any kind of lifestyle but couldn't stand not knowing if, when I said I was going to class, that was really where I was going. We agreed that from that point on we would be open and honest with each other.

I saw this as a chance to start fresh and was determined to spend as much time with him as possible. It seemed like a good chance to be alone and get to know each other again. We've drifted so far apart.

It was a physically exhausting schedule, and sometime when I got back to East Lansing on Sunday my spirits would be really low. That's when I seemed to slip back into my negative thoughts.

One Sunday when I walked into the house, a girl whom Mike had been involved with for a couple of years was there. She had borrowed Mike's drill and was returning it. The thought that came into my mind was, "Will this girl never stop borrowing tools from my house?" I had just enough energy to keep from saying it.

It was Mike's decision to quit playing in Atlanta. He had major back surgery in January for a herniated disc and, by all rights, shouldn't have been able to pitch at all. But Mike knows more about conditioning and rehabilitating muscles than anyone I know, so he practically performed a miracle by being ready to start the season. Still, he had a long way to go before he'd be back to 100 percent effectiveness.

Mike kept asking the manager, Dave Bristol, to put him into games that they were losing so that he could get as much work as possible. Bristol ignored the request. Mike got more and more frustrated, and finally, in a game against the Dodgers, he lost his cool. When Dave removed him from the game, Mike threw all the bats from the rack onto the field.

I was waiting for Mike in the tunnel under Atlanta Stadium, and when he came out of the clubhouse, I asked, "Do you have your bags packed?"

He answered, "I'm going to think about it overnight." And he decided to leave. He had worked too hard to be irritated by a manager he just couldn't work with in a decent manner. It meant walking away from $150,000, but that just didn't seem important.

After being home for a couple of weeks, Mike and I met with Eddie Robinson, general manager of the Texas Rangers, when the team was playing in Detroit. Mike pitched some batting practice and eventually signed.

I've been spending most of my spare time working on my book. My baby-sitter, a really super lady who's a bit older than I, read the manuscript (such as it is) and told me she couldn't put it down. She had stayed up until three A.M. reading it. Since she's not a baseball fan, I found that encouraging. Are you still keeping your journal?

I did something rare and went on an extended road trip to California with Mike. We saw our good friends Ron and Cathy Woods in Inglewood. Actually, I planned to spend a few days with them after Mike went on to Oakland. But the season has been difficult, and when it came time for him to leave, he was a bit down psychologically, so I went with him instead.

There was a doubleheader in Anaheim on the last day of the series with the Angels. Since I had to check out of the hotel early, I took a book to the stadium and sat high up in the stands and read. I was rather amused when I felt a tap on my shoulder and the woman who was sitting behind me asked, "Do you belong to one of the players?"

I'm not sure how I felt about admitting I "belonged" to anyone, but since I knew what she meant, I said yes. I guess only someone who has seen one (at least) too many baseball games would read throughout the game.

During the break between the two games, I had a drink with the woman and her husband. I found myself explaining for the umpteenth time what had happened at Michigan State when Mike was charged with trespassing. They kept saying things like, "Why didn't we read that in the papers?" or "We didn't know that's what actually happened." Tell me about it.

Toward the end of the second game, when it looked as if Mike would come in to pitch, I got up and went to the car. I knew there was going to be a lot of negative fan reaction, and, frankly, I wasn't in the mood to listen to the obscenities one more time. I was right, too. The boos made it all the way to the parking lot.

Someday I'd like to figure out why it is that no matter where Mike plays, within a couple of months, the fans are against him. At the end of the season in 1974, although he had pitched superbly, the fans in L.A. booed him on Fan Appreciation Day. Mike doesn't have a lot of charisma—that I know—but that doesn't account for the strength of the fans' dislike.

I feel as if I have come full circle in relating to the other wives on the team. I started out in 1963 with a bunch of young women who were just starting their families. Now in 1977 I'm ending up with a bunch of wives who are just beginning to have their families. These women won't even leave their kids to go out to dinner together. I remember being like that once myself, but that seems light-years ago.

There is one wife who has been around about as long as I have. She found out her husband had another girl living with him before his family joined him for the summer. She threatened to throw the stereo that she was sure belonged to the other woman over the balcony. I suggested she pawn it and pocket the money!

One more term at Michigan State and I will graduate. I can't say I've learned anything that will prepare me to do any job in particular, but it was important for my self-esteem that I finish. The nice part was I met some really good people and had a ball doing it.

One of those people whom I particularly enjoy is Gerald Miller, a professor in the communications department. Gerry has my kind of sense of humor. During a recent lecture he made the statement that any boob could do his job. After hearing that, I drew a picture of a very detailed, sumptuous tit and labeled it "Miller's Replacement."

Since the class lasted three hours, we always took a break. As Gerry walked past me I handed him my artwork. When he came back down the aisle to start the second half of class, he bent down and whispered, "I thought your picture was tit for tat."

Keep in touch.

NANCY

Englewood, New Jersey

DEAR NANCY,   December 1977

I feel as if I've been on a roller-coaster ride this year. Unfortunately, merry-go-rounds are more my speed, and I don't see an end to this topsy-turvy ride.

After Jim was unexpectedly released from Durango on July 4, we returned to New Jersey with about three dollars in our pockets. We spent the money on milk and bread. Then, while Jim called minor league teams, I gritted my teeth and drew the kids' savings out of the bank. Later, we also borrowed on our life insurance to help us through the winter.

We could be sitting pretty from the book and TV show money, but we lost a lot on Baseball Brain, put too much into our Maple Street house, and bought things like a motorboat that we used exactly once. Also, after taxes, agents, and splitting with Lenny Shecter, Jim's partner, there wasn't as much as you'd think.

This summer both the Mecca lake property and this house were on the market, and if we had been able to sell one, we'd have been okay. But, boy, did we scrounge meanwhile. I don't mind scrounging, but I hate being the one stuck with the worry of balancing the money.

In August Jim made a deal to pitch with Portland again. Dave, Laurie, the cat, and I flew out to join him a few weeks later. (Michael went to camp.) It was lovely being in Portland with the May crew again.

This group keeps me in stitches. One game the ump warned them to stop using four-letter words, and if he heard any bad language, he would clear the bench. The rest of the game the poor ump could hardly keep a straight face because the players were yelling, *"poo-poo, ca-ca, doody,"* etc.

This team is so "loose" that I guess nothing they do should surprise me. Except that there was an exhibition game, and Jim warmed up on the sidelines in his underwear and jockstrap and embarrassed us with his lack of decorum.

Before the first game that the pitching coach, Rob Nelson, played, infielder Kurt Russell told him not to worry because he had gone out

152

and bought a new tape measure. Steve Katz, the trainer, also told Rob not to worry about the two umpires who threw players out early: "They suffered from premature evacuation."

Steve helped Jim this summer when he was having trouble with his asthma because of the air-pollution levels. Steve showed Jim how homeopathic remedies work; we were amazed at how quickly Jim felt better. Jim told Steve that if he succeeded in his comeback, he'd become a "religious figure" and help make Steve famous also.

Comeback-wise, things don't look too good because Jim called everyone after the season and couldn't find anyone interested. Finally, we sold the Mecca lake house. (Moving the furniture and cleaning it for the last time, while hiding my tears, was tough.)

With the money left over from paying back loans, we took a trip to the Netherlands to check out the baseball situation over there. As much as I enjoy seeing new places, the trip wasn't as terrific as the scenery. We had an argument in Holland because I told Jim not to say he wasn't interested in making any money playing ball. He conveniently forgets we need money to live and doesn't care as long as he can play ball.

Later in the trip, he got into an argument with a waiter who wouldn't let him take a bottle of soda back to our hotel room. An American tried to explain the rule, but Jim got even madder. When I told Jim that the guy was only trying to help, Jim got furious with me for not supporting him. Our translator shook his head and said that's why we get nicknamed ugly Americans. I was really embarrassed; maybe it was a stupid rule, but the waiter didn't make it.

Perhaps the memories of working my way through college as a waitress returned. It wasn't my fault if the steak was tough; people would either let me know in a nice way or be complete jerks. I had no love lost on the jerks and felt that was exactly how Jim was behaving.

After those blowups, it got better, and we actually had a lovely time until the day we left. This had been a shoestring-budget trip. We flew Laker, and stayed at El Cheapo Hotels. (Seeing Europe on fifteen dollars a day.) We were going home, having spent very little, except that Jim went wild buying clothes in London. He bought several velvet suits, which were nice, but he also got carried away and purchased things he's never worn, like a multiprinted velvet smoking jacket. I reminded him we were trying to cut down expenses, but heard the old "I deserve it" bit. (What you deserve and what you can afford are two different things. I didn't buy anything for myself, except a book for about fifteen dollars.)

What really bothers me is my own reaction to Jim's behavior. Have

I been partially blinded into thinking everything Jim does is fine? Why am I afraid to protest? I'm not sure I can handle this problem right now. I'll just have to be thankful that the problems are few and far between.

Few and far between, like the argument he had with his brother, Bob, a couple of months ago. Jim was telling him to quit his job and try acting if that's what he really wanted. Bob countered that he had responsibilities, but Jim kept at it till Bob and his wife walked out. Later they made up, but it certainly ruined the evening. I kept clear of that one.

I did the same during his next fight. We went to one of Dave's hockey games, and Jim asked a couple next to us not to smoke. (Jim's asthma bothers him in cold places.) I agree that smoking in public places should be banned, but the man politely informed Jim that they enjoyed smoking and Jim could move. They got so heated that the referee stopped the game and asked them to simmer down or leave. Dave and I wanted to hide.

For the next fight, I was right in the middle: We were having a bite to eat with a builder, who suggested we live free in his houses so that he'd get good publicity. The drawback was that we'd have to move every year. Jim was interested, but I certainly wasn't and pointed out the drawbacks. I know about the work involved and don't like losing my roots every year. I pointed out these drawbacks. Jim was really annoyed with me and stormed out. When we got home, he grabbed my arm and slapped me, in front of Laurie. She started crying. (This slap was a first.) He said it shouldn't bother me because I didn't do the moving. He conveniently forgot that we didn't have professional movers when we moved to Englewood. We (mostly me) collected boxes, packed everything, and had two college students do the heavy stuff. Moving from Mecca was worse. I physically helped load heavy stuff, besides cleaning the place. This time we had the help of a friend. Where does he get off—you don't have to move? My back ached for days after both moves, and carrying boxes of books up and down two flights of stairs is not a picnic.

That was the worst argument, but we're still having problems. We bought a smaller house that needs "mucho" work. We're redoing the kitchen and trying to save money by doing most of it ourselves. Sometimes I get depressed, but Bob warned me that remodeling is a strain on a marriage and to try and keep cool.

Right now we're fighting because I won't agree to having the refrigerator seventeen feet across the room from the sink and stove. Jim said I never compromise and don't deserve such a nice house. He's right! I never compromise—I give in, but not this time. Do you know that the only time I remember saying no was the time he was going to buy a child's coffin to use as a coffee table?

I hope we'll sell the Maple Street house soon and that our money problems will be solved. That will help the domestic situation immensely. Also, if Jim can hook up with another baseball club, we'll be sitting pretty. I know these pressures are getting to him, and I try to stay out of his way when he's in a bad temper. The other day he blasted a telephone operator because Ted Turner didn't return his call.

My fingers are crossed that Turner calls and agrees to give Jim a chance. I know this would make things copacetic again.

Hope things are copacetic with you. Your last letter was about as depressing as this one. I understand why you're trying to spend as much time as possible with Mike, but with your school schedule, those trips to Atlanta were above and beyond the call of duty. Take care.

Fondly,
BOBBIE

There was more to the argument of where to place the refrigerator than meets the eye. My rose-colored glasses were slipping, and I wasn't saying yes unilaterally. A big step for me. We had so many arguments about changing things in the house that I used to think of it as "house of hate."

After Jim left it was up to me to make the house comfortable, and I've put a lot of elbow grease into making it a home. Now my kitchen's nice enough to be listed with Great Locations *and has been used for some commercials, including Pepperidge Farm and Lipton.*

B.B.

Eagan, Minnesota
August 1978

DEAR BOBBIE,

This has been a year of change for me, mostly good, I think. First of all, I was graduated from Michigan State last December—with high honors, no less. (Mike was very quick to point out that had they counted my grades from Eastern Michigan, my grade point wouldn't be nearly so impressive!)

I have to share with you one of the last bits of wisdom I picked up by going back to college. One of my last classes was a communications seminar. My friend Gerry Miller was one of the professors in charge

155

of the class, and whenever he wasn't lecturing we sat together in the back of the room. One day Gerry sat at a desk that had some poignant graffiti carved on it and he was conscientious enough to point it out to me. Someone had inscribed the following: "If God didn't want man to eat pussy, why did He shape it like a taco?" Remember Edith Brownstone's advice to her daughter? I say it's just as easy to fall in love with a rich man who likes to eat out and don't forget to make sure he likes Mexican food!

In mid-February my good friend Carol Gallagher called and asked me if I had meant it when I told her I'd like to find a job. I said yes, and she told me about an opening at a travel agency. I made an appointment with the manager. (I did this only after Mike assured me he had no plans to return to baseball again.) When I met with Terry, she was on hold with an airline, and looking over her half-glasses, she said, "I have only one question to ask you. Are you crazy? You have to be crazy to want to work here."

I assured her that I was amply qualified, took off my coat, and started answering the phone. I worked three twelve-hour days and every other Saturday—and loved every minute of it. One of the things that I liked was that Terry didn't tell a soul whom I was married to. It was weeks before I told anyone, and by then the girls I worked with couldn't have cared less.

The women in the office are all a little crazy but also bright and interesting. There was no time to talk babies and diapers. We were too swamped with work. Friday night was always the best time to work; that's when we dipped into the wine fund and had a sip of the grape during the last hour of the day. Occasionally, we all gathered around a table at the nearby lounge and had a drink and laughed until the wee hours of the morning—an act that justifiably did not endear me to Mike.

One of the things travel agents not only get to do but are required to do is go on "fam" trips. "Fam" is short for familiarization. In May, I had my first "road trip"—to Jamaica, for a week. The first five days were filled with seminars and hotel inspections. I hardly had a minute that wasn't planned by the Jamaican tourist board.

However, the last two days were all mine. Originally, I was to spend them in Negril, but I ended up being there only a few hours and in Kingston the rest of the time. I'm not a particularly religious person, but those two days had to be a gift from someone who is looking out for me. I got two days of incredible peace—food for the soul. It actually crossed my mind not to get back on the plane.

I don't know why I believed Mike when he said he was through with baseball. He may never quit. Mike frequently came out to have lunch with me, and usually he had just come from throwing. Day after day, he kept saying, "I can't believe how good I'm throwing."

There were rumors that Pittsburgh was interested in him, but in early May he still didn't seem to have any solid prospects for returning to baseball. I knew Mike would be happy only if he was playing with Gene Mauch as his manager. So one day, after having lunch and listening to how excited Mike was about how he was pitching, I called the Minnesota Twins and asked for Gene Mauch. When Gene answered the phone, I told him how surprised I was to get right through to him. He said, "When you're a clean-living person, you have no reason to hide."

I asked him if he had any use for a short, chunky, right-handed relief pitcher. He quickly answered, "Boy, do I ever!" I didn't know it at the time, but his number-one relief pitcher had a sore arm.

Gene asked, "Is Mike interested in playing again?" I told Gene I was sure he was, and I knew he would be happy playing only for him but that he would never call Gene himself.

Gene said, "Yeah. I know Mike Marshall's pride. I'll call him."

I hated the thought of giving up my job, but I figured that Mike needed to get back into baseball, if for no other reason than to prove to himself he could still pitch. I wanted him to end his career voluntarily, not because of an injury.

After lots of haggling with the Twins' officials, Gene arranged for Mike to meet the team in Chicago to throw batting practice. Mike and I took the train from East Lansing. Seeing Gene in the lobby of the hotel brought back many good feelings. I do care for that man.

Mike threw very well, but the Twins' owner, Calvin Griffith, vetoed the idea of signing him. He said he didn't want a troublemaker on the team. Rod Carew, the Twins' first baseman, publicly blasted the Twins by accusing them of not doing anything to improve the team. We heard that Gene threatened to quit, but that is strictly rumor. We had given up hope when Gene called and told Mike that Calvin had changed his mind.

Mike is incredibly pleased to be back with Gene, and professionally it has been a good season. Personally, it hasn't been so hot. First of all, it meant being a single parent again, and this time I was working full-time besides. Even though the girls are eleven, thirteen, and fifteen now and quite capable of taking care of themselves, I didn't like leaving them alone. On the days that I worked I saved up my breaks and added them to my lunch hour and went home to fix dinner. It still meant the girls were alone for a couple of hours three evenings a week, but I was only ten minutes from home and they kept in touch by phone. Perhaps it was selfish of me but I didn't want to give up my job any sooner than I had to, so I called on the girls to cooperate until we joined Mike for the summer.

We started the summer out horribly, and it hasn't gotten much better since. As soon as the girls were out of school, we headed for Minneapolis. Since the Twins were on a road trip, we met Mike in Chicago. Within hours I was faced with a bit of evidence that our "open-and-honest" agreement wasn't working very well. I packed the girls in the car and drove back to Michigan.

That night Mike called and said he would quit unless I came back, so with a firm knot in my stomach I reloaded the girls in the car and drove back to Chicago the following day. It will be a miracle if the girls survive this without some severe emotional scars. They don't understand what's wrong, and I can't tell them.

I have been totally bored all summer. After working full-time and loving it, sitting around in one more two-bedroom apartment just hasn't been very stimulating. (I figured out the other day that we've been married approximately one hundred and eighty-eight months, and one hundred and forty-one of those we've lived in two-bedroom or less apartments. But who's counting? Me.) Fortunately, my boss (and friend) has assured me that I can come back to work as soon as I get back to Michigan. I can hardly wait.

Mike will be a free agent at the end of the season. For negotiating purposes he's acting as if he'll consider all offers, but he has told Gene he'll be back with the Twins even if it means taking less money. Peace of mind and good working conditions can be worth more than money.

Personally, I think the timing is rotten. For years I've wanted to get out of East Lansing and live in whatever city Mike was playing in. I'm really sick of moving. It appears that Mike will sign a multi-year contract, and since he has finished getting his Ph.D. (some nineteen years after he started school), he'll undoubtedly want to move. Now that I have a job that I enjoy and have settled into the lifestyle of my neighborhood, I don't want to give it all up. I can always find another job, but it takes years to establish the network of friends that I have now. And to think I picked up the phone all by myself and got us back into the rat race. For a recent college graduate, I certainly ain't too smart, am I, lady?

Keep in touch,
NANCY

Part 3

REALITY SETS IN DECEMBER 1978– NOVEMBER 1982

East Lansing, Michigan
December 1978

Promise yourself to be so strong that nothing can disturb your peace of mind.

To talk health, happiness and prosperity to every person you meet.

To make all your friends feel that there is something in them.

To look at the sunny side of everything and make your optimism come true.

To think only of the best, to work only for the best and expect only the best.

To be just as enthusiastic about the success of others as you are about your own.

To forget the mistakes of the past and press on to the greater achievements of the future.

To wear a cheerful countenance at all times and give every living creature you meet a smile.   •

To give so much time to the improvement of yourself that you have no time to criticize others.

To be too large for worry, too noble for anger, too strong for fear and too happy to permit the presence of trouble.

—CHRISTIAN D. LARSON

161

DEAR BOBBIE,

Jim told us of your separation; of course, we were sorry to hear of it. The kind of lives we have led aren't terribly conducive to smooth and peaceful marriages. Although Mike and I are still together, the strains are always with us—at least, they are with me.

I know you may not believe it now, but you'll get through this just fine and probably come out of it in better shape than Jim. Baseball wives are generally a sturdy, solid bunch of women. We're used to change and dealing with stress that a lot of women never encounter. And you've had lots of practice at being alone. That should help.

You're in my thoughts,
NANCY

Englewood, New Jersey
December 1978

DEAR NANCY,

I've saved the card you sent because the words are very meaningful to me, and heavens knows I need to be optimistic. It's extremely hard for me to believe things have turned out this way. If Jim hadn't told you about our separation, I don't know when you would have heard from me, as I can't bring myself to tell anyone. It took me over a week before I could write to my own mother.

In the past, I've prided myself on "hanging in there," but this has got to be the pits. Fortunately, I'm seeing a marriage counselor (in our case, a divorce counselor) twice a week, and she is really helping me.

This past year was a terrible strain. In February, when the kids and I joined Jim in Florida, he told me he liked being alone and would make a good bachelor. Since I'd been knocking myself out fixing up the new house and taking care of the kids by myself, this bothered me more than I could say. I'm sure I cried—probably in the bathroom —it's hard for me to show when I'm upset. I still have that old "hang tough" midwestern background. Even though Jim said he liked being alone, before we left he admitted he loved me and had no desire to go out with others.

Later in March, when I went to Florida alone, he was sweet and said that I was a good person, and, besides loving me, he really liked me. He said we'd work things out; we'd persevere. I said, "I'm good at persevering," I've had to be. After these visits I went home and continued painting, scraping, and spackling the new house. Also, there were the bills to be juggled, and the financial problems kept multiplying. We had buyers for the Maple Street house, but they kept putting off the closing. We were struggling to handle two mortgages

162

and trying to fix up the new house. We bought it because the price was good, partly because it needed a lot of fixing and decorating.

Sometimes I ached so much from working that I couldn't sleep. One night I dozed off, exhausted, and didn't remove my contacts. Since I slept only from one to seven A.M. there wasn't any permanent damage.

Jim finally landed a "job" as batting-practice pitcher for the Braves AAA team in Richmond. He was happy because he could work with Johnny Sain, his former mentor and coach extraordinaire. When I aksed how much he would be paid, he said, "We didn't discuss that." I probably said something that Jim thought of as a downer, but I didn't let him know what I really felt. How could I tell him that I thought he was being irresponsible? He's provided for us so well over the years, but now it's the other extreme. Since I didn't want to upset him, I shouldered the burden again.

Maybe we shouldn't have spent as much money as we did on traveling to be together, but I felt that it was extremely important, both to me and the children. I cut expenses everywhere else I could.

We drove down to Richmond in April. I was beat because the night before, when we were working at the new house, Dave blew the lights and Michael flooded the toilet, which dripped down through the bedroom ceiling. A note in my diary says, "You know it don't come easy." The minute we arrived at the motel, Jim wanted to make love. I was happy that he felt this way, but I wanted to shower and square the kids away first. Jim got mad and ignored me half of the evening. Later, he apologized, but I felt rotten. I could see his point of view; I just wish he could have seen mine.

The next day Michael found some pot in Jim's bag. We discussed it and decided not to tell Jim because we didn't want to bother him. However, later that day, Michael told Jim and he blew up at me because I didn't inform him about finding the pot. Maybe I was wrong, but I was just trying to keep things smooth. That's been my philosophy—keep things smooth—even if you get kicked in the teeth.

These days my therapist is helping me see that it isn't good to keep it all inside, and I have to let people know how I feel more often. She's right; I know there were problems that I just swept under the carpet. (Nowadays no more nice guy.)

Shortly after we returned home from Florida, my grandfather died. I was very fond of Grandpa Mohney and had been especially close to him. My mother was divorced when I was around eleven, and my grandfather was my father figure. He was a terrific gentleman, a retired minister who turned to farming and carpentry. We often corresponded, and I had tried to get home and visit him every year. Feeling as low as I did, his death really hit me like a hammer. Also, I knew it was impossible for me to fly out for the funeral. We just didn't have the money, and we were moving in a week and a half.

When everyone in your family is a pack rat, moving the contents of a twenty-room house is not easy. Every time I went over to work at the new house, I took several boxes in the station wagon. But when I returned to Maple Street, it seemed I hadn't made a dent. The kids and I moved at least sixty boxes of Baseball Brain alone (not to mention all of Jim's fan mail and scripts from TV).

Early in May I was talking to Jim on the phone—probably looking for some encouragement, since I felt so tired and blue. He said he could move out this fall, and I'd have less stuff to worry about. Later, he called and apologized, but this happened so much that my stomach was in constant turmoil.

A few days later, he called and asked me to come to Richmond early. He wanted to make love before his big start against the Atlanta Braves in an exhibition game. He felt it would help him relax before the game. I said there was so much to be done before I could leave, but I'd try. We got there early enough but couldn't find his apartment. I felt so guilty at letting him down.

It turns out he didn't need me anyway, since he pitched beautifully, and Ted Turner promised him a spot on a team somewhere. Turner told Jim they had a lot of good pitchers, but good pitching was like pussy—you could never have enough.

On May 15 the Braves called and offered Jim a spot in Savannah. Jim was upset that it was only AA, but Turner told him that if he did well, they'd bring him right up to the biggies. Jim packed his car and left.

Early in the morning of June first, Jim called and wanted us to fly down to Savannah that night. I busted my tail and made all the arrangements. Later that day, he called and said not to come. When I told him that we would be disappointed and asked why the cancellation, he said, "All you had to do was make a few phone calls."

Not only was I disturbed for myself but for the kids as well. It was like dangling a plum in front of us and then taking it away. Even though he called a couple of days later and apologized, the damage was done.

To make up for the aborted trip, he flew home the following week and surprised us. He stayed only overnight because the following day he had a speaking date. (Thank goodness for the money from these lectures.)

The rest of June was hectic. Dave—a typical fourteen-year-old riding a bike with no hands—was hit by a car—nothing serious, fortunately. Laurie graduated from sixth grade. I found time to make her a dress, and she looked adorable as she accepted all her awards —everything from top athlete and top student to most talkative. I was also able to fix the new house enough to rent it for the summer.

When we arrived in Savannah, Jim was still in the little apartment by the beach. On my last visit I had pointed out to him the sign—NO PETS—and how crowded we'd be; then I had suggested he find another place. But he told me not to worry. Well, it's easy to spot a fifty-five-pound Belgian sheepdog going up and down apartment stairs. We were asked to move.

We wound up moving eight times in two months. From the beach we moved to a house for two weeks—it didn't have air-conditioning, and Sauna-vana (as the players call it) wiped out the kids and me. We had trouble sleeping at night, and we'd go to a movie during the day to cool off. Since Jim was on the road half the time, it didn't bother him much.

The big argument came when we were looking for a place to stay in August. I said, "I have only one prerequisite—A/C." We found a perfect apartment, but when Jim went to pay for it, it wasn't available. He then took another place without consulting me. It was lovely and right on the beach but no A/C. When I hedged, he blew up and said I'd complain if it were the Taj Mahal. Later, during counseling, Eva pointed out that the real reason I was upset wasn't because of the A/C but because I felt he didn't care about us.

Looking back, I realize I should have driven home then and there. I didn't complain about moving eight times and living out of a suitcase with three kids, a dog, and a cat. But I should have reached my limit when Jim told me I made him feel common. He feels he's a thoroughbred, but he can't be with me—I hold him back. I took it! Is lack of backbone contagious?

Because of a combination of things, I didn't leave. I didn't know about the other woman then. I thought the problems were due to the stress of making it back and to the lack of money. I figured we'd work things out in time. When Jim told the kids he might move out in the fall and try a separation, he said we'd have counseling. I remember Michael saying, "You don't argue. Why do you have to separate?" Dave knew parents of friends who separated and worked things out, so he wasn't worried. Laurie was like me; she really didn't believe it would happen.

The main reason for not leaving was that I didn't want to do anything to spoil his comeback. I believed he could make it and wanted to feel that I had not held him back in any way. I wanted to have a clear conscience.

Overall, parts of the summer weren't bad. We had stretches where Jim was almost his old self and we enjoyed each other. And, luckily, I had a terrific aunt and uncle living nearby, with whom we stayed when we didn't have another place. The best times of the summer were when Jim was gone and we stayed in Beaufort. We went crabbing, visited the beautiful beaches, saw the water festival, and had a good time being there. Besides, Charlestown and Savannah are lovely areas and have architecture that knocked me out.

For parts of the summer, Jim was having trouble breathing and kept blaming me. He said, "You don't keep the place clean enough, and we should get rid of the cat." He was also mad because, even though he was pitching well, other pitchers were being called up to Richmond instead of him.

Some days Jim would talk about how, when he made it back, he'd be the *Time* magazine Man of the Year. It seemed to me that his ego was incredible, but I still tried to encourage him without going overboard. I suggested *Sports Illustrated* instead.

He also seemed to me to be trying to regain his youth. He played practical jokes on other players and set off firecrackers under the opposition's bench. He was concerned about his tan and hair coloring; also, smoking pot was new. I really couldn't understand how he had changed so much this year.

During the summer, Rob Nelson from the Mavs visited us. It was good to see him; he's a bright young man. One night he told us about some of his ideas. His best idea is to shred bubble gum and put it in a pouch (like tobacco) and call it major league chew or something like that. He thinks kids will love it. He also has an idea for a batting range that lights up like a pinball machine. Jim liked the bubble gum idea so much that he wanted a part of the action. In fact, that night we wrote a check so that Rob could patent the idea. Hope it's not another Baseball Brain.

The first part of September was tough. We didn't know if and when Jim would be called up. First, Jim wanted us to stay down; then he wanted us to drive home immediately. He said he felt like a bird in a preserve, that I had him tied down. I did have enough nerve to tell him that if he tried 10 percent as hard at our relationship as he does at other things, we'd do great.

While deciding what to do, we stayed with my aunt and uncle again and then at a motel—making a total of ten moves in two and a half months. The kids and I left Savannah on September 6. We drove straight home, but the car wouldn't start in North Carolina and we were late getting to Jersey. We stayed with Jim's folks until our boarder moved out.

Jim was brought up to Atlanta and called to have me tell all our friends and invite them to the game and a big party afterward. He offered to pick up the tab for half of them. (Where he was going to get the money was beyond me.) Most of the people I called couldn't make it, but Jim was confident that hundreds of friends would fly to Atlanta to see him pitch.

The game was on a Sunday and Jim's family and I wanted to fly down Friday, but Jim said he wanted the time to adjust and asked us to come on Saturday instead. We bowed to his wishes, but his brother Bob and his family went on Friday. The real reason, as it turned out, was that Jim didn't want us there so he could have some time with his girlfriend, Paula.

Bob happened to fly on the same plane with Paula. He recognized friends of ours, Pete Golenbock and his girl friend, Rhonda, sitting with her. Bob went over to say hello to Pete and put two and two together. Told me later he was floored. He didn't think it could be serious. She wore a lot of makeup, and was totally impressed by the event.

My mom and sisters and brother-in-law flew in from Michigan. My aunt and uncle drove up from South Carolina. Jim's whole family, Nancy Smith, Kathy (Jim's secretary from CBS), Pete, and Rhonda flew from New York. And the Mavs' Rob Nelson and Steve Katz came all the way from Oregon. Jim paid for all the flights, except the family's.

It was a very confusing time, with me trying to juggle rides and tickets for everyone. In between interviews, Bob and I took the kids to *Six Flags Over Georgia*. That night Jim and I went to Pete's room so that he could interview Jim. It was almost as if I weren't in the room, a nonperson. Rhonda said she was tired and curled up in bed, and Pete and Jim didn't include me in any of their exchange. Even though I had known Pete for a long time and had been in on a fair share of interviews, I felt like the fifth wheel and went back to our room around one. By the time Jim returned to our room, it was so late that we didn't have any time for ourselves. I was quite upset because he had always shared his feelings with me in the past.

The next day, in the big comeback game, Jim pitched well for three innings. It was obvious to me that one of the Dodger hitters was upsetting Jim by taking too much time and arguing with the umpire. I predicted for the *Sports Illustrated* reporter who sat with me that Jim would lose his concentration. He did and was bombed. The party was short because Jim had to catch a team flight. He left when I was looking for Laurie, who had done gymnastics on the field, so I didn't even get a good-bye.

After making it back to the majors, Jim was mad that he wasn't on the cover of *Sports Illustrated*. He also expected all kinds of job offers that didn't materialize. (He at least expected a vitamin commercial.)

The kids and I had barely moved back into the new house when Jim called and wanted me to put it on the market. This was right after I had a call from a sportswriter friend, who tried to warn me about Jim's affair. Instead of putting the house on the market, I looked for a marriage counselor. This doesn't sound like me, not going along with Jim's wishes, but I just didn't have the energy to move again. Also, I was starting to be concerned about my future.

Shortly after the call, Nancy Smith and I made plans for a carefree weekend in her hometown of Cincinnati, which included seeing Jim pitch. After the game we had dinner with Nancy. Then while he walked her to her car, I went to our room and changed into one of his favorite nightgowns. When he came back, he laid the news on me. He said, "You made it easy for me to move out by not putting the house on the market." Then he agreed to go to counseling, but he'd let the counselor know that he didn't want to change. Finally, he confessed that he thought he was in love with another woman he had met last fall. He didn't look at me when he started telling me these things. Later, when I still balked at selling the house, he got mad and did look at me.

I was a mess. I hyperventilated, then shut myself in the bathroom and cried. I curled up, hugged my knees, and rocked myself on the bath mat, slowly letting it all register and trying to understand what had just happened.

I honestly don't know how I was able to spend the rest of the night and fly home with him early the next morning. I certainly didn't sleep; I was stunned. When you trust someone and he pulls the rug out from under you, it's a bad fall. (Jim had received special permission to fly home, since the season wasn't over. I guess everyone knew what was going to happen except me.)

It had only briefly crossed my mind that there might be another woman. This was when I read in the papers that during a road trip Jim had flown to New York. I asked him about this and he claimed he had gone to see a doctor and didn't want to worry me. He swore there wasn't anyone else. (This should have been a clue because I hadn't accused him of anything.) This trip bugged me because he said we couldn't afford to get counseling during the summer and could wait till fall.

Looking back now, more things fall into place. One time I found a Macy's bag in his Richmond room and kidded him about going to New York City. He exploded and was furious with me for the comment. You can also tell by looking at the Master Charge every time she met him on the road. It used to upset me to see thirty dollars for room service when we couldn't pay our insurance bills, but he'd get angry if I said anything.

It's ironic that when a reporter in Savannah asked me if I was worried about other women chasing after Jim, I laughed and said, "No. With all those young bachelors on the team, why would they be after Jim?" It's humiliating to know that the team and everyone else knew but me.

Now I also understand the hotel clerk's expression when I checked in at Atlanta. Surmising that Paula had slept with him in the same bed as I had in Richmond, Savannah, and Atlanta really makes me sick.

Jim told me that her husband saw them together in a restuarant, and that's how he found out about the relationship. He claims her husband shook his hand and wished them well. It turns out that they met at Bloomingdale's (shades of *Unmarried Woman*).

At the counselor's, Jim said that I didn't dress sexy enough for him. It's true he had tried to get me to go braless a couple of years ago, but I wasn't comfortable. I don't think it's a lack of confidence in my body because it's not bad (except that now I'm down to ninety-four pounds from my regular 108). It may be the upbringing; nice girls wouldn't flaunt it. Except that I know some nice women who are sexy dressers, but they're comfortable that way and I'm not. My other main fault was that I didn't keep the house clean enough. I'm sure that he'll come up with more, but should these faults break up a marriage?

We took the children to Eva, the counselor, only once. I'm worried about their reactions to the separation. Michael said he was almost glad it happened because now, for the first time, he had his father. God, how sad. Poor Michael has been dying for attention from Jim for most of his fifteen years, and now that we're separated, Jim is finally spending some time with him. David is very quiet and hostile; Eva pointed out that he had already lost one family. Laurie is visibly the most shaken. In spite of her distress, she has been a real comfort to me, trying to cheer me up. I'm trying for the sake of the kids to keep up a front, but I'm hurting.

After the family session with Eva, she warned me not to push for family counseling. She pointed out that I'm being scapegoated and would be put on the defense even more than I am now. There's no way I can counter what Jim's doing. He's having parties, taking the boys to "Saturday Night Live," and backstage afterward. He's also blasting me in front of the children quite often. When I refused to sign something without letting my lawyer see it first, he called me sick and a liar in front of the boys. When I asked him to get out of my car (we were in Paula's driveway), he wouldn't. I finally got out and started walking. The apology the next day was worthless.

Naturally, the following day, David gave me a hard time and called me "sickie." The manipulation of the boys doesn't end there, unfortunately. I am also being accused of everything from Michael's not doing well in school to the money crisis. Eva says to concentrate on me and tell the boys how I feel and how they hurt me when they call me names. I'm in a tough spot, and it will take a while to get better. Sometimes I think it's a bad dream and hope to wake up.

Jim's family has been terrific. They are as upset as I am and have offered any help they can give. Also, friends who know have been supportive, and this really means a lot to me. I need all the help I can get! Most of them think Jim will eventually return and I should just be patient. (Rob told me it was the first inning and the game wasn't over yet.) As much as I want to believe he'll come back, it's hard to be positive. Was it just a year ago that I received forget-me-nots in Durango?

Laurie and I are going home to Michigan for part of the holidays. I don't think I could handle staying in New Jersey. The boys have plans and will stay with Jim. Keep in touch. How are you doing?

Fondly,
BOBBIE

East Lansing, Michigan
January 1979

DEAR BOBBIE,

After reading your letter, I ended up with an all-too-familiar ache in my stomach. I know you never thought of the possibility that your problems with Jim had anything to do with another woman. It's so easy not to see reality when your world consists primarily of the kitchen. You've had to leap suddenly from stage one to a stage I haven't even thought of yet.

As I'm sure you have guessed, I came upon my theory of the stages from firsthand experience. While I think I have put the on-the-road infidelities in their proper perspective, that hasn't seemed to have helped much in squaring away my own marriage.

One of the things I think you and I both did wrong from day one was to act like puppy dogs at our husbands' feet. They had all the success, all the glory, the notoriety. It was only natural that we fell into the trap of idolizing them much as their fans do.

When I talk with friends about the way Mike and I view our relationship, I use the following analogy: Think of relationships in terms of a wheel. I think that for years Mike was the hub of my wheel and all of my interests were spokes that originated with him. On the other hand, I think I was just a spoke in Mike's wheel, along with his career, his education, and lots of other interests. Frankly, I now think Mike's approach is best.

You, too, have made Jim the hub of your wheel. You're going to have to change all that now, and it isn't going to be easy. It's time to become self-centered, but in a positive way.

I recently saw a photo in the *Sporting News* of a pitcher who had received some award. His wife was in the photo, also. He was looking straight at the camera with a big smile on his face, and she was giving him a big kiss on the cheek. I no doubt overreacted, but I felt like vomiting on the spot. It's not that she shouldn't have been proud, but what was she in the picture for, anyway? It was his accomplishment; she had nothing to do with it. Apparently, her role was to play adoring wife. I wondered at the time if he would have settled for a profile shot of him pecking her on the cheek, if the situation had been reversed. I think there is too fine a line between being supportive and being subservient.

Being married to someone who is very good at what he does and very famous besides makes it easy to sell yourself short. After all, no one applauds when you clean the toilet bowl. You should take an honest look at what you have accomplished, but not by comparing yourself to Jim. Compare yourself to a lot of women you know. You'll see value there that you never recognized. While it's great to have a man in your life who validates you, it's so much better to do it yourself. The trick is to become independent without becoming insensitive and indifferent. Work on getting strong but keep that softness, too, kiddo.

NANCY

DEAR NANCY,

Englewood, New Jersey
March 1, 1979

Recently I reread your chapter on stages; boy you had me nailed as a "true believer" all right. Overall, being in the first stage isn't that bad, that is until you're out of it; then you groan and hate yourself for being so stupid. In my case, it was certainly lovely protection for a long time.

Now that I'm out in the real world and exposed, I have to adapt to a whole new stage. This, I think, is my "transitional period." I have been reading every book on the market that helps you deal with divorce, middle age, being single, teenagers, male menopause, and getting your act together.

One book suggested drawing a picture of a pie and sectioning the pieces where your time goes. See how much time is spent on what you want to do for yourself. Boy, did I realize that my old pie had only a minuscule piece for me.

This is certainly still a time of turmoil for me, but I think I'm going to make it. My weight is now up to ninety-eight! Only ten more pounds to go. I just hope it goes to the right places so that I can fit back into my old clothes.

One of the things some separated women do is to buy a new wardrobe, but I'm not ready for that yet. I have splurged on buying new sheets, a blanket, and a comforter—just didn't want stuff we had shared still on my bed. I'm going to sell the bedroom set, too. It was our first purchase of good furniture, and I don't want the memory.

Taking my memories is the worst thing Jim has done to me. While sorting out some photographs the other day, I realized that I can no longer enjoy thinking about things we did together. Maybe time will change my feelings; they say time heals all wounds, except it's hard to imagine that I'll ever have good feelings for Jim again.

I'm just now getting over feeling that I wanted him to come back. It wouldn't work; there has been too much pain. I could never trust him; for that matter, I will probably have trouble trusting any male.

At least I'm not bitter. I dated a recently separated man who said he was surprised at my not being bitter. What a waste of energy that would be.

My energy is channeled into dealing with the kids and the divorce process. Also, I've been seeing an interesting man. He's an ex-mayor of a neighboring town who made national news a few years back by turning down a bribe. The FBI then wired him to help trap some Mafia members. He's a few years younger than I am and decidedly good-looking. Burt is just what the doctor ordered.

My ego was at rock bottom. After all, being dumped and stomped on can do a number on anyone's head, and I was not an exception. Burt really gave me a much needed pickup; his sense of humor is great, too. We knew each other slightly before Jim left. Burt had known Dave, and we had used his travel agency.

It was sheer luck finding a male friend so soon. My friend, Alice, had taken me to a singles concert in the city: I felt as if I was back in high school. It was so depressing watching the men trying to get up enough nerve to say hello. At least the music was good, and Alice and I had a nice chat. You should probably go alone and force

172

yourself to mingle. It's so rotten knowing that there's no one to go home to.

Fortunately, baseball road trips prepared me for being alone at nights. Pity the poor wife who is thrown into this situation even more unprepared. I've really been doing a lot of work around the house. I guess it's a kind of therapy. What a treat not to have to argue about choosing a color to paint the bathroom or what type of window treatment to use.

Eva is rather pleased with how I'm doing. She is seeing only me now. Jim stopped some time ago. He tried to manipulate her several different times; however, she stood her ground. I felt so good seeing someone not crumble; it gave me hope. He once called her and bawled her out because I left the office smiling.

Jim isn't doing too well. He signed to go back on TV, but he just isn't very good. He always seems uptight and frazzled and doesn't do light pieces anymore. Of course, I know he really wanted to play ball again, but doubt that Paula, who teaches at a local college, would schlepp around the country with him. Also, even though I think joint custody is best, the court could give me full custody if Jim is in Atlanta or faraway.

It's ironic, but Jim called me before the announcement of his signing with CBS. He wanted to coach me on what to say if the papers called. One of the papers already had a little blurb—BOUTON STRIKES OUT—saying that we had separated. Later, I found out that my terrific sportswriting friends had kept the lid on the story because they didn't want me hurt.

Right now, beside the emotional hurt, my mouth is killing me. Braces, can you believe it? As if things aren't bad enough, the dentist told me last year to start getting my teeth straightened or there would be future trouble with my gums. My orthodontist was very understanding and devised a retainer for the top, that can be taken out for a date, but I have railroad tracks on the bottom. Just what any single woman approaching the big four-oh wants.

God, do I hate the legal hassle! I know I'm lucky that my ex-neighbor, Jerry Levien, has taken me under his wing. But just having to try to estimate all my expenses and future ones, and be reasonable and yet not be strapped, is a pain.

Jim is throwing in loving little reminders like, "You don't deserve any luxuries anymore." He told me that I overestimated my contributions to our life together and didn't deserve enough money to continue to live this way. I told him I had weeded the garden and deserved some of the fruits of my labor.

Finally, I'm starting to stand up for myself. Eva helped me realize that things had been fine with Jim until I started to assert myself. Possibly I didn't push too much because I was afraid I'd lose him. Later, I grew uncomfortable being submissive and didn't like being dependent on him. Also, the reason I didn't spend money on myself was because I felt I didn't deserve it, that I was unworthy in some way. It's important to love yourself and remember that it's not bad. In my family, we were raised to think you were conceited to think of yourself. Examples: I never spent more than forty dollars on a dress, even when we could afford it; and I didn't have a cleaning lady at Maple Street in that twenty-room house—dumb, dumb, dumb!

One thing I've got into the habit of doing is raising my arms, like Rocky, after a phone conversation with Jim when I feel that I haven't been intimidated. It just makes me feel good; two can play this game. Just wish it weren't still so much of a game with him. I told him that a book I read said that if one person had to win all the time, a breakdown in communication is the outcome. He said that I always had to win. Well, at least I can joke about it now, and not have the sinking feeling in the pit of my stomach all the time. Now, if I can just hang in there until all this legal stuff is over. . . .

You hang in there too,
BOBBIE

Shorewood, Minnesota
July 1979

DEAR BOBBIE,

As you can see by the new address, I made the decision to move. Mike said he wouldn't play ball anymore unless I did, and I guess I'm not ready to be blamed for the premature end of his career. Frankly, I don't think the move is good for me, but, unfortunately, I'm not the only person I have to think about these days.

We bought a very large but informal house on Lake Minnetonka, which is about thirty miles west of Minneapolis. We are out in the boondocks, which means that I'll play chauffeur a lot, I'm afraid. I've started looking for a job. Now that I've had a taste of life outside of the house, I'm not willing to go back to just cleaning toilet bowls again.

Because Mike was playing ball in Minneapolis, the responsibility of moving fell on the girls and me. He came back to East Lansing one day and packed a lot of his books and tools, but, unfortunately, much of what he packed had to be redone. He put so much in one box that when the movers tried to put the box on the truck, the bottom fell out of it. And he flew home and drove Deborah and Kerry to Minneapolis in my car. (I had driven the Ford up to him earlier in April.) When my boss and good friend, Terry Olson, came to pick Becky and me up to take us to the airport, there was a row of very sad-looking kids sitting on the curb waiting to say good-bye to Becky.

This is a move only Mike and Deborah wanted to make. When Deb found out I was considering a divorce, she told me she would never forgive me if I left Mike. Becky, on the other hand, put her arm around me and said I should do what was good for me. Now if someone could just tell me what that is I would appreciate it.

Just before I left my job, I went on a "fam" trip to Key Biscayne with Terry. Mike has been accusing me of having affairs with everyone from the superintendent of schools to the teenyboppers I went to school with at Michigan State. Well, he doesn't know it, but I finally did spend the night with another man.

Apparently, when Terry and I checked into the hotel, we must have switched room keys, because when Terry's seventy-eight-year-old dad arrived, they gave him a key to my room. It was a bit of a shock to walk in and find a stranger in one of my beds. He had been sick recently, so he was rather drawn and pale. In addition, he was lying there with no shirt on, and his pacemaker was clearly visible.

Since he was all unpacked, he ended up staying with me. That first night I got no sleep at all. Every time he made the slightest sound, I woke up. I was convinced the man was going to have the big one at any minute.

The next night I was in the Delta Airline hospitality suite celebrating their fiftieth anniversary. Since I had been out on the beach and was wet and sandy, I was sitting on the floor trying to hide. I felt a tap on my shoulder and turned to see a very attractive man sitting next to me. He said, "Do you know any good jokes?" Well, he didn't know what he was getting into by tapping me on the shoulder. We told jokes, sat on the beach, and talked until seven in the morning. I figured I wasn't going to get any sleep anyway, so why go back to the room?

I have to tell you what Terry's dad said to me the last morning he was there. Papa-san (my name for him) had arranged to have breakfast on the balcony. As we were getting ready, he said, "Toots, I want you to know I think we could have a good relationship, but I don't move fast with my women." I thought he was really sweet and resisted the urge to tell him that at his age he couldn't afford to take too much time!

As I sit here typing this to you, I'm looking out my picture window. Night after night, we have the most breathtaking sunsets over the lake. Tonight is no exception. There is a hot-air balloon floating silently over the lake. With all this peacefulness around me, why do I have this knot in my stomach?

Take care,
NANCY

Englewood, New Jersey
DEAR NANCY,   October 1, 1979

Thought I'd drop you a line and let you know how things are progressing. Right now the settlement agreement is still up in the air; I've signed, but Jim keeps vacillating. I really wish he had signed because after a year's negotiation, we may have to start from scratch. The reason is that Jim is no longer at CBS. He quit to start his own production company and will sell pieces to TV. There was an article and a poll published in *The Daily News* stating that he was the most disliked sportscaster in New York.

It doesn't surprise me. Back in June, I attended a party where there were a lot of old friends from ABC. Several asked me what had happened to Jim; he seemed lost. I agreed, and at one time since the separation when we were on fairly cordial terms, I had given him the idea for a piece on a university band that performed on skates at hockey games. This is the type of offbeat thing that he would have grabbed at before. This time he got mad at me and said he didn't have to prove himself anymore and had always succeeded at anything he tried—end of conversation.

After the party, I decided to try again. I told him I didn't mean to be critical, but he had done so well before that I felt he should try to bring back some of his old style. He became very defensive and complained about his working conditions. Said he didn't have to prove himself. Truthfully, I'm not even sure why I tried; I guess there's a little spot somewhere that still feels for him. After he split, sort of subconsciously, I think I wanted him to fail, so he would realize what a mistake he'd made. Now that he isn't doing well, I have mixed emotions.

The production company he's setting up should be interesting. Michael said that Jim is broadening his horizons with this new venture, and they're doing it together. (Paula is his producer.)

But then Jim is the leader in everything, from what I'm told. Jim communicated that the reason his family is having trouble adjusting to his new lifestyle is because Jim is a leader, and the other women

176

are afraid their husbands will follow. Jim is not happy that his family continues to be close to me, and even though they have met Paula, they still haven't ended the "mourning period" (Jim's term).

I've met Paula, too—indirectly, of course. Once I dropped off something for the boys, and she was the only one there. My first impression was that she was big—tall—and older than me and dressed to the teeth.

Actually, the first time I saw her was at one of Dave's hockey games. I was watching the game with the Leviens when Michael came in and said, "Mom, I want to warn you, so you can leave, that Dad is bringing Paula." My first response was to leave, and then I got mad and thought, "Why the hell should I leave?"

I thanked Michael and stayed and was grateful that Jerry and Lisa were beside me. I almost gagged at the way Jim helped her up the bleachers. I could rarely recall him giving me a hand, but he held her arm and walked up slowly, step by step, to the top. She was dressed to the max (as Laurie would say). Spiked black boots so she was taller than Jim and a stylish black outfit, not nearly warm enough for a hockey game. Probably that's the reason they left early. I thought to myself, well, if you wanted someone to help call attention to yourself, you got her: definitely traded *Better Homes and Gardens* for *Vogue*.

The boys are now living with Jim and Paula in Teaneck. They usually have dinner with me during the week and stay a day over the weekend. Laurie is with me full-time, except Wednesday dinner when she is at Paula's.

When Jim was renting in Englewood, we tried half and half with the boys, but it was such a hassle. They'd forget something that was at Jim's or vice versa. One day Dave was furious with me when he couldn't find a new tape. He called me every name in the book— "incompetent" was the mildest—and later found it at Jim's and apologized. (I thought of doing a sampler: "I don't need this aggravation.") Jim's brother, Pete, suggested shortening it to "I don't need this shit."

Fortunately, I still see Eva, so she helps me deal with these dilemmas. The main problem now is that since we still haven't signed an agreement, I get called "heartwarming" names like "leech" by my sons. Not too long ago, Michael started in on how I was bleeding Jim, that I was hiding stuff, that Jim showed him a contract for $30,000 that I had refused to sign. When I mentioned that it shouldn't be Michael's concern, he said, "Oh, yes, it is my business. Dad even lets me listen when he talks to the lawyer."

The crowning glory is when I hear: "Paula didn't take any alimony from her husband. Why do you want it from Dad?" They don't realize that Paula has her house and a Ph.D.; that she has been working; and that she received child support from her first husband. I doubt if she asked anything from her second husband. (Also, I agreed to take money as alimony instead of child support to give Jim a tax break.)

I'm starting to look around for a job, and have sent away to have my college transcript evaluated for a teaching certificate. I'd like to go back to school and pick up whatever I need to qualify. It's been hard trying to figure out what to try to do. Certainly, there isn't good money or the chance of meeting eligible men in teaching. However, at this point in my life, I feel it's important to do something that I'd enjoy. My volunteering in the school library for eight years has been a rewarding experience, and I like working with youngsters, so why not continue along these lines?

Marilyn Peterson and Alice are teachers and have encouraged me while warning me about the problems. I've been seeing them both quite often. Alice had had a close relationship with a separated man who just went back to his wife. (She deserves a better deal.) Marilyn is having her ups and downs. We went to a singles bar, and boy was it the pits! It's not that men didn't come over; it's just that we were so out of place and uncomfortable.

Burt and I have changed from dating to being very good friends. We were good for each other for a long time; in fact, we even took David and his buddy, Brad, on a fishing trip in Canada. Burt knew I was unhappy with my relationship with Dave and thought going fishing together would be good for us. It was a terrific trip. I even caught a thirteen-pound pike. I hope that by sharing this experience with David, we can become closer. My counselor has said that he may still blame me for not holding the family together. Also, because of the negative things going on, he hasn't had the perspective or the maturity to see things another way.

My sister Janet and her daughter came out this summer, and we drove back to Michigan together with Laurie. We stayed and visited for a while. It was so good to get back home. My mind is still racing so much that it was good to relax.

Once I returned to New Jersey, it was back to the same old grind —Jim wanting me to sign stuff without my lawyer's approval, telling me I'd better change the gas and electric service to my name because he wasn't responsible, informing me there would be no more money until he had the rolltop desk (my lawyer said not to give it to him). Jim also wanted me to itemize everything I bought for the kids on graph paper, listing color, size, price, and where and when I bought it. I finally told him to get off my back. True, he's paying my expenses, but I have to justify every little thing. When I bought some dishes for twenty dollars, he had a fit. This is one reason I hope to work soon. The lawyer says I have to wait until we sign; still, I hate being so dependent on Jim. I know there's no way I can get a decent job without going back to school, but Jim says I should go to work right now as a clerk.

At least I've had time to get my head back together and organize the house pretty well. Boy, I can understand why they say don't date someone who has just separated. It takes a lot of time to get over the rough spots. Even now, I remember things that were warning signals and feel stupid because I missed them. Even little things like when Jim sent me a check after he made it up to the Braves; the envelope was addressed to Ms. Bobbie Bouton. (It's hard to believe I once devoured Sherlock Holmes.)

Ms. Bobbie Bouton isn't so bad. Except when I tried to change the credit cards to my name. Fortunately, when we moved and changed the address, I signed the forms Barbara A. Bouton, and these charge cards had my name. The other companies wouldn't issue me a card —no credit rating, you have to have a job! Lovely! I've read about this problem, and now it hits home. Maybe I should be bitter, well, not bitter, but definitely teed-off.

As much as I want these credit cards, I hate it when I purchase something and the clerk says, "Bouton? Oh, are you any relation to—?" My head starts shaking no before they get halfway to his name. Once upon a time, I used to enjoy saying yes.

Once upon a time, there used to be a happily married woman who would send wedding gifts with a note that read, "I hope you'll be as happy as we are." I hope I didn't jinx any marriages. I feel a bit guilty about it now. I have a friend who says there must be Jewish blood in me somewhere to feel so much guilt. He says, at least I don't have original guilt, or I wouldn't be able to sleep at night.

When my mother was divorced, I promised myself that my kids wouldn't have to go through that scene. I'd be such a perfect wife that there wouldn't be a chance for a divorce. I failed to live up to my expectations. However, it's not the end of the world, and I can't punish myself forever. I certainly didn't blame my mother. I'll feel a lot better when this settlement is signed. Right now, I feel like Atlas, hoping Hercules will come along soon.

Hope everything is smooth at your house, keep me posted.

Fondly,
BOBBIE

DEAR NANCY,

Hallelujah! Jim signed the agreement on October 30. There was some last-minute negotiating, including Jim wanting Paula to be named as the insurance trustee for the children. (I thought my lawyer would fall over on that one.) Jerry also wanted to delete the section that says if I live with someone, Jim can cut down the money he pays me. I didn't care about that; chances are slim, and none that I'd live with someone anyway. The only thing I didn't get that I really needed were my legal fees. Jim refused to budge on that. He was mad that I had a New York lawyer. It will take me quite a while to square this debt away, even working full-time.

After we signed, I started working in a local book/stationery store to earn some money for Christmas. Now Burt has decided to run for Congress and has asked me to work full-time managing his campaign office. This should be exciting. I'm not sure if it's my thing and I don't have any experience, but Burt says no sweat. He was impressed by some research I did for him, but then research is right up my alley. He has some good people to help, so I can learn from them, and, most important, Burt would be a terrific congressman.

This last week has been nice because my mother, who was widowed this year, and sister Fay came out to visit. I certainly wasn't looking forward to this time because it's tough being single during the holidays. It hurts going shopping and seeing couples hugging and holding hands. Statistics show more suicides by people living alone during the holidays, and I can see why. I miss not having the boys around. Jim wanted them to go to school in Teaneck, and I didn't fight it. They have programs that Englewood doesn't that the boys will enjoy. Also, Michael is rather infatuated with Paula's daughter (a very pretty girl who is also sixteen), and I knew he would choose to stay with Jim and that Dave would follow. Fortunately, I have friends and family besides my kids, and the boys still come over, but not as much as I'd like.

A new friend, Jane, whom I met through Burt, was alone on Christmas, so she came over. We always used to have extra singles at our house during the holidays; now I'm the extra single. *Ugh!*

Thanksgiving wasn't bad. Other new friends—the Woods and Lustbergs—asked me, but I had already accepted an invitation from Burt. It worked out nicely because I had the kids for brunch, then went to Burt's for dinner with his family. Jim's family also made sure I was busy, or I could have joined them.

Having friends that you've made since the separation is important.

It's good not to slip into talking about when you were together with your ex. I met Jean Anne and Arch Lustberg through the kids, and Jean and Charlie Wood through the Lustbergs. They are terrific people. They live nearby, and I've taken to dropping in on both families frequently. (Charlie Wood's stage name is Osgood; you may have heard him on CBS.) Both women are writers and avid readers, and we have many interests in common. It just makes me feel good to know I can make new friends on my own, that they like me for me and not as an extension of a celebrity.

Even though Jim and I have signed, and the weight of the world has been lifted, it's still a pain finalizing things. Jim called and wanted me to clean and organize the garage and basement so that he could come and just pick out what he wanted. I asked him if he wanted it gift-wrapped.

He came, and I was expecting him to help me arrange the garage (I can't lift half the stuff), but he just took mostly tools and said I could have the rest and he wasn't going to help me sort things out. The same in the basement. It will get cleaned out little by little. I'm not looking forward to dividing the artwork, paintings, books, etc.

Jim has also been calling me at work and upsetting me. I asked him to wait till after hours, but he called several times to argue about the kids. It was embarrassing, but the people at the store understood and said, "Tell him off."

He also accused me of controlling his family. Certainly we talk, but controlling six adults—he must be kidding! It seems he wants them to have a big Christmas gathering and all exchange gifts—even adults. The family has never done this—they were never even able to get everyone together until after Christmas—but Jim's pushing and upsetting everyone else's plans.

Social events seem to be very important for Jim now. For Michael's sixteenth birthday, they rented a room at a very nice restaurant overlooking New York City and invited part of the family. For his fifteenth birthday, Dave received a $150 gold chain that I can't help contrast with the hockey stick he received when we were still married.

It seems impossible that Jim's tastes have changed so much. When Michael wanted to buy him a sweater for Christmas, he was instructed to buy only cashmere. Come to think about it—Jim started to get into good clothes a couple of years ago, and now even his jeans have creases. He used to have me patch his favorite stuff, and he enjoyed wearing it around the house. Now you'd never catch him with a patch. Well, I like patches. In fact, I remember that Warren Beatty had patches on his pants at the McGovern get-together. That was terrific, a man worth a mint wearing patches.

Now that you're filled in on the latest here, how are you doing? It was good getting together when you were in town. But after seeing you so animated, it was strange how much you changed when Mike entered the room. You seemed to tighten up, and there was an uncomfortable feeling in the air. That's why I bowed out so quickly. Hope the rest of your trip went well.

Take care of yourself and be in touch,
BOBBIE

The Players Association held their winter meeting in New York in November 1979 and I went along with Mike. While he was in his meetings, Bobbie and I met for lunch and then took in the matinee of "The Most Happy Fella."

It was a strange day in a way. We walked the streets of New York, grabbed an ice cream cone at a small hole-in-the-wall store near Broadway, stood in line at TKTS to get half-price tickets. And all the time we talked about why Bobbie ended up separated and how I probably should be. Even though we were in the middle of hectic, crowded New York City, it was as if no one else existed. We trusted each other with thoughts and feelings that we had never been willing to risk sharing previously.

I remember telling Bobbie that I was continually frustrated because no matter how hard I tried, I never seemed to be able to do enough to please Mike, there was always one more test to pass.

Bobbie observed that all she'd ever wanted to do was be a good mother and wife. She had had no desire to be a career woman and now suddenly she had to switch gears. I told her it was too bad she wasn't married to Mike!

N.M.

Shorewood, Minnesota
DEAR BOBBIE,   April 9, 1980

Good news for the kid! The ice left the lake last week. It's the first time in seventy years that it went out this early. I was also relieved that Minnesota winters are not what the natives would lead you to believe. We didn't have a single snowfall that warranted firing up the John Deere.

I'm in the midst of a new experience. The manager of the travel agency where I work is on maternity leave, so I'm playing surrogate manager for three months. It means working more hours, but I saw it as a good opportunity to see if I like this kind of responsibility. I don't! Managing at this agency means doing a bunch of paperwork and listening to customer complaints all the time. Since the baseball season has started and Mike is on the road half the time, it also means doing two full-time jobs by myself.

Mike is not pleased with my new status. I was hoping he would have a tinge of pride that I was asked to take on this job, but that was not to be. I know it means we don't see each other a lot—I leave before he gets up, and he's at the ball park when I get home. But it is only temporary.

He called me during the last road trip, and after talking for half an hour about how he had pitched that night, I started discussing a problem I was having at the office. It was a recurring dilemma that I didn't seem to be able to solve, and I had talked with him about it before. After just a short time, Mike said to me, "I know you have this on your mind and want to talk about it, but frankly I'm not interested."

After we hung up, I thought about his statement for a long time. I wondered if he thought that I was always interested all those nights he would call and relay every pitch he had thrown for the past week, particularly when he called at two in the morning.

Must be I've had the wrong idea all these years. I figured that if someone you cared about was troubled, you did whatever you could to help them out, including listening to their thoughts. I remember Mary Gosger saying to me one summer in Montreal, "I wish just once when Jim calls he would ask how my day is." Amen.

Ann comes back to work the first of July, and I'm taking the summer off. Much as I like working, I don't think the girls should be home alone when they are out of school.

Last February I escorted a group of one hundred and thirty people to Cancun, Mexico. Once I got there, I didn't have any official responsibilities; I was merely on call, so I had a lot of free time. I had asked Mike if he would like to go with me, but he declined. Turned out there wasn't room on the airplane anyway. He is now accusing me of having an affair while I was there.

The Jim that you describe these days is so unlike my recollection of him. In my memories, I see him with that enchanting, almost boyish smile. It sounds as if he's angry a lot of the time now. After all the years you were together and all the moving around you did so he could do his thing, I can't imagine why he now has such unkind things to say about you.

It's stupid to be angry because he found another woman whom he cares for more than you. Those things happen. However, I can't accept the way he is treating you now. It's hard to understand how the one person who was his good friend for years can suddenly turn into the enemy. People should be able to divorce without slicing each other apart. Haggling over money does rotten things to people, it seems.

A friend of mine, who works in Miami for a cruise ship company, has suggested, that I apply for a district sales rep job that is open. Whoever gets it would be based in Minneapolis but would have to travel a lot. I don't believe I would stand a prayer of getting the job, but I can't even see any sense in applying. Who would take care of the girls when Mike is on the road? When you're not the main bread-winner, there is no such thing as equal opportunity.

Always,
NANCY

Englewood, New Jersey
DEAR NANCY,   May 12, 1980

I don't think being a campaign treasurer and running an office is my thing. Fortunately, Burt's campaign manager, Lew, is Mister Efficiency. His wife, Sylvia, is also a pro at working in politics, so I have great help.

The hours are long, and when you're not used to working outside the home, it's hard to get everything done. Seems as if I never have time to give my house a good cleaning. At least I've used my new-found "assertiveness" and told Burt that Ivy Baker Priest didn't vacuum the oval office (his cleaning lady was ill). We also have a sweetheart of a college worker, Scott. Burt takes all kinds of advantage of him. Several times I've told him to "give him a break." For me, this is a big step!

Much of the work is interesting, but much of it is tedium of the highest level. Addressing mailings is the pits; on the other hand, the telephone poll has been fun. Luckily, Burt's former secretary does much of the typing; however, I always have plenty to do.

After some trepidation, I've started back to school. Signed up for a master's special education class and am enjoying every moment. It was a bit scary going back after almost twenty years; you might have heard my sigh of relief when I discovered that half of the class is around my age.

The professor, Dr. Stoia, really helped my confidence when he told the students he was sorry he didn't have time to read one of the essays to the class because it was a model paper, with excellent analysis. I recognized my cover and almost slid out of my chair. Being in a large class of teachers and doing well meant a lot to me. The kid can do it! Think I'll have a soft spot for Dr. Stoia for sometime. (Although, I must confess, Alice looked the paper over and caught the glaring mistakes.)

Unfortunately, I'm not seeing Eva anymore. Part of the settlement set the limit of visits; however, I felt she had done yeoman work, and it was time to solo. Now I use Alice for outpouring sessions; actually, it's mutual. We ponder such important topics as, "What are the psychological implications of our picking the men we do?"

We also tried the singles concert scene again. This time we had drinks afterward with someone Alice had met before and his friend. The friend was interested in seeing me, but he was in his early thirties and I demurred. It did give my ego a boost that he couldn't believe I had a thirteen-year-old. (Of course, I didn't mention she was the youngest of three.)

Maybe I'm being too narrow-minded about younger men. My mom called and told me that a schoolmate just married a twenty-seven-year-old guy. The time I did go out with a younger man, we were talking about baseball, and he didn't remember Dizzy Trout. I later figured, of course not: When Dizzy finished playing, my date would have been around six years old.

Burt is dating a very young woman, and the other day he told her he had a crick in his neck. He said he felt like Ed Sullivan. "You do know who Ed Sullivan was, don't you? Don't try to lie to me." (I know the feeling and had to laugh.)

It's not that I don't like younger men; I do and I feel a good rapport with them. Scott is my good buddy. The guys on the baseball teams used to come and have a cup of coffee and chat with me even when Jim wasn't home. I even remember an Ingrid Bergman movie when I thought she was foolish in choosing the older man over the younger one.

The Bouton family was dealt another marital misfortune. Jim's brother, Bob, has left his wife, Dee. This was very upsetting to me, particularly since Bob had been so comforting after Jim left. Bob had really been shocked by Jim's behavior and felt that that was the blow that split their close ties. Now it seems he brings a girl friend to Jim's frequently.

Dee is doing quite well; she's going back to school for her master's. She is confident that Bob will come around and has put a rock in the family room and told him she'll be there, like the rock. I don't envy Dee being in limbo and hope things work out.

Somehow I'd expect this situation to happen to an athlete; after all, it's hard for them to avoid the overtures. Let me qualify that: It's not impossible for ballplayers to be the way they expect their wives to be, except that they can be influenced by crowd psychology. You do things in a group that you wouldn't do alone (like businessmen at a convention). But Bob had been honest and loyal; he was approaching forty, too. Did that trigger Jim, too? Can't people try to work things out anymore? Right now I feel for all women and men that get dumped on. Wish I believed in a hereafter where people received their just deserts.

Not that people who aren't getting along should stay together at all costs. It's just that there are right ways and wrong ways to end a relationship, and a person should have the decency to try to empathize with the other partner. There were times in our relationship when Jim would have been a basket case if I had left him. Not that I thought about leaving, but it's true that the blow to his ego would have been fatal. I couldn't have done that to anyone, much less someone I had ever loved. Cripes, I sound like a sentimental fool. Gotta remember to keep looking out for myself.

Boy, if I don't look out for myself, no one will. Lately, David has been complaining about this house. It's too big, you should have a smaller place, one of the reasons I don't like to visit is because this house is big and ugly, etc. He wants me to go and look at some of the houses advertised in the paper. After thanking him for his concern, I tried to explain that financially it wouldn't be a good move. He argued, "Oh, no, I'll show you why it is." Groan. Wouldn't it be nice to be fifteen again, and know all the answers?

Dave also was annoyed when his buddy Brad and I admitted we were lukewarm about the newspaper column that Jim just started writing. Dave said Jim wasn't used to doing short pieces and can't be expected to do a great one every time. We didn't even bring it up; he asked us what we thought. I'm not going to say anything bad about Jim's work, though I won't lie either. Michael is all enthusiastic, says Jim will be like Jimmy Breslin, syndicated all over the states, maybe world. He will never be a Breslin, but he has the potential to do well as a writer.

Laurie complained to me that whenever she visits, Jim spends his time writing and not with her. She calls me a lot from Teaneck when she visits there. I'm glad she stays there sometimes. It's important that she develop a good relationship with Jim. However, I wish he would invite her when he has time to spend with her. My time with her has been cut back so that I feel guilty. Well, I guess she was lucky to have it for so long.

There's that guilt again. Well, I'm working on it. How are you doing?

Keep in touch,
BOBBIE

P.S. Thank Mike for the complimentary tickets he left at Yankee Stadium for the campaign crew.

Shorewood, Minnesota
DEAR BOBBIE,   August 20, 1980

This could be the toughest letter I've ever written to you. So much has happened this summer that I hardly know where to begin. Even more important, I don't know if I can find the right words to describe what I've been thinking and feeling.

I just came back from being in Michigan for two weeks. It was not a pleasure trip. There was so much tension in our house this summer that I finally short-circuited. I woke up early one morning, showered, packed a suitcase, and drove nonstop back to East Lansing. Even though Mike was home all day to take care of the girls, leaving them was hard. Considering my state of mind, it was probably best that I was gone. Going to Michigan really made no sense at all, but I just couldn't stay in the house one minute more.

When I came back, Mike had emptied my desk of all my personal belongings. He also had the girls go through my closet and drawers and told them to take whatever they wanted. It was almost as if I had died.

The Twins released Mike in June, and the parting wasn't pleasant. Mike and Gene Mauch have always been such good friends, but by the time Mike left they weren't even speaking to each other. Mike took a strong stand in the players' fight with the owners over compensation for free agents, and Gene has no use for the Players Association at all. I tried to get Mike to talk to Gene, but he wouldn't. I have such warm feelings for Gene that it hurt to have our families on unpleasant terms. I have no way of knowing, but I suspect that since Gene had fought so hard to get the Twins' owners to let Mike play here, he may now feel that Mike let him down.

We had company for the entire month of July, sometimes as many as nine people at once. Becky was dating a boy whom Mike didn't like, and it seemed as if I was in the middle of that battle all the time.

Mike spent much of the summer secluded in his den. He didn't want to sail with me, didn't want to ride around on the lake in the speedboat either. In early August, after I had been home for a month, one of the girls at the office got sick, so the manager called to see if I could fill in for her. When I told Mike I was going in to work for a couple of days, he hollered, "See, you lied again. You said you wouldn't work this summer." I couldn't see why he cared.

I've thought about what it must have been like for you to hear out of the blue that Jim was leaving. I don't know which is worse: to get dumped on all at once or to pass through the stages bit by bit. I was eight months' pregnant with Kerry when I first knew Mike had been with another woman. I can still recall the pain that I got in my stomach when I found out. At the time, I thought I could just put it out of my mind. In retrospect, I can see that I didn't. I just started a pile of emotional crud, a pile that I'm only now trying to unload.

After that first incident, there followed another and another. While I confronted Mike with the first one, I kept silent about the rest, but I kept adding to my stack of resentment chips, and never let Mike know I was doing it.

And that resentment influenced some decisions I made. Mike wanted more children, and while I halfheartedly agreed, I know I sent the message across loud and clear that I didn't want more. I remember when I was pregnant with Kerry and hurting very badly, I said to myself, "Why should I carry his baby while he's out screwing another woman?"

Why Mike and I ever got together in the first place is a real mystery to me. From day one, we've had a love-hate relationship. Despite the fact that we have very different personalities, I was always attracted to him. After we were married, those differences became even more glaring to me. I'm a very social being; Mike loved to stay home. Throughout our marriage, we've never had a circle of friends whom we've seen on a regular basis. We rarely go out and seldom have anyone to our house. And up until I discovered that Mike was having a gay old time on the road, I accepted our lifestyle. I wasn't nearly as accepting after I realized that Mike was dancing up a storm on the road. Stack on another chip.

Then other problems started to appear, problems totally unrelated to Mike's infidelities, although I'm not sure you can ever separate cause and effect totally. Just because of our lifestyle, I became very independent. I had total responsibility for running the household, caring for the girls, moving from place to place. I started challenging Mike's authority bit by bit. I don't really know if it was because of my independence or because I was subconsciously angry. Maybe both.

I'll give you an example. Remember when I got to Montreal in 1973 and the apartment was a disaster? I didn't tell you the whole story.

Mike was coming in that night. I was to pick him up at the airport at 2:30 A.M. When I mentioned getting a motel room, Sam and Mary Schirelli (my baby-sitter's parents) wouldn't have it. They realized I was exhausted from the long drive. They insisted that we stay with them that night. I didn't hesitate in accepting. I just wasn't up to hunting for a motel room, getting the girls to sleep only to have to wake them up again to go to the airport and then getting them back down again. Instead I set the alarm in Mary and Sam's bedroom, got up by myself, and went to the airport to pick up Mike. When he finally arrived, I told him what the situation was. I still can't believe what happened next.

As best I can recall his words, Mike said, "You know goddamn well I don't want to spend the night at their house. How can you be so fucking stupid? Why didn't you just go to a motel?" He then drove from motel to motel looking for a room. He planned to go back to Sam and Mary's, drag the kids out of the house in the middle of the night, and go to the motel. Since there weren't any rooms available anywhere, we silently drove back to the house. The next morning he sort of grunted hello to everyone, then got everyone dressed and out the door in record speed.

The really terrible part of this story is that the entire time he was hollering at me and dragging me from motel to motel, I sat there. I didn't say a word. Of course, what I should have been saying was, "How could you have signed a lease for an apartment without even seeing the inside of it?" Why didn't you call and check with the woman to make sure everything was still okay before I drove all the way from Michigan?" "Did it never occur to you that I was tired from driving eleven hours with three kids and a cat?" I should have said a lot of things.

Sometime many years after this, Mike and I were recollecting this incident. You know what he said he was thinking that night? He felt I was just toying with him, that I wasn't satisfied with the apartment he rented, but instead had to have something much nicer. I found the thinking incredible. If there is anything I have never been, it is pretentious. I have lived on next to nothing. Each year that we've gone away for the summer, I've taken only what I could get into the trunk of the car or a car-top carrier.

When we finally did move into our apartment the next day, you know what I used as curtains? Sheets. I bought flowered sheets. Good old practical Nancy figured that she could use them afterward. (I still have them, in fact!) Doesn't quite jibe with the demanding shrew that Mike saw me as, does it?

After that night, something clicked inside me. I think the sound I heard was one-too-many resentment chips being added to the stack. Still, I never confronted Mike with any of my thoughts. It never seemed to do any good to try to talk with him; he didn't understand. Now I'm not so sure I even tried.

Add all of this to the fact that Mike was always in the midst of some controversy. (One TV commentator said that Mike could stir up a controversy in an empty room.) The fans in Montreal booed him. The plain truth of the matter was that life was a lot of work and not much fun—that is, not until Mike went on the road. A good friend of mine recently pointed out to me that as long ago as 1973 I would breathe a sigh of relief when Mike left. I realize now that I've always led a Dr. Jekyll and Mr. Hyde existence. I was one person when Mike was home, and another, a much gayer person, when he was out of town.

All of that caught up with me in 1974. After discovering that Mike had another woman at the All-Star game (I used to refer to her as Pretty Polly from Pittsburgh), I kicked my stack of resentment chips over. I put up a total smart-ass front about being left behind. Then, when I learned he was not alone, all I could think of was "Why do I get the work and the responsibility, while another woman gets the good times?" It was at this point that I stepped into stage three. I became very emotionally detached from Mike.

I think I can best demonstrate my frame of mind at that time by telling you a story of something that occurred during the World Series in 1974. JoAnn Wynn (Jim's wife), Brenda Yeager (she was married to Steve at the time), and I were riding on a bus to the last World Series game in Oakland. I started telling them about a friend of mine who had recently called me in the middle of the night. She was crying because she thought her husband had been with another woman while he was out of town for a few days. I was explaining to Jo and Brenda that my friend had trouble understanding why I didn't see what the big deal was. I had said to her that she shouldn't get bent out of shape over a piece of ass that undoubtedly meant next to nothing to her husband.

JoAnn has a slow, lazy way of talking, and she very quietly said, "Doesn't she know it isn't a whole lot different than if he came in his hand?"

I was tough on the surface. But what was going on inside of me was different—there I was really vulnerable. My fragility caught up with me that fall—1974. I went back to East Lansing in early September to put the girls in school. The first night back I met some friends and sat around, talked, listened to music, and drank some wine. Eventually, there was only myself and a man whom Mike and I had become friends with the previous winter. From day one we found our relationship to be very comfortable. Each of us seemed to know what the other was going to say before anyone spoke a word.

I'm sure you've figured out what I'm about to tell you. I ended up spending the night with him. I remember being scared to death and not understanding why I was doing it. I know now that I was incredibly lonely and in need of some emotional support. At no time was there ever a thought of trying to get back at Mike by playing his game. That wasn't what it was about at all.

What has happened since that time has been a horror story. As I relay it to you, keep in mind that I'm telling it in retrospect. Most of the time while it was happening, I had no idea what was going on in my life.

First of all, I have to tell you that my "affair" lasted twenty-four hours. However, we continued to be good friends; in fact, he is still today one of my best friends.

That fall when Mike returned, his behavior toward me went from bad to worse. He was rarely home, and when he was, he locked himself in the study. He flaunted the other woman he was seeing at me. He acted as if he couldn't stand to look at me, let alone touch me. Whenever I tried to talk to him and questioned him about why he was acting the way he was, he would say, "If you don't like my lifestyle, get out." Or, "If you want another man, why don't you just leave?"

I didn't find out for a couple of years that he thought I was having an affair. Obviously, he sensed the good feelings between me and our friend. He was correct in believing something had gone on between us, but he was incorrect in thinking that it had continued. Since that one twenty-four-hour period was long ago put from my mind, it never dawned on me that Mike was convinced I was being unfaithful.

I sort of hung in there as best I could all winter, but as soon as possible I left East Lansing and moved to Los Angeles. Usually I waited until May to take the girls out of school and move to wherever we were that summer. Not that year. I felt I had to get away from that city and try to spend some time just with Mike and see if I couldn't put the pieces back together. Instead, I think I lost some of the pieces permanently.

One afternoon in early May, I was sitting in an auditorium on the campus of UCLA taping a speech that Mike was giving on his kinesiological study of pitching. As I was sitting there, I couldn't help but hear a young lady behind me talking about how wonderful Mike was. She did go on and on. After the speech, Mike, a friend of his, and I were standing in the aisle when this young lady approached us. Mike introduced her to Charlie but apparently forgot I was in the area. It seems that at the end of the 1974 season Mike had helped her with a kinesiology paper. That really struck me as funny. Mike has stead-fastly refused to help any of the students with their research, saying that it was important that they dig the information out on their own.

The next day I began what was to be the start of a long career in detective work. When Mike left for the ball park, I did something I had never done in my life. I searched his briefcase. Laying out in plain sight was his little black address book. I paged through it to see if the girl's name was in it. It wasn't. Then I started looking through the compartments of his briefcase. Zingo! Little green address book with a plethora of ladies' names in it, including several I knew. Searching further, I found hundreds of dollars that he had stashed away.

My immediate reaction was to pack the children up and drive back to Michigan. I called my father and asked if we could stay in his cottage until I could get back in my own home. I had just plain had it. It wasn't as if I hadn't known all along. I was just tired of the duplicity and dishonesty. And I was tired of being accused of some-thing I wasn't doing, particularly in light of the fact that he was doing it a hundred times over. I was plain sick and tired of the double standard he was tossing at me. Looking through the briefcase and finding what I had known all along was just a catalyst to get me off my ass and do something—anything.

When I confronted Mike with what I had found, he denied that the address book was his. He said he was keeping it for another ballplayer. And he maneuvered the conversation to where we were discussing our problems as if they were entirely my fault. I remember sitting on the couch and listening to Mike. I felt as if I were dealing with a mechani-cal man, someone incapable of feeling any warmth and understanding for me.

In retrospect, the best thing I could have done was to pack up and leave. But I didn't. I stayed. And I got harder and harder. I cared less and less. I became more and more sarcastic. Ultimately, I became someone I didn't care about very much.

After this major confrontation, I did try a few times to reconcile our relationship. Later in May, I asked Mike if I could go on the road trip to San Diego with him. I explained that the winter had been really rough and that I wanted to spend some time with him by myself. Also, I wanted to get away from the girls for a couple of days. You know what his answer to me was? "What the hell is wrong with staying home with the girls?"

When the Thursday came for him to leave for San Diego, I dropped him off at the airport. The next day at nine o'clock at night I got on a plane and flew to Las Vegas with a United stewardess that I had met earlier that year. What an incredible weekend I had. I don't think I got more than two hours' sleep at a time. Saturday morning I got up at five in the morning to play tennis with the man who ran the baccarat table at Caesars Palace. That afternoon we met a bunch of people by the pool who were there for a business gathering; we partied with them until four in the morning. In other words, I had one hell of a good time. And I didn't fall into bed with anyone either.

When I got back Sunday night, my baby-sitter informed me that Mike had called Friday night. Thought I would die laughing. You see, Mike never called the first night he was gone. He might call once during the road trip, somewhere in the middle, but never the first night. I had instructed her to tell him she didn't know where I was. And she didn't. I checked in every day to make sure things were okay, but I had decided this was my weekend, and I wasn't going to be interrupted or harassed by anyone.

Sunday night, after the kids were in bed, I went up to Jo Wynn's apartment and was drinking some wine when the phone rang. It was Mike. Was I there? Yes, I was. I told him I would call him when I got back to my apartment. Then I talked to Jo for another hour or so. Calling Mike back was not of tremendous urgency, as far as I was concerned.

I don't remember much of the conversation we had that night. In fact, we talked a couple of times. I think I called him a second time at about four in the morning and let him have some more of my infinite wisdom. The only thing I remember about that conversation was telling him, "You know what, Mike? You still think you're married to a naïve twenty-year-old who has no confidence in herself. Somewhere along the line, I grew up and you missed it." I thought of the line in Lillian Hellman's *Toys in the Attic:* "People change and forget to tell each other."

The rest of the summer I did nothing but play tennis. I'd get up hours before Mike would, leave the house, and come back only a short time before he left for the ball park. I stopped going to the games. I stopped listening to the games. I'll never forget the time Mike called me from San Francisco and asked what I thought about his interview. I said, "What interview?"

He replied: "I was on the pregame interview on television today. Didn't you see it?" He was quite shaken to find that not only had I not seen the interview, but I hadn't seen the game either. I could understand his dismay. This is the girl who used to stay up until three in the morning listening to his games.

That was the summer I also started hitting the streets. I had a baby-sitter more that summer than I had in all the previous years combined. I just went crazy, that's all. I think I knew that the only way I was going to stay within this marriage and survive was to get really tough. I had to get to the point where I didn't give a shit. Of course, I now see that I was caught in a catch twenty-two. If I kept that attitude up, Mike would never cope. If I stayed the soft touch, I'd end up in the funny farm.

When I went back to Michigan in September, I took two changes in direction. One, I went back to school. Somehow I suspected that in a couple of years I would have to get out of this marriage, and I wanted to be able to support myself and the girls. And, if you recall, I started doing telephone sales for my friend who had written and published the sewing book. I sure wasn't about to sit around the house another winter and put up with the total rejection I had experienced the year before. It was a matter of self-preservation. Of course, both actions put another nail in the coffin.

In January of 1976, Ginny and I took her book down to a convention in Miami Beach. Ginny was a marvelous public speaker, but she felt she lacked the ability to communicate one to one. And since a lot of sales are made at the hospitality parties and around the pool, she took me along as social chairman. I don't know how many books we sold, but we worked very hard, and in the process, I had one of the best weeks of my life.

The first night we were there, Ginny and I went to dinner with a man I had met earlier that day at a seminar. Although I was miserable with menstrual cramps, the man had me laughing so hard that I cried through the entire dinner. And it continued that way through most of the week.

One morning at 5:00 A. M. I got up, threw on some jeans, went down to the lobby, and called his room. I pretended to be the hotel operator and informed him that this was his "five o'clock wake-up call." After a few words of protest, he figured out what was going on, threw on some clothes, and we went out on the beach and talked until the sun came up. He didn't know who I was, if I was married, or if I had children. And I knew absolutely nothing about him, other than that I smiled a lot when he was around.

For the next two months he called me once a week and talked to me, never talking about wives, husbands, kids, or problems. Just talking—and laughing.

I began to realize that as much as I still cared for Mike, there was something very important missing in our relationship—companionship. I also realized I liked being someone other than "Mike Marshall's wife."

Eventually, I spent a weekend in the country with this man whom I knew mostly as a voice on the telephone. It was a weekend of total joy. I laughed and played and laughed some more. Now I regret a lot of the things I did in that time period, but to this day I don't regret that friendship.

Maybe I had never been observant before, but all of a sudden I discerned that all kinds of men seemed to find me attractive. I played it pretty straight when Mike was around, but I'm afraid I have to admit that as soon as he would leave town, I was out and about. At times I felt as if I were acting out my own version of *Looking for Mr. Goodbar*. I would stick close to home for weeks at a time. Then the pressure cooker inside me would blow and I'd backslide. If I made a list of all the times I was with another man, it wouldn't be that impressive, and all of this took place over the course of about a year. But by the time I got myself squared away, I had done irreparable harm to our marriage.

Remember, in early 1977, my telling you that Mike and I had talked out our problems and decided that from that point on we would be "open and honest?" That was Mike's idea. He was convinced that every time I left the house I was seeing another man. The truth was that only once did I ever go out with anyone else when Mike was home. His imagination was really working overtime. Finally, he couldn't take it anymore. He told me that he could live with whatever I was doing, but he couldn't live with the suspicion and doubt.

For a while after our conversation, things seemed pretty good. In fact, I felt as if I were on my honeymoon. I don't know when we slid back into our old noncommunicative pattern, but that's what happened. I think Mike expected things to go back to the way they were in the beginning. I'm guessing, but I suspect he thought I would revert back to the little old *haus frau*, and when I didn't, the old suspicion started up again. Or maybe he just got disenchanted. I was so busy going to school and being involved in the girls' school functions, as well as some community activities, that I never noticed Mike was slipping out of my life again.

The worst mistake I made was calling Gene Mauch in 1978. Maybe Mike would have joined another team; I don't know. I do know for sure that I regret his returning to baseball and all its accompanying complications.

When Mike joined the Twins, it had been a year or more since I had even thought about Mike being with anyone but me. It just wasn't something I looked for or concerned myself with, and it wasn't that I suppressed it. I had made the decision to trust him, and I stuck to it. After all he had told me in 1977 about the women in his life, I couldn't see any reason for him to lie to me ever again.

However, just before the girls and I were to leave East Lansing and join Mike for the summer, I learned through a friend that Mike had supposedly told one of his old girl friends that things were back to the way they were prior to our talk in 1977 and that if she wanted to get away for a weekend to just call him. *Ouch!* That one hurt.

Instead of driving straight through to Minnesota, the girls and I were driving to Chicago to spend three days with Mike, then on to Milwaukee to complete the road trip, and then on to Minneapolis for the summer. We arrived in Chicago at about two in the afternoon. Mike greeted me ever so warmly. Of course, I had the question in the back of my mind about Mike's openness and honesty.

When Mike left for the ball park, I turned into Nancy Drew again and hit the briefcase. Once again, we had the case of the "Duplicate Address Books." One for general consumption, with all the legitimate names and numbers in it, and then the really important one. This time he had it all sectioned out by American League cities . . . and in alphabetical order to boot! You know what I did? In between Kansas City and Milwaukee, I inked in LANSING and wrote in my name and telephone number. Then I repacked the car, and the girls and I drove the four hours back to East Lansing.

Mike, of course, was at the game, so he didn't even know I had gone until he came back to the hotel and found the rooms empty. About five minutes after I walked into the house, the phone started ringing. It was Mike.

"Why have you done this?" he asked. "Why are you doing this to me?"

Once again, it was me doing something to him. He certainly had no responsibility. I was being ridiculous. He had just bought the address book to go along with the guys. Bullshit! This was a situation where no matter what he told me, he lost. If he was seeing other women again without telling me, it was Katy-bar-the-door as far as I was concerned. There was no way I would ever trust him again. If he wasn't and was indeed just trying to act like one of the guys, that disgusted me also. Here was a grown man who prided himself on being a freethinker, trying to tell me that he was just "being one of the guys," "playing the game." As far as I was concerned, the game was over.

By the end of the conversation, he was just about in tears. He was going to quit the team and come to Michigan the next day. I remember thinking, "Oh, great. Now he'll blame me for ruining his baseball career." So, once again, I caved in. The next day I threw the girls in the car and drove the four hours back to Chicago. And when I got there, he never mentioned what had happened. It was as if the previous twenty-four hours were nonexistent. That's always been Mike's philosophy: Ignore something, and maybe it will go away.

The entire summer was a disaster. I walked around with a chip on my shoulder most of the time. The apartment didn't have hot water, and I pissed and bitched about that. I missed my job, and, I constantly complained about being bored. In other words, I was a royal pain in the ass.

As always, I returned to Michigan before school started for the girls. But, as I had promised, I flew back to Minneapolis to spend a weekend with Mike. However, I made a very big mistake and flew in a few hours earlier than originally planned.

Originally, I had reservations to leave on Friday morning and return on Sunday. Thursday, at about three in the afternoon, I was just sitting around the travel agency doing nothing. The phones were quiet, and since I hadn't been there all summer, I didn't have a backlog of work to do. So I hustled up to the loft and asked my boss if she cared if I left work. I explained that Mike had the night off, and I thought it would be much nicer to be with him than sit around the office doing nothing. She suggested that I call him and tell I was coming early. I remember saying, "There's no need to do that. It will be a nice surprise. He'll be tickled to think I want to be with him for the extra day."

I reticketed myself, dashed home, called my baby-sitter to come a night early, fixed the girls some supper, packed, and made it to the airport with just ten minutes to spare. When I got to Minneapolis, I hopped on the Marriott bus and rode to the hotel. Mike wasn't in the room, so I got a key from the front desk and went up to the room. Since I hadn't had anything to eat all day, I decided to go downstairs and have some supper. The lights were on in the room, so I figured Mike hadn't gone out for the night.

When I walked into the restaurant, the first thing I saw was Mike and a young lady having dinner. I calmly walked in and sat down at their table. Between wiping the sweat off his brow and stammering, I learned that she was "some doctor's, some doctor's, ahh, this is . . ." Finally, she bailed him out and told me what she did for a living. I never did find out if she had a name. I sat there and put on my "Everything-is-just-fine-because-Mike-and-I-have-this-open-and-honest-relationship" look. I thought I carried it off fairly well, but I lost it when he turned to her and asked if she minded if his wife had dinner with them. I thought the classic line of the evening was when he turned to her and said, "Obviously, I didn't know my wife was coming tonight or I wouldn't have invited you to dinner." He really knows what to say to make everyone feel good, doesn't he?

If Mike had done one of any number of little things, I could have kept up the game. Had he just touched my hand and said he was glad to see me. If, when he followed me out into the hall a few minutes after I arrived, he had said, "Look, I hope you're not upset. I'm just having dinner. I really am glad to see you." If he had given me a kiss on the cheek even. But, instead, he sat with his back turned to me most of the night and put all his efforts into making the girl feel comfortable.

Finally, I couldn't take the mindless chatter anymore (twenty-three-year-olds are not particularly interesting). I had a tremendous headache by this time, so I excused myself and went up to the room. Twenty minutes later, Mike swept in, brushed his teeth, whipped off his clothes, climbed into bed, and, without a single word, started to make love to me. I suppose it was his way of telling me he was glad I was there. You know what thought zipped through my mind? I said to myself, "Well, Nancy, he paid for the girl's dinner and didn't get the piece of ass that goes with it, so you better make sure he gets his money's worth."

I didn't sleep all night. I just lay there and stared into the darkness. The next day Mike didn't say a word about what had happened, and neither did I. By Saturday morning the pain in my stomach was so bad that I could hardly stand up straight. I hadn't eaten anything for about forty-eight hours. Despite what had to be clearly obvious signs to Mike that I was very upset, he continued to say nothing.

Finally, Saturday morning, as Mike was leaving for the ball game, he asked me if I was coming to the game. I said, "No, I don't think so." When he asked me what I was going to do, I answered, "I'm going back to Michigan."

"That's what I was afraid of," he replied. Then and only then did he talk about it at all. He admitted he had handled it terribly and insisted that he would have told me about having dinner with her had I not turned up before he had the chance to do so.

I might have believed it had it not been for one little thing that had to do with the layout of Mike's hotel room. During our week of pouring out our hearts to each other, I asked him how he met girls and within a matter of a few hours talked them into his bed. One of the things he told me was that he would invite them up to his room, and he always made sure he had a bunch of magazines like *Oui, Penthouse, Forum, Playboy,* and *Playgirl* fanned out on the table in the room. Now, normally, Mike is a real slob about these things. When he gets done reading something, he tosses it. He never stacks anything up neatly on the table beside the bed. One of the first things I noticed when I walked into the room that night was the half-moon of magazines spread out ever so neatly on the table. After all that had gone on before this weekend, he expected me to believe that he intended to just have dinner.

I finally said to Mike, "Look, I think it's clear that you and I have different definitions for the words *open and honest*. As far as I'm concerned, our agreement is off. What you do is your business, and the same goes for me. I don't want to hear any more lies."

I'm afraid that all this discussion puts too much emphasis on our extracurricular sex lives. None of that is the real reason this marriage is in trouble—it's only a symptom.

I've tried to sort out the real problems and have come up with several answers. First of all, our society rears men to believe they are superior to women, and we women have bought into that in exchange for being taken care of by men. They are used to being right, to being in control. I don't buy it anymore, and that's a problem.

I believe Mike when he says I wasn't taking care of his physical needs, and that is why he sought out other women. I'm not sure it's a valid reason for risking ruining your marriage, but I do accept the fact that he saw that as a legitimate excuse to behave as he did. And I can believe him when he says he still cared just as much for me as ever.

The problem I have is that he can't, in turn, see that he wasn't fulfilling my emotional needs; consequently, *I* turned to someone else. Just because my need was different doesn't make it any less valid, nor does it make it any more acceptable. Mike's inability to see my point of view is a problem. He doesn't have to agree with it—he just has to recognize it.

When I got back to Michigan after that disastrous trip back to Minneapolis, I took the advice of a dear friend and made an appointment with his psychiatrist. I needed help in understanding what was happening in my life. I wanted to make sure I wasn't short-circuiting. After three sessions, he told me that I was asking him to treat a marriage with only one person attending the sessions. So I asked Mike to go with me. Mike took the approach that he was going for the sole purpose of helping me get myself straightened out. He didn't see that he had any responsibility for the state of our marriage.

During one of our sessions with Arnie, Mike told him that no matter how late it was, I used to always pick him up at the airport when he'd come in from a road trip. But in 1972 I stopped doing that. (Mary Gosger would leave their car at the airport for Jim and Mike to use to get home.) Mike said he felt that meant I didn't love him anymore. Arnie pointed out to him that I could have continued to haul the kids out of bed and pick him up, but that wouldn't have meant I loved him, since I could have done it grudgingly. I don't think Mike saw the point.

When I heard Mike tell that story, I realized that I probably never could convince Mike I loved him. There wasn't enough I could do. Mike may never be able to understand that because I like to be outside of the house working doesn't mean I dislike being with him. It's not a case of liking oranges and therefore not liking apples.

Arnie told me something that gave me some perspective on our problems. He said that Mike and I may as well be speaking two foreign languages to each other. We have entirely different meanings for the same words. So now when I say I've compromised and Mike says I haven't, I realize it's probably because we don't even agree on what the word means. Unfortunately, Arnie didn't give me a solution to the problem.

I put away my roaming shoes quite some time ago, but our problems still persist. Mike wants a wife who is content to be in the kitchen all the time, just waiting for someone in the family to need her. I know that and blatantly refuse to be that woman, so I guess the responsibility for this failing marriage ultimately lies with me.

I frankly don't see much hope for us. Mike doesn't believe he should have to change, and my trust in him is at such a low level that I'm wondering why I should bother to change either. Even more important, I like myself as is and would really like to be cared for as is. I may be asking too much.

Fondly,
NANCY

In trying to explain to close friends why our marriage didn't work, I used to say I changed and Mike didn't. I think the part about Mike not changing is true. He's more mature now and has expanded his interests, but his basic approach to life and his personality are very much the same as when I met him in ninth grade. He was always a strong-willed maverick.

For many years, I don't think I knew who or what I was. I could and would be whatever someone wanted me to be. As I grew more self-confident, I became less willing to wear the mask. I gave the appearance of changing, but in reality I just allowed the real me to stick around for all the world to see.

That was a dirty trick to play on Mike. He thought he had married a girl who would be content to be the adoring wife, who was only happy barefoot and pregnant. I can see all of this clearly now and wish I had been more honest with him and myself, but I refuse to feel guilty about it. Wonder who it was that said, "If God had wanted us to operate on hindsight, he would have put an eyeball in our asshole."

N.M.

DEAR NANCY,

Englewood, New Jersey
September 15, 1980

Just how much is it possible to hide inside? If you don't deserve a medal, I don't know who does. If I had known all along that Jim was fooling around (now I know), it would have been terribly hard to handle. In counseling, I asked him if he had been with other women before (wanted to punish myself, I guess), but he wouldn't say. Maybe I wanted to dislike him even more so that I wouldn't want him back.

I remember once saying to Pete Golenbock that if I knew Jim was being unfaithful, I'd leave. Pete, who was quite taken aback, said, "Why?" I said, "It's a matter of trust, and it wouldn't be the same feeling anymore." But then, after Jim left, I still tried to give him "the talk of my life" to persuade him to return. Now that I have a little perspective, I see that it would be impossible to live with him again.

Keep yourself together as best you can. You should continue seeing the psychiatrist, even if Mike won't cooperate. Jim didn't want to change, but he went to the therapist to help me. After a while I was glad he didn't come because it gave me more time to work on myself. That's what you have to do: Think about yourself!

My situation here has me uptight also. This summer would have been lovely, except that Jim refused to sign some papers for my lawyer the day before I left on a trip back home to Michigan. Said he'd type up his own statement.

It's rather a mess, but Jim wanted to claim all the money he's given me as alimony. I told my lawyer that we should help him out as long as we didn't lose anything. Then Jim started pushing—wanted to claim the car and add an extra one thousand to the cost. Wanted me to pay the income tax and he'd reimburse me. When he wouldn't sign the paper guaranteeing to pay the extra money, my lawyer said no deal.

Jim was really furious; he threatened me with going back to court. He said that my lawyers had fucked up and that I'd pay. Also pointed out that I was an ungrateful bitch and had better agree and say thank you. Later, he mentioned that he was setting up Big League Chew (Jim and Rob formed a corporation and sold the idea), so I'd never see a cent of the money.

This little hassle kept me from completely relaxing on my trip home, but I felt a special closeness for my family. It was as if my feelings had been so wrapped up in Jim before that there wasn't room to spread them around.

Jim and I also divided the artwork in July. I had feelings of trepidation and just knew Jim would try something. We made a list beforehand, and we were choosing from the list when, out of the blue, Jim chose something not on the list. (A stained-glass castle he had made for me.) After catching my breath, I objected. He started getting red, and I wondered why I really wanted it now anyway. This scene would be remembered, and any enjoyment from the castle would be spoiled. So I said, "Take it." The one painting I really hoped to keep that Jim took was one of Mt. Rainier. Some of the prints I chose I'd like to sell or trade for something different. I realized that Jim had chosen almost all of our artwork; only a couple were actually my choices. Not that I disliked his taste; still he always determined the selection.

This lack of confidence in my judgment was my fault. Wanting to please him and not trusting in my own discernment were part of my old problems. Now I trust my taste more but lack the money to buy anything! Thankfully, my new friend, Jean Anne, introduced me to bazaars, and they help stretch my money even further than before. At least you don't have this problem.

Hang in there,
BOBBIE

Englewood, New Jersey
October 1, 1980

DEAR NANCY,

No joy in Mudville here. We almost pulled it off, but Burt lost the election by a narrow margin. Everyone involved in the campaign was drained. I was really pooped, even though this summer I had just relaxed and done a little work on the house. Now I'm taking two classes and doing substitute teaching.

In my last letter, I mentioned that Jim was threatening me with going back to court. Well, my lawyers weren't surprised. It seems that Jim has changed lawyers, and it looks as if he is trying to stick me with the income tax and may take me to court, saying that he was ill-advised by his first lawyer. He had been so worried I'd get a big chunk of his action—and I had worried about being protected if things weren't flourishing—now Jim's hurting financially and I'm protected. Since we negotiated for a year, Jim will have a tough time proving he was ill-advised, especially since his lawyer has a fine reputation.

Maybe I was wrong in not taking a property settlement and choosing alimony over a long period. Not that there was that much cash. I just wanted not to move and to have time to get back on my feet. Now, if Jim doesn't live up to his end of the deal, I'm out everything.

Just the idea of more legal fees and more hassle depresses me. Meanwhile, Dave is on me to get a smaller house again. And Laurie is saying that she'd never take alimony and that Jim is paying me more than he makes.

I'm still stretching my money because Jim says he's not going to give me any more until he gets his income tax returns. Good thing I had a job for six months and have a little left after paying some debts. It sure won't last for long. Hopefully, I'll make some money subbing.

A couple of weeks ago, we visited my soon to be ex-sister-in-law Dee and the kids in Connecticut. She's still in limbo. We went to the beach club, and people were asking, "How's Bob? Haven't seen him lately." She answers that he's been busy. She's keeping the separation under wraps, hoping he'll return soon and that others won't have to know what's been going on. Boy, can I empathize! I even wore my wedding rings for months after Jim left. Just couldn't face taking them off. Putting them in the safety deposit box was quite traumatic. They were made for me by Jim's jewelry instructor at Western Michigan University. I never wanted them removed, even when I was in the delivery room. It's sad, but denying that things have happened won't change them back.

Discussing how vulnerable we are is one of Alice's and my standard philosophical discourses. So far, our only solution is the possibility of being healed by time. Hang in there, Dee and Nancy. Hang in there, Alice and Bobbie. Jeeze, this seems like a soap opera.

How are you doing? You can lie if you want. I'd love to hear some good news.

Best,
BOBBIE

Recently, I read The Cinderella Complex: Women's Hidden Fear of Independence *by Colette Dowling. I felt that she really hit home with the following: "Women don't know it, because just supporting ourselves seems so radical an effort, but hanging in is not, in and of itself, a noble occupation. It is marking time, treading water. Ultimately, 'hanging in'*

*is a retreat from challenge. Women need to do more. We need to find
out what it is we're afraid of, and go beyond."*

*How many times did I say, "I'm hanging in there?" The sad thing
was that, at the time, it seemed a real accomplishment. From now on,
when I talk to friends who need help, I'll tell them onward and upward
—no more of this hanging-in-there crap!*

B.B.

Englewood, New Jersey
DEAR NANCY,   December 23, 1980

First, the good news. My braces are off. Hurrah! There is a retainer
(actually two) to be worn at night, but that's a cinch. What a joy to
have a bagel again and not to worry about chomping on an apple.

It's also good that my psych-testing class is so satisfying. I've been
giving different tests to friends' children and am enjoying this class
thoroughly. My psycholinguistics of reading, on the other hand, is a
bear. Since it's my first reading class, it's like starting with one foot
in a hole, since most of the students are planning to be reading
specialists. It's interesting but tough!

If I knew how to teach reading, it could be helpful now. My
baptism-under-fire started when I got my first subbing job in October.
The job turned out to be six weeks in the fifth grade. Luckily, the
teachers I worked with were great, and they helped me stay afloat.
The whole experience seemed like the last week of the campaign,
really hectic. However, I survived and now sub two or three times a
week.

After twelve more credits and practice teaching, I'll qualify for a
teacher's certificate. Next semester, I'll take the twelve credits and
practice-teach in the fall. I want to be qualified for a job as soon as
possible because things are not going well on the homefront.

Jim hasn't paid me any money since July and he has changed
lawyers again, so it doesn't look good. He wants to go to court and
cut me back. He informed me that maybe he'll prove that I'm an unfit
mom and nuts. I'm trying not to take what he says personally. My
lawyer points out that it's a game. Give me a break!

For Michael's birthday, we had plans to go into the city to see a
play. When I called to finalize the pickup time, Jim blasted me with:
"You're irresponsible—Michael has SATs tomorrow." I argued that
he had been studying all week, I'd have him home by eleven, and a
break wasn't a bad thing. Also, if he felt that way, why didn't he tell
me a week ago? I told him that I was also taking tests and last-minute

cramming wouldn't matter that much. He said, "I'll call you back." Then he okayed it.

Calling me irresponsible in front of the kids wasn't as bad as when he informed Laurie's guidance counselor that I was a bad influence and was trying to keep her a little girl. He said he was engaged to a Ph.D., who was working on the problem. I hit the ceiling.

I worry about switching her—not schoolwise—but it's in the back of my mind that Jim will use it against me, change of circumstance or something, since she stays with him two or three days a week now. She wanted to go to school in Teaneck; the boys and Jim pushed, and I gave in. Now Laurie's not doing well. She had been a top student through sixth grade and made the honor roll once in seventh, but after that her grades went down and her social life went up.

I'm sure one of the reasons Jim accused me of trying to keep her a little girl was because I refused to buy her makeup. Told her she'd have to pay for it herself. Paula was a model and showed her how to use eye shadow, etc., and since I prefer the natural look, especially on a fourteen-year-old, I'm accused of repressing her. Wish I could figure out a nice way to tell her it's too much.

Jim is currently on the outs with his folks. Knowing my family was in Michigan, they had invited me for Christmas. When Jim found out, he was furious. The boys said they wouldn't come because they didn't want to "punish" their dad. When the folks invited me, they also had planned on having the rest of the family another day. But Jim called and vented his anger on them and had his mother so upset that she didn't care if they got together at all.

Can't blame Jim's folks for not wanting to be pushed around; I know the feeling. It turned out that I didn't go to their home and had the kids here Christmas afternoon; Jim had them Christmas Eve. Holidays can be a hassle! Especially when my starter froze and I couldn't drive the boys home. Because of this, the boys called me irresponsible. Wonder where they heard that? (Not from Frank Sinatra.)

I'm still fortunate to have so many good friends looking out for me. Must admit that going to the Woods's over the holidays was a treat. They have four children under six years, and little ones at Christmas are a delight. Now that my nieces and nephews are growing up, it's good to feel like an honorary aunt to other children.

It's really good to have an old friend like you; hope the new year will be the best ever.

> Fondly,
> BOBBIE

Sometimes I despair of ever reaching a safe port in this storm. Things have gone from bad to worse. Thank God, I put some money away for a rainy day because it helped save me from being swamped.

You knew that Jim hasn't given me any money since last summer and that he's contesting the settlement. Well, he filed a motion to require psychiatric examinations for me and Laurie. He states that I caused her emotional harassment and put pressures on her to try to keep her from visiting him. He mentions the warmth and friendship in his house and says, "I am overjoyed that Laurie can spend as much time with us as she does . . . my front door is always open for her to enter." At least, he does point out that he doesn't want to deprive her of my company, and he always wants her to have two parents.

He also expresses "great concern" about Laurie's not always sleeping in her own bed, and he wants this problem investigated. Just seeing how things have been exaggerated against me really hurts. Maybe three or four times I let Laurie sleep in my bed—when she wasn't feeling well and asked if she could stay with me. I know it wouldn't be good to make it a habit and wouldn't want to anyway.

Probably I relied too heavily on Laurie for the first few months after Jim left, but later I almost felt guilty at my relief when he would have the children. Eva and I discussed why Laurie identified with me and how important it was for her to have a good relationship with Jim. I want all my children to have good relationships with the whole family, including Jim.

In order to be able to testify for me, my New York lawyers, Jerry and Bill, arranged for me to have a New Jersey lawyer. This transfer meant filling out more forms. Also, Jim's lawyer requested new information, such things as "Set forth each and every expense you have paid for the benefit of the children during 1981, 1980, and 1979, and the source of each such payment." "Itemize all items of personal property in your possession today, whether to be retained by you or relinquished pursuant to the alleged property settlement agreement." I also went through my diary and every time Jim threatened me or something happened that might be pertinent I pulled out the reference and gave it to the lawyers.

As if this crap wasn't bad enough, wouldn't you know another one of my professors says, "Bouton, are you any relation to . . . ?" I felt like answering, "God, I hope not."

Moneywise, I'm hurting. Except for the sum earmarked to pay my income tax, the money saved from working is gone. My boarder may be leaving, too—rats! Good thing that for Christmas I made many gifts. (Almost "O.D.'d" on elves and scarves.) Also, I just had another garage sale and sold my bedroom set. Since I'm attending school almost full-time (twelve credits), it leaves me only a couple of days to sub, so I've started quilting for a friend. The pay isn't much, but I can make my own hours and it helps me relax.

Since I'm an old pro at juggling the books, the bills get paid, slowly but surely. When I didn't have enough money and the insurance was going to expire, I sent a check minus my signature. By the time they sent it back, I had enough to cover it. Wish my creative juices could be channeled toward school.

Also, wish the kids were more understanding financewise. When I took them out for pizza and asked the price of something, they let me know that they were embarrassed by my asking the cost. They also informed me that they didn't go to pizzerias anymore. They preferred Tavern on the Green or Windows on the World. I told them that I was happy they could afford that, but when they were with me we'd have to keep it under three dollars per person.

Actually, things have been a bit better with the kids. Michael has been stopping to see me more often. He'll come by to watch a hockey game or HBO or listen to music or just chat. This helps pick me up. Michael and I used to do a lot of things together, and I have more interests in common with him than with the other children. I miss the way we used to attend the theater, ballet, or museums. Eva said I should give them time to mature, and they'd come around. One small step.

The other day Michael mentioned that Dave went to Boston with Jim because Jim was passing kidney stones. Once he had passed out in his car, and he wants Dave with him in case he has a problem again. Michael mentioned that they're caused by stress and are very painful. I can guess who's fault this stress is.

Mike also told me that the reason Dave isn't playing hockey this year is because Jim can't afford to pay me and also pay for Dave's hockey. Maybe I would feel guilty about this, but when I took Laurie to the dentist to have some teeth pulled, Jim and Paula came to the office—they were outfitted in the latest. I wore my thirty-five-dollar bazaar coat.

While we were waiting for Laurie, Jim questioned the necessity of current college expenses and whether I really needed to have practice teaching. I should have told him to bug off. Instead, I said I'd check. The agreement says that I receive the grand total of two thousand dollars to apply toward college credits pursuant to a career. Even though I'm attending the cheapest school around, the money is almost gone. Why in the world would I waste it? Why do I still justify things to him?

Socially, I'm not doing very well either. Burt still lifts my spirits when we get together. He says if all the women in the world were drowning, he'd save me. (He's not having any luck meeting anyone either.) With my school and this legal paperwork, I'd have trouble finding time to socialize anyway. Besides, the grapes are probably sour.

Some people do get lucky. Marilyn Peterson just married a terrific guy on Valentine's Day. Hurrah for Marilyn, she deserves a good guy. Now she won't be alone either, becasue her new husband has four children.

Burt's friend George, an Englewood policeman, knows I worry about being alone and has taken to stopping for coffee on his break. He's a real sweetheart, and I feel good knowing that he keeps an eye on me. Right now a little TLC is all I need. As long as I'm wishing, having the court business over would be what I *really* need. My theme song is the same as Annie's: "Tomorrow."

Haven't heard from you in ages—how are you doing?
BOBBIE

Shorewood, Minnesota
DEAR BOBBIE, May 1, 1981

After reading all the tales of your divorce, I've decided it's not fair that you have all the fun, so I'm joining you. I figure I'll capitalize on your experience and expertise.

I don't know why I'm being so flip. There's nothing funny about it. I hate the thought of throwing away the last eighteen years, but things have deteriorated to the point that even if the marriage could be salvaged, the relationship couldn't. Someone recently asked me when our marriage started falling apart. I got a good laugh when I said, "Ninth grade." But I was serious.

Now that we've decided to separate, I've looked back and tried to figure out where things went wrong and what I would do differently. A lot of things have contributed—our contrasting (and frequently conflicting) personalities, our lifestyle, and our immaturity.

I used to be so insecure that instead of confronting Mike with all the things that bothered me through the years, I just stacked up a whole bunch of resentment chips. (I didn't want to rock the boat, or —God forbid—have him accuse me of not supporting him.) Now the only resentment I have is with myself for being such a gutless wonder.

208

It was things like giving up nursing Deborah because Mike wanted supper at the same time that she had to be fed. It was coming home from the hospital after having Becky and finding all of Mike's dirty dishes left in the sink for me to wash—and doing them. It's years of scraping Mike's shit off the toilet bowl—a mess I wouldn't think of leaving for someone else.

After I came back last August from my whacko trip to East Lansing, things sort of stayed at a stalemate until December. Then one day something happened that put me over the edge.

Since Mike resented my working, I rarely brought anything home with me, but I was so swamped with work that this one time I brought a file home. I had the following day off, and since the work load had been so overwhelming at the office, I decided to just crash for the entire day. I sat in the TV room and watched soaps. While I was sitting there, I called Club Med to find out the information I needed for my client and then left a message with his secretary for him to call me. About 4:30 P.M. Bill returned my call. With the phone cradled between my ear and my shoulder, I explained his options to him as I continued to fix supper. Suddenly Mike appeared in the kitchen (the first I had seen of him in four hours) and said very loudly, "Tell him not to call here. This is your day off." I totally lost it at that point. I got off the phone as quickly as I could, found Mike, and asked him who the fuck he thought he was that he could decide whom I talked to. Can you imagine how he would have reacted if I had done something like that when a reporter called the house? He didn't want to be with me that day; he had holed up in his study for hours. But he didn't want me to work while I was sitting all by myself watching television. He was just generally mad at me all the time and merely took it out on my client.

Everything reached an all-time low when in mid-January Deborah told me that Mike had said I was having an affair. At the time I was sitting in the dark crying my eyes out and she was trying to comfort me. I was so upset that when Mike came into the room, I said, "How could you tell Deborah I'm having an affair? Even if it were true, which it is not, that's a terrible thing to do." I would've screamed it but I'm not a screamer. I couldn't believe that after all the times I had covered his ass for him he would tell her that. When I confronted him with what he had done, he wasn't sorry, just mad that Deborah had told me. That's when we started negotiating our divorce settlement. What a horseshit way to live, for him, as well as for me.

In the process of putting together a financial statement for my lawyer, I discovered that starting in January Mike had transferred every cent we had in joint accounts into ones in his name only. I now see that was just good business, but at the time I was furious. While he was making sure I had no access to any money, I was handing over my paycheck (paltry sum that it was) to him each week to use as petty cash (very petty). I stopped trying to negotiate with him and told my lawyer to file papers. Among other things, we asked the court to have Mike leave the house.

Mike says that kicking him out of his own house was a very vindictive thing to do. I'll admit that it wasn't very nice, but it was no worse than living with someone and continually sending messages that clearly said, "I don't like you," which is what he was doing.

I just couldn't live in a situation any more in which, as long as I was horizontal, I was okay, but the minute my feet hit the floor, I couldn't do anything right.

Mike asked for a trial separation until the end of the year. He said he thought it would be a shame to do something as drastic as divorcing only to regret it. Since I have no urgent need to be divorced (only need that if you want to get married again—shudder), I agreed.

Mike is living just yards away in our apartment behind the house. It's a rather awkward situation, to say the least.

I'm approaching this separation as the one last chance to put it all together, but I'm not optimistic. In his affidavit, which he filed with the court last spring, Mike stated that I'm not the woman he hoped I would be. True. In the early years of our marriage, I had little or no self-confidence. I was too busy being a wife and mother to think about the "woman." When she finally did emerge, the product was not to Mike's liking. And since I find myself very much to my liking, we have a real dilemma.

My mother is flying in for Deborah's high school graduation in June. Just last week I was organizing some pictures and found the one of your kids and mine sitting on the make-believe turtle at the Storybook Apartments in Houston. They were all little then—Kerry was only three, now she's thirteen, and Becky's fifteen.

If you could come visit, I'd love it. There's nothing more mindsettling than jumping into the boat at seven in the morning and cruising quietly around the lake. I'd love to share the peacefulness with you.

Fondly,
NANCY

P.S. On a more positive note, I have applied to two local law schools. With my mouth, I'm a natural.

One of the things I've worried about while writing this book is that I will put too much emphasis on the extramarital relations Mike and I had, that it will appear that they are the cause of our marriage falling apart.

From my point of view, although those incidents didn't help, there were other things that were more influential. I'm not sure Mike would agree.

One time during an argument he licked his hand and slapped it to his forehead, thus giving the impression he was planting a gold star there, and said, "I've been a goddamned Boy Scout for two years." At the time, it dawned on me that apparently he thought all would be well if only he gave up the other women in his life.

I've always been frustrated by the fact that I could never find the right words to explain to Mike what was troubling me. He kept bringing the center of conflict back to our sexuality. Long after we were separated, I read a book called Women's Reality by Anne Wilson Schaef. The author discussed the different ways men and women view sex and intimacy. She described a situation where a man has been on the road, and as he heads home, he fantasizes about his wife meeting him at the door. He sweeps her off her feet and carries her to the bedroom, and they make love. On the other hand, the woman's fantasy was quite different. She would pour a glass of wine for both of them, sit on the couch close together, and share the things that each had been doing during their separation. Probably they would end up making love but maybe not.

That's a lesson I wish I had learned when I was much younger. I had an inner sense that Mike and I were misconnecting, but I never thought it through enough to recognize the problem.

When I read that passage, it brought back memories of a conversation I had with a friend in East Lansing whose husband had played professional baseball at the minor league level. She said, "I remember the times my husband would come home at five in the morning from a road trip. He'd been riding in a smoky bus for hours and smelled like a two-day-old cigar. He'd always briefly say hello, whip off his clothes, and want to screw. It never dawned on him that I'd been up twice with the baby already that night, that he stank, that it might be appropriate to tell me he missed me, to say anything for that matter. He'd just want to screw, get off, and go to sleep. I, of course, would have to get up for that early morning feeding. You know, he never could understand why I wasn't more enthusiastic."

Those different value systems, different perspectives, can really foul up a relationship. My friend might not have been nearly so disgusted

*with her husband's behavior had she recognized that he was telling her
he loved her in the way he thought was most valid.*

*In October of 1982 I picked up my daughter, Deborah, from college.
On the way home, we stopped and had dinner, and while we were
waiting for our food, I asked her if her dad really still felt that I had
ruined our marriage. She said yes.*

*That night in recollecting my conversation with Deborah, I remem-
bered a story that "60 Minutes" had done in early January of 1982.
It was a piece on Moya Lear, now president of Lear Jet. Bill Lear, just
before his death, had asked her to follow through on his idea for the
fan-jet (a new plane that is built from very lightweight material and,
as a result, gets fantastic fuel mileage). Since the plane was ready to
go into production, CBS covered Moya and her role in turning her
husband's concept into a reality. During the show, the reporter approached the delicate subject of the notoriety Bill Lear had as a woman-
izer.*

*Moya admitted it was true, and that although it had bothered her,
she had received so much other good stuff from Bill that she never
considered leaving him.*

*People who know about Mike and my years together find it hard to
believe when I say that the women in his life have very little to do with
our getting a divorce. If that were the case, I would have gotten divorced
years ago. It became an issue only when I no longer got the other good
stuff—the warmth, the caring, the understanding.*

N.M.

Englewood, New Jersey
June 12, 1981

DEAR NANCY,

It really didn't surprise me to hear that you and Mike are having
a trial separation. After the letter you sent me last year, I was surprised you stayed together as long as you did. Believe me I understand
some of what you put up with through the years. It seemed a separation was almost inevitable.

Naturally I hope you are able to work things out between the two
of you. But I must admit that my breakup, in the long run, was a good
break for me.

The first year or so was rotten, but now I feel pretty good about
myself. No longer am I just an appendage of Jim. I was so wrapped
up into trying to be a good wife that my own personality was completely lost. Even though I had outside activities, they were so second-
ary that they didn't count.

212

When we were together in New York the last time, I had the feeling you were ready to be on your own. You were so alive and vibrant, but you seemed held down by some invisible strings.

It's funny because Jim said I held him down, even though I felt I bent over backwards to support him. Now I feel I was held down; perhaps he was, too, but in a different way. Maybe if we had received help soon enough, things would have been different. I hope you're getting counseling. I once thought that because I had a social work certificate I should be able to deal with every problem on my own, but outside help is a real plus.

Another friend has separated, too. Randy has moved out and left Barbara with two small children (be thankful your girls are teenagers). That's the end of our old Sunday dinner gang, first Alice, then me, now Barbara. (Ironically, Larry Ritter got married to a lovely young woman from Brazil.) We're all concerned about Barbara. She's young and very pretty, but starting over with a two-year-old and a physically handicapped four-year-old will be a tough row to hoe.

You should really enjoy law school. You have a quick mind and you're inquisitive; being a lawyer should be right up your alley. Also, knowing what I've paid in legal fees versus what I'll be earning teaching—the money is in law! By the end of this year, I'll have finished my student teaching and have the credits needed for my teaching certificate and a leg on my master's. Going back to school has been great. It's good to know my brain is alive and well.

Things are looking up. When my lawyers went to court to contest the psychiatric exam, we got everything we asked for. No exam, some money to live on, and some legal fees (one big sigh of relief).

Unfortunately, it didn't end there. Jim claimed he signed the original settlement under duress. Are you ready for this? He also said that I threatened to shoot him and Paula and that I had her kids followed. (It's hard to believe that I once loved this man.)

The kids also keep telling me how I'm financially draining Jim, even though he hasn't given me any money since last year except the money the judge recently ordered. Also, the court date kept being postponed, and Jim kept telling me he'd take it out of my hide if we didn't settle.

I had to give my deposition in the midst of my finals. We just missed going to court by an eyelash, settled outside the judge's door, then verbally in front of the judge. Now we'll sign papers when they're ready. Even though my lawyers have all been nice, I'll be so glad when it's over.

On the beautiful June day, when the judge said we were divorced, I didn't feel bad, just relieved. It had been such a strain, and going to court would have meant the back page of the *New York Post*. It was also a help that I'm seeing a nice professor and feel comfortable and happy about this relationship. (Just when I thought there weren't any more men around, a bright, attractive man tells me he's been trying to get my phone number for ages, gasp!)

The children are doing well. Michael is excited about starting George Washington University in the fall. Dave will be a high school senior and Laurie a sophomore. How are your girls handling the separation?

These six months will be hard on you, but it should give you time to sort things out. Let me know if there's anything I can do to help, and if you need a break, come and stay here for a while. Keep your chin up and stay in touch.

Affectionately,
BOBBIE

Shorewood, Minnesota
DEAR BOBBIE,   August 15, 1981

Mad as I was when I read your letter, I couldn't help but laugh. You know if anyone is incapable of shooting someone, it is you. Now if someone accused me of that, I might buy it! I have trouble thinking of you even raising your voice, let alone being violent. I can understand why you didn't want to go into court and have it dragged into the papers, but there's a part of me that wishes you had taken the tough line and fought. I guess you had to weigh the monetary outcome against your peace of mind. I suppose another way of looking at it is to just treat it as business. Jim probably never thought all those rotten things at all, but he had to use something to get out of the contract.

It's been just about three months since Mike moved out of the house. Oddly enough, we are getting along better than we have in years. However, I know he is seeing a couple of girls in Minneapolis. Although I don't think this is a very positive way to be putting a marriage back together, I'm trying to keep it in perspective. When we wrote up our separation agreement, we never discussed whether or not we would see other people. But I feel that since I asked him to leave, he is free to do whatever he wants.

Every once in a while, something happens to give me a little more insight into both myself and our problem. A few weeks ago, a charitable organization that I belong to was having a fund-raising event at the house of the woman who is our president. An hour or so before I was planning to leave, Mike came over to the house. I was standing at the kitchen sink, and he came up behind me and put his arms

214

around me. I sensed something was wrong and asked him what it was. He replied that he was just feeling down in the dumps. I asked him if he wanted to go with me, but he said no. So I stayed home with him instead.

It seemed important to me that he know I cared how he felt. I didn't think it would help us out if I ignored his feelings that night and left him alone while I partied.

The following Saturday I was helping Mike work on the trailer that he was fixing up. It got to be about five in the afternoon. I asked him what he wanted to do next. He said he had to quit because he was invited to a barbecue at a friend's house. My stomach knotted up because I knew what this friend's parties were like.

That night Becky decided to violate her curfew, and since I was waiting up to greet her, I saw Mike's car pull in at three A.M. I didn't know whether to be mad or sad. I knew for sure that if we were married I wouldn't have been able to get him to a party, let alone stay after midnight.

I felt cheated, frankly. I'd given up a party to be with him, and he wasn't willing to do the same for me. Then I started thinking about that, and I realized I was being unreasonable. Mike didn't ask me to stay home. I did it voluntarily. And just because I did that for him is no reason to expect him to do the same for me.

I think women frequently give "gifts" like my staying home and follow it up with anger because the gift isn't appreciated the way we feel it should be. Maybe it's a technique we use to control people. I'm planning on throwing out my ribbon and wrapping paper.

Although I have enjoyed living by myself and don't have the knot in my stomach anymore, I am thinking of asking Mike if he wants to move back in and give it one more try. It's more a decision of the head than of the heart. I just think if we could cooperate with each other the way we have this summer, we could at least get the girls raised. Then four years from now, after Kerry graduates, we can take a good look at our relationship and decide what to do. I've come to accept the fact that ours will never be a marriage made in heaven. Too much has happened to expect the romance to return.

Incidently, I told Mike about your letter. He said, "That doesn't surprise me about Jim. He always was very self-centered." That about cracked me up because when I filed papers on Mike last April, he submitted an affidavit about me that was incredibly vindictive. He took things that had actually happened and twisted them out of context, like you wouldn't believe. One time, when we were having a terrific fight, Mike told me that he hadn't loved me for seven years. I walked over to him and said that if I was so fucking worthless, why didn't he shoot me between the eyes the way they do a horse that's broken its leg. He put in the affidavit that I had baited him to shoot me! And he went on to say that my psychiatrist (I guess he means the one we were seeing together in Michigan) had told him to allow me to have these episodes. Don't you love it?

Mike will soon be flying to New York to join the Mets. You know, I wouldn't be a bit surprised if he calls you. In fact, I'd lay money on it that he'll not only call you but will ask you to come into the city to spend some time with him.

Write soon.

NANCY

Englewood, New Jersey
DEAR NANCY,   September 1981

You were right. Mike did call me! He sounded very smooth and self-assured, and I felt one step behind and very uncomfortable during most of the conversation.

He started by telling me that you were separated and that the marriage really ended when you had an affair with his best friend several years ago. That you had also done something devious financially—not his words—but confiscated his money by a court order or something. He was mad at you but still sounded very much in control.

He mentioned that he had always found me a warm woman with a lot of sensuality hidden just below the surface, and this was partly why he clammed up when he was around me. He didn't use these exact words, but he said it in a way to make me feel rather flattered.

Then he told me that when he roomed with Jim, Jim had told him about our sex life. Since Jim was proud that it was good, Mike knew that I was a sexually warm person.

I must admit from this point on, half of the conversation went over my head. The thought that my husband, the one I would have walked through fire for, was telling about our intimate life stunned me. I was mad and upset. And mad and upset with myself for feeling mad and upset! It didn't seem fair that Jim's past actions could still hurt me. I thought I was over being hurt by him. Fortunately, it took me only a couple of days to recover my equilibrium, but, at the time, I had a sick feeling in the pit of my stomach.

Something was said about Jim fooling around on the road—and hadn't I cheated, too? Mike was surprised that I had never even thought about cheating on Jim and had felt that Jim wasn't cheating on me. Mike said, "Even after *Ball Four*"?

216

I remember telling Mike that I still was old-fashioned and wanted a real relationship, not just a sexual one. He pointed out to me that these were hang-ups I should work on, and I said I was trying. I admitted that after Jim left, it had really been hard for me to sleep with someone, but, fortunately, I had found someone sensitive to my needs.

Mike told me that in a casual relationship, I should think of the guy as the one-night stand and not me. I said I wanted to feel special. How would he feel if I said, "I'm seeing someone, but maybe I can squeeze you in on Tuesday." He said, "Well, you would have squeezed me in, wouldn't you?" He really was very convincing and had ready answers and made me feel that I was wrong or, at least, should be more receptive.

In the back of my mind, I was thinking of the times when I look at myself in the mirror and think—what a waste! Why am I being such a monk? But I just can't separate my head from my body. Born a few years too soon maybe.

Mike said he thought we could have a very warm experience, that I shouldn't be wasting myself. He mentioned he was seeing many different women and would probably never be monogamous again. He gave me a number to call if I changed my mind. I said, "This means I can't just call you to have a friendly dinner, doesn't it?" He said, "Right." He then asked me if Marilyn Peterson might be available. When I said she was happily remarried, he said, "What did she want to do that for?"

I couldn't sleep that night. I wasn't upset that Mike had called. You said he would. In a mixed-emotions sort of way I was complimented. But when he told me that Jim talked about our lovemaking, it really hurt. I felt naked, as if I were in a class with the baseball Annies—For a good time, call Bobbie.

He really didn't say much about your breakup. It was basically a conversation directed at my changing my moral hang-ups. Mike probably had some valid points, too. It's just that I have this feeling in the back of my head that someday, somewhere, I'm going to meet someone who will appreciate me for what I am. And I can't force myself to change some feelings. Others I'm working on changing but not gut feelings.

Why do I feel so drained after writing this? Maybe because I'm not going to be seeing my "nice" professor much anymore. He's backed off because the relationship was too intense for him. I suspected this, but my previous suggestions to slow down were ignored. He certainly did give me a big rush in the beginning, and just when I was starting to feel something special was growing, it was "pruning time." Well, if the roots are strong, it will survive the winter.

Hang in there on the homefront,
BOBBIE

Shorewood, Minnesota
DEAR BOBBIE,   October 2, 1981

After reading your letter, I realized how kind you were to Mike. Since I talked to you on the phone the day before I got it, I know how upset you really were. You know, for a while I was angry with you. Mike was offending you right and left with his propositions, and all you worried about was being too tough and possibly hurting his feelings.

After we hung up the other day, I got more and more angry. When this kind of thing occurs, I like to inspect why I react as I do, and I've come up with some thoughts I'd like to share with you.

First, I thought he was being incredibly insensitive to your feelings. You didn't need to hear any more shit about Jim. I don't know about you, but when I first had to face the fact that Mike wasn't all I thought he was, I was hard on myself. I questioned how I could be so fucking stupid and blind. Every time I hear something more, such as what you related, I get the same feeling all over again.

Second, it infuriated me to think Mike thought he could make all your troubles go away by giving you however many minutes it took to get you off. Is that a little harsh? I just think the ego involved is incredible.

Apparently, Mike's attitude toward sex hasn't matured since we were in junior high. I recall sitting on my front step with him and listening to him tell me that he felt it was his obligation to take as many girls' "cherries" as possible. He said it was important that a girl's first sexual experience be a good one, and he knew how to do that.

Third, I'm really pissed because I don't think Mike gives a rip about you or me or any other woman he has anything to do with as people. I think we are all pieces of ass, first names and telephone numbers to gaze at with pride.

I feel obligated to warn you that Mike has a tendency to embellish his stories. Jim might not have even said the things Mike claimed. In 1977, when we had our hour of true confessions, he told me a lot of things he had done. I later found out that some of it wasn't true. Hard to understand why he would want to make his behavior out to be worse than it was, but he did.

Unfortunately, Mike came back to Minneapolis right after the

218

season ended (just after you and I talked), so I have had to contend with him every day. It takes all my energy just to be civil to him. I have kept my promise to you and haven't told him you relayed his conversation to me, so he thinks the reason for my hostility is because he didn't move back into the house.

I wish it had been me instead of you who received that phone call. I would have ripped him a new asshole, with questions like, "And you kept your cock in your pants all those years, right?" I find it intriguing that Mike takes a period of my life that occupied less than twenty-four hours and blames our failing marriage on that. I've had to face the fact that he still believes that; therefore, anything I might have done all those years to overcome it would have been in vain. When someone has you nailed to the cross, it's tough to get your feet on the ground. I've decided I've been crucified long enough.

The one accurate observation Mike made was that he'll never be monogamous again. My flip side wants like mad to say that the only time Mike was monogamous was during his prepubescent years.

I think I'd better wait until I'm in a more positive frame of mind to write you again.

Take care,
NANCY

DEAR NANCY,

Englewood, New Jersey
October 6, 1981

Maybe I shouldn't have written so much in my last letter. I really didn't mean to upset you; my anger was more with myself than Mike. My response was basically geared to one comment Mike made, and I didn't analyze the rest of our conversation.

Things have been so hectic student teaching that I still haven't had time to reflect on my reaction or Mike's or yours. As soon as there's a break in my schedule, I'll drop you a real letter.

Meanwhile, hang tough,
BOBBIE

DEAR BOBBIE,

Shorewood, Minnesota
October 10, 1981

Fret not. I have since realized that my anger was really with myself, too. You see, just a week before I talked with you, I had suggested to Mike that he think about moving back into the house and our giving it another go. I seem to have this incredible knack for ignoring

219

the fact that the man has a value system that I can't understand or condone. Yet I keep going back for more. Why?

I've thought about the statement Mike made about my ruining our marriage. You know, he's absolutely right. Despite the fact that Mike the physiologist would make such profound statements as "Our sex drive is innate, and under the right circumstances with the right person present, anyone has the capacity to be unfaithful"; and despite the fact that Mike had been sleeping with a whole bevy of women for seven years before my first indiscretion, he fell apart at the mere suspicion that I had been with another man.

I think back to last January when we first started to talk about getting a divorce. At the first sign of trouble, Mike was on the phone talking with a woman whom he's known and apparently cared about for years. (I knew this from our telephone bill, on which I saw her number. Checking out our phone bills, I had quite accidentally come upon this strange number and by doing a little detective work, I'd figured out what was going on.)

When we signed our separation agreement on April 28, I agreed that Mike could stay in the house until May 15. If he hadn't signed to play baseball by then, he was to move out into the apartment in back. That same night, he left the house without telling anyone he was going, and he didn't come in until eleven-thirty. The next night he did it again; only he came in at one-thirty. I met him at the door and told him that this was not a fucking hotel, and if he wanted to come and go as he pleased, he should get out.

A few days later, he told me he was going jogging, so when the phone rang, I answered it. Usually, I let him get it. He was down in his study and answered it at the same time as I did. All I heard was a sweet voice say, "Michael, how are you?" I knew he was seeing a woman who worked for a mortgage firm in Minneapolis, and I figured it was her. When he got off the phone, he came up to my bedroom. I blew my stack.

I said, "Do me a favor. Tell her my days off, so she knows not to call here." Then I got real cute and asked, "Tell me, does she always call you Michael? Does she say 'Michael, can I get on top?' "

I was storming around the bedroom naked, saying such witty things as "How typical of you to have someone who makes loans by day—odds are you figured she'd give it away at night." Even Mike had to laugh at that one. He told me, "God, that's a funny line! You really missed your calling. You should write monologues for Johnny Carson."

It was funny. But then again, it wasn't. The not-so-funny part was that Mike could hardly wait to hit the streets. It seemed he was all-too-anxious to trade family for fanny! I also thought it was ironic that for the past year he's been falsely accusing me of having an affair and on the first night after we've signed our separation agreement, he has a date! Did this relationship just appear out of the blue? How convenient that he found someone so quickly.

I think I've always known that Mike could never be a one-woman man (at least with me), and I've tried hard to live with that. But I've also really kidded myself. Although I've asked Mike to think of giving it a go again, I know it's an ill-fated attempt. I just won't live in a less-than-monogamous relationship, and I think Mike was being honest when he said he could never be that way again.

Years ago, Mike used to tell me that if I didn't like his lifestyle, I should get out. Scared as I am to start all over again, I think I have to take his advice. I'm not interested in living with a man who values a woman primarily for what lies between her legs.

Frankly, I don't think you are the one with the hang-ups. Some people call them principles or morals. There was a time when I tried to change my moral code and "swing." I wasn't comfortable, and I regret that I allowed myself to get sucked into it because everyone around me was. There's no ego trip in getting laid. It's easy to do. Don't get me wrong. I consider sex a delightful part of my life and have had some marvelous experiences, but only with men I like more for their head than their sexual apparatus. Actually, some of my better moments have been when I've been alone!

Stick to your gut feeling!

Fondly,
NANCY

Eventually, I did confront Mike with his phone call to Bobbie. His answer to me was, "Bobbie doesn't know anything, and neither do you."
I haven't to this day figured that one out. What's not to know? Maybe he had some wonderful insight that neither Bobbie nor I had, and was really thinking about her welfare somehow.

N.M.

DEAR NANCY,

Englewood, New Jersey
November 5, 1981

Sorry I've been so busy and haven't had time to drop you a line. Besides my practice teaching, I almost ended up back in court, when the lawyers couldn't agree to some wording in the contract.

Don't believe everything that comes out during the settlement talks. It seems to be a time when each partner tries to justify his side, and you will both say things you don't really mean. I was called a "leech" and told I didn't deserve a "fucking" thing, but I'm sure Jim didn't really feel that way. He just figured he was being overly generous and I wasn't appreciative enough. Actually, our settlement now is probably pretty fair, although some friends can't understand why I didn't go for the jugular. But I only wanted a fair share and security for the children.

Thank God, we avoided court, not just because of the publicity but also because the lawyers requested a list of possible people who would testify on my behalf, and it was terrible having to ask them. They were all wonderful and said they'd be happy to help, but I put myself in their place and thought how I'd hate to testify against an old friend. What was really upsetting was the possibility that Jim's father might have had to give some financial testimony.

Jim hasn't talked to his parents since last November, and the boys haven't seen them either. I'm very upset by this. Jim's dad was ill in the spring, and had it been serious, Jim would never have forgiven himself and the boys would have felt guilty, too. When I tried to get the boys to go to their grandparents for a cookout, Michael said, "No way, because then they would win." (God, is everything a game?) Finally, Michael did at least call his grandparents and invite them to his graduation, though he waited till the night before.

Boy, Michael's graduating from high school made me take stock of the difference the years make. Must admit I felt removed anyway, since I haven't involved myself in the Teaneck schools. I feel it's Jim and Paula's turf, and I have only attended a couple of parents conferences for Laurie.

A friend of mine (also going through a divorce) thinks that newlyweds should be able to purchase divorce insurance. Since money is needed for legal fees, etc., and a majority of couples do split, it should be a routine investment. If you make it through thirty years, you'd receive a bonus or something.

I'm not ready to be that cynical, but heaven knows it's been depressing having so many friends separating. Actually, I'm rather optimistic. I think I've learned a great deal about myself by going through this breakup, and I would avoid many of my mistakes the next time around.

Keep that in mind, kid. Think of what you're going through as a learning experience. Above all, keep your sense of humor. If I hadn't been able to laugh at some of the absurdities, it would have really been the total pits.

The thing that is bothering me now is the way Laurie is manipulating me. If I won't buy her something, she says, "Well, Dad will buy it for me." She gave us a bit of a problem this summer because she wanted to run away and join some friends at the beach. At least Jim and I handled the problem together and agreed to Laurie's receiving counseling because she is often unhappy and hostile.

Right now, she's doing fine. In fact, the "family" in this house is now an extended one. Jacqueline, twenty-four, a children's librarian, has been rooming upstairs for several months, and we've just added two more boarders. Brad (Michael and Dave's friend and a favorite of mine) is staying with us during the school year because his family moved to Connecticut. He wanted to finish his senior year here, so I'm sort of his temporary guardian. Last but not least, Sam Surprise, who lived next door to me in Michigan, is staying until he can afford an apartment. Sam was just graduated from Michigan State in communications, so you probably know some of the same people. He is twenty-eight and reminds me so much of my brother (they're good friends) that I told him he could stay as long as he wants.

Sam has a way of rubbing off on people, and it's easy to pick up some of his expressions. He works for Warner Communications, scheduling TV movies. His job includes seeing as many films as possible. Last week he was telling me about a foreign film in which a stripper is performing on stage with a remote-controlled tank that has a dildo on the end. She becomes intimate with the tank, but Sam assured me that it was "tastefully done." This is currently my favorite expression.

Next week I'm having a party on Friday the thirteenth. I'm sort of celebrating two certificates (divorce and teaching). This will be the first party I've had in this house, and I figure it's about time. So cheer up, kid. It takes only three years to indulge in some festivity.

Affectionately,
BOBBIE

DEAR BOBBIE,

Shorewood, Minnesota
November 30, 1981

Every time I get a letter from you, you sound better and better. Does that mean there's hope for me, too?

Any hope I had of a reconciliation with Mike has vanished. I went over to his apartment a couple of weeks ago, and when I got to the top of the stairs, I couldn't help but hear him talking on the phone.

Since he is a bit hard of hearing, Mike always talks very loud. Before I could let him know I was there, I overheard him tell another woman (at least I assume it was a woman) that he loved her and had for years. I don't know if he meant it, but frankly I don't care at this point. Either he's toying with her or with me, and at my age I'm not interested in game-playing anymore.

Since I have lost all trust in Mike, I feel the need to defend myself somehow, and have resorted to playing Nancy Drew a lot of the time. When we signed our separation paper, Mike agreed not to conceal any of his investments. Now he refuses to tell me where he is putting our money, so I'm doing whatever I can to keep track of things. I'm getting so good at subterfuge that I'm beginning to enjoy it.

I recently discovered that Mike changed the lock on the apartment door. He walks in and out of my house at will, but apparently he doesn't want me in his place. He left a few days ago to spend Thanksgiving in Michigan. Supersleuth hired a locksmith to open his door, then I took the doorknob off and had a key made for it. I had to be careful about how I put the knob back on because Mike had installed it upside down.

There's a part of me that feels really shitty invading his privacy like this, and I also think I have more constructive things to do, but I'm having too good a time to quit just yet.

Somehow, despite all of the garbage, I have maintained my sense of humor. I'm not sure Mike thinks I'm so funny, however. Since he agreed to keep the girls for a few days while I went out of town, I decided I should give him a thank-you gift. Have you heard about the parties that people are having to promote the sale of marital devices? They are kind of like Tupperware parties, only they sell things like edible panties. Well, I knew Mike would enjoy those, but didn't have time to order any, so one night after consuming far too much wine, I got a wonderful idea. I drove to the grocery store and bought half a dozen fruit rolls. Do you know what those are? They are round, thin, sticky pieces of gelatinlike substance. You can tear strips off and chew them, and they come in assorted fruit flavors. You're ahead of me, aren't you?

I made a pair of panties out of them. Had to stuff them with paper towels to keep the front and back from sticking together. I put them in a shoebox, tied it up with a ribbon and wrote a note apologizing for the fact that they were so small. I pointed out that I thought they might only fit someone who weighed one hundred eight pounds. I left the box on the kitchen counter. He never even acknowledged it. Think maybe he can't take a joke?

On a more serious note, I'd like to tell you that I take great comfort in our friendship, and am particularly grateful that you have shared some of the things that you have gone through in the process of getting your divorce. Just recently Mike told me that I didn't deserve any of *his* money because, after all, I did have room and board all these years. I passed up the urge to point out the fact that the room and board was pretty skimpy for several years! He also told me that I had no reason to be upset because he had another woman at the All-Star game in 1974, since, and I quote, "you had my name three hundred and sixty-five days out of the year."

Reading that Jim called you a "leech" gives me some measure of comfort—makes me think these kinds of statements are just par for the course during periods such as we're going through.

Take care,
NANCY

DEAR NANCY,   Englewood, New Jersey
                                                December 10, 1981

The party was terrific. I'll have to find some more excuses to celebrate. Mostly old friends and Englewood people came—and Englewood has some interesting people. You must come and visit soon.

I was still basking in the afterglow from the party when Jim called and asked if I'd be home that Sunday morning. He wouldn't discuss why, just said, See you then.

Sunday morning he pulled up and dropped off Laurie and all the stuff she kept in Teaneck. He said, "She's living with you now. She doesn't love me or respect me, so you win!" I said, "What do you mean, 'win'? This isn't a game; can't we discuss this?"

But he wouldn't look me in the eye, just said, "There's nothing to talk about. We'll switch her back to school in Englewood." I said that it wasn't good for children to be estranged from their parents, and that she often told me she didn't love or respect me either. I asked him, "What would you do if we were still married—still kick her out?" He said she had lied to them, gone to a party that was unchaperoned, and wouldn't abide by their rules. Now she could have her wish to live full-time with me, and with that he left.

I was stunned, to say the least. Here I thought we were cooperating when the children had problems, and then boom! Laurie was obviously upset, but all she did was let loose at Jim for leaving. She said, "Why don't you just leave again?" This, I fear, is the real root of the problem. Laurie had been the apple of her daddy's eye and his adorable little clone. When he left me for another woman and wouldn't return even when she begged him, she was badly hurt. After Jim left, Laurie said, "Paula told me she was going to try to convince dad to send me here full-time."

I suggested that Laurie try to be on her best behavior and that she make up with her dad and try to get along with Paula. I also pointed out that if she improved her school grades, it would help mend her relationship with Jim and also make me happy.

This situation reminded me of a quote from *The Bleeding Heart* by Marilyn French.

Male ego was so fragile, because it made everything into a game and then has to win every game. Or shatter. That man who wrote a letter to *The New York Times* about his tiny children, and kept saying "She won," or "He won."

She came into my study and disturbed me at my work and she knows she's not supposed to, so I was going to spank her but she was so cute I couldn't: so she won. Man like that shouldn't have children.

Boy, did this hit home.

It's tough having teenagers. I'm not sure how much of the kids' problems are related to the divorce and how many are just normal growing problems. Laurie is the toughest to handle because she's so much like Jim, and they didn't call him Bulldog for nothing.

Speaking of bulldogs, you're hanging tough. Your last letter really made me laugh. I can just picture you fashioning fruit rolls into panties. I'm just sorry you have to go through the pain of hearing unwelcome remarks. Maybe it will make you stronger in your resolve to seek a new life. Hearing that Jim had fooled around before helped me not want to live in the past. I also didn't blame myself as much as I think you do. Eva helped me to realize that blaming myself wouldn't do any good then and certainly wouldn't help me in the future.

Meantime, Alice and I are trying to help our social lives. We put a personal ad in the *New York Review of Books*. Alice had done this before and had about thirty replies. This time we decided to put in something light that only someone with a sense of humor would answer.

The ad read: "Two women recently returned from Asbestos, Canada, interested in meeting men (35–45) who have been to equally exotic places." We figured this would be a change of pace from the regular: "Attractive woman, 39, desires to meet intelligent, sensitive, single male." When I told Burt, he laughed and came up with a great ad for himself. "Tall, dark, rich, handsome Harvard graduate, quarterback for the Pittsburgh Pirates, interested in meeting Scandinavian woman." P.S. 75 percent of this is true.

We received about a dozen answers, unfortunately, most from men living too far away to consider dating. The one local man we called told me that he was extremely passionate—was I? I said, "Only after feeling close to someone special; I wasn't interested in one-night stands." We decided not to meet. Jeeze, it is difficult meeting someone. Sam has a friend he wants to introduce me to, but he's younger than I am. Maybe I'm ready for that.

During the holidays my social calendar is fairly full, and it's good getting together with friends. I just hope the boys will agree to visit with Jim's folks; they've moved to Connecticut.

One nice family occurrence is that I've been in closer touch with my dad. We drove down to Philly to visit over the summer and plan on going again over the holidays. He's been very supportive during the whole divorce.

It's too bad that your family isn't nearby. When you're having these emotional ups and downs, it's so good to have a parent or sibling nearby. Jim's folks and I are still close, and even though they have moved, we keep in touch. And my ex-sisters-in-law and I have lunch together when we have a chance. I'm glad we're still friendly; after all, we've been together almost twenty years.

Friends can help the most, Nancy. I'm sure you have some that you can confide in and they will be happy to give you a hand. Wish we weren't so far apart because we could have a good time going out together.

You're going to do just fine. The best is yet to come—I'm sure of it.

Affectionately,
BOBBIE

DEAR BOBBIE,

West Palm Beach, Florida
December 24, 1981

It's Christmas Eve. Becky, Kerry, two of their friends, and I flew to Florida to spend the holidays. I rented an apartment that Mike and I stayed in twice before—once when he was in Montreal and again in 1976, when he was with the Braves. Because Becky and Carissa are asleep in the living room, I am writing this by the light from the back-door patio. I just can't sleep.

I've been thinking about this past year and all that has happened. I think I've felt about every emotion it's possible to have, and all too strongly.

When Mike asked me to agree to a trial separation instead of getting the divorce, we agreed to continue to spend a good bit of time together. I did it with the hope that a little time and space would help us come to at least an amiable understanding so that we could finish raising the girls. When, halfway into the summer, I discovered he was spending three or four nights a week with me and the other nights with other women, I felt the same old hurt of 1967 all over again. I couldn't understand how he could think that was any way to make a serious effort to put our marriage back together. Then when the incident with you occurred, despite the fact that I predicted he would do it, I was incredibly angry. I guess I hoped I was wrong about his value system.

But I guess the worst was overhearing him tell another woman he loved her and had for the past twenty years. I realized he never had any intention of working things out. It reminded me of Jim saying you had won when he brought Laurie home to you. It was all a game. Do you suppose that since they've played games since childhood, they can't do anything else?

I felt such total sadness because Mike rarely said such kind and loving things to me. I've thought about that and come to the conclusion that (1) maybe he never really cared for me, so he couldn't say those endearments, or (2) maybe in his younger years he didn't have the ability to express himself, and now that he can, the feelings aren't there. Actually, I think there is a third possibility. I believe he still cares, but too much emotional crud has built up for him to take the risk of saying them to me. I can understand that, since I could never trust him again either. Trust is believing that someone will not only do the right thing but do it for the right reason.

I've been rereading Marilyn French's *The Women's Room*. She developed a character named Kyla who reminded me of myself in a small way. In the end, after going back and forth to her husband, struggling to make the marriage work, trying to be what he wanted her to be (unsuccessfully), she finally left him and offered the following explanation. "This time I understood what my problem was. Because I did love Harley. I do love Harley. I think he's great. But he crushes me. He's great for himself, but he's bad for me."

In a conversation I had with a good friend last week, I explained why I had to get this divorce. I said I feel like a person who absolutely loves to smoke but is giving it up no matter how painful it may be, and no matter how much I may miss it, because I know it's going to kill me if I don't.

The papers will be served January 5. I feel less and less sad and more and more strong. I get up each day and tell myself not to think about the past nineteen years and all the mistakes I've made, but to look ahead and not fuck up again!

I'm sure you're right. The best is yet to come, good friend. Happy 1982.

As always,
NANCY

DEAR NANCY,

Englewood, New Jersey
February 14, 1982

The holidays went well this year—considering. Laurie didn't go to her dad's; she chose to go to her boyfriend Adam's on Christmas Eve. When she told Paula of her decision, Paula informed her that families have Christmas plans from the day they're born. She said that "this is an interesting game you're playing. I'll wait till your father gets home, and you can play it with him." Gee, I wonder if they ever win one for the Gipper?

The boys didn't go to visit their grandparents with me. Later during his vacation, Michael went up alone for a visit, which I was very happy about. Michael and I also went into the city and visited the Whitney and Guggenheim museums. It was good spending the day together, except that he must have talked about Jim half a dozen times. "Dad can paint as well as this artist. Dad's as funny as the new 'Saturday Night Live.' That table is reserved for celebrities; they always put Dad there." After that last one, I asked if he realized how much he talked about Jim. He smiled rather sheepishly and said, "Yeah, does it bother you?" I said only in that I worried about him overidentifying with Jim.

He then told me about his reoccurring dream about a man shooting Jim; he tries to warn Jim, but is too late. I suggested that he read some books on dream interpretation, but he said Paula was an expert and would tell him what it meant. Later, he said that Paula told him it meant he was angry at Jim. I asked if he agreed with that interpretation; he wasn't sure. We had many interesting chats and visits during the holidays, and I realized how much I miss his company. He has always been an engaging person to converse with. Can't believe he's a college freshman already.

Dave visited a little more, too. I let him have a "little" New Year's

229

Eve party here. When I returned from dinner at Burt's with my friend Jane, there wasn't room to park anywhere near the house. Later, I had to call the ambulance when one of his friends went into insulin shock. Hope my next New Year's isn't so hairy.

After the holidays, the Woods had me over when they invited the Ittlesons, a couple I had known from ABC, for dinner. Betty complimented me on looking much younger. She mentioned that before I had looked tired, as if I were supporting Jim. She said I had been given a gift with the divorce. The more I thought about it the more I thought she was right. True, I subordinated myself, but it was my choice. Now I couldn't do that again. Feeling good about myself does show through. Now, to sustain the feeling!

I just finished taking an ESP holistic health class through the local adult education school. It was taught by a psychic. The class was fascinating. I even started seeing auras, which shook me up.

After the semester was over, one of my classmates and I went for a private reading. We wrote seven questions, and the psychic answered them without looking. Of course, he knew a bit about us from class, but we were still impressed. He told me that I would publish three books and that there would be some legal problems with one; that I would remarry within eighteen months to three years to someone in the medical field; that I'd probably meet him in grad school; that Laurie and her dad would make up by Easter; and that April 17 would be an important date for me.

He told Rani, the friend I had gone with, to be sure to attend her company Christmas party because she would meet someone there. She hadn't planned on attending because those parties are usually boring, but she went—and sure enough—is dating someone she met there. Hope he's right about me, too!

Happy Valentine's Day! I sent one card—to Michael. Not many cards are appropriate for your teenage son. Figured I'd bake cookies for the rest of my "valentines." Brad was a sweetheart and gave me roses.

Thinking back—Jim was never much on holidays. I always had to remind him when my birthday was near. (That was easy because it's the same day as his dad's.) I'd say, "What should we get for your dad's birthday next week?" One time Jim gave me pierced earrings, although my ears have never been pierced. Do you know I've received more flowers from men friends since the split than during my whole married life. Does this mean a rosier future?

Affectionately,
BOBBIE

Shorewood, Minnesota
February 20, 1982

In case you've forgotten, let me remind you that getting divorced is the pits. We'll make our third court appearance next week, and we're still dealing only with temporary maintenance. But that isn't the bad part.

Mike won't even speak to me these days. If I call him to discuss something pertaining to the girls, he'll answer one question before he hangs up on me. He recently said that if I have more than one question, I should say so up front, or else he will hang up after the first one.

When I asked Mike last October to make a settlement offer, I was shocked at what he expected me to take. Clearly, he has an entirely different perspective on what my contributions have been.

I can't help but think about the early years of our marriage. I have a ledger in which we wrote down every penny that we spent for the first five years of our marriage. Rarely did we spend more than $200 a month, and that included rent. Even when Mike was making $150,000 a year, we lived very modestly and deferred most of his income until after he retired. Now he says I'm not entitled to any of that savings. I hate battling over money, but I'm not going to give in, either. Mike may not place much value on the caring and nurturing of the children, but I do.

Someone asked me recently if I regretted having been married to Mike, and I could honestly say I didn't. I had some terrific years and experiences that most women never even get to think about. Living as we did forced me to become strong and independent. And I learned a lot from Mike. One of the things I learned was not to worry what other people think about you. As long as you believe what you're doing is right, what anyone else thinks is inconsequential. It is this thought that is getting me through these difficult times.

I'm working on getting out of the "pit" stage of the divorce. I've been playing Nancy Drew a lot for the past couple of months, and I really don't want to do that anymore. Mike's phone line still comes into the house and I don't want to be tempted to listen in to his conversations so I've asked Mike to get his own phone in the apartment. I've also had it with sharing the kids' phone with them.

The last Nancy Drew discovery was a real bombshell. Mike must have sat down one day and listed all the things I had done wrong and reasons why I ruined the marriage, because I found an eleven-page grievance list on his desk. There was a section marked "1975 rib injury" with the following subheadings:

231

1. On April 17, 1975, I broke a rib while pitching.
2. The best theory why this rib break occurred is that stress reduced the calcium level in my body, making the rib suscepti- ble to break.
3. The stress was my wife's infidelity and injury to children caused by marriage breakup.
4. This internal turmoil severely hampered my concentration and performances for several years.

Now let me get this straight. My one night of indiscretion—which was all I was guilty of at that point—put so much stress on him that he broke his rib, right? Ye gads, after the years of his "affairs," it's a miracle I wasn't in a total body cast!

In addition, he complained because I wouldn't have eight children. Can't you see me driving from East Lansing to Los Angeles with eight kids? Me and my Greyhound bus!

In a later conversation, I asked him how he managed to put the blame on someone else for everything that went wrong, and he said, "Reality is reality."

When we were in court the first time in early January, the referee suggested marriage counseling. After we were out of the courtroom, Alan, my lawyer, asked me how I felt about the idea. I told him that we had tried it once before and that Mike had gone into it with the idea that I had to get myself straightened out. Further, I said that Mike likes the way he is and that I had no right to ask him to be anything else, just to make me happy. I felt I had two alternatives. Either I could accept him as is and do without the things that I needed or I could get the divorce. Mike likes to play with people's lives, but I don't. That left me with but one choice. It is an attitude that has also allowed me to go through this divorce without anger—most of the time, at least.

John Denver has a lovely song out called "Seasons of the Heart." I thought some of the lyrics particularly appropriate. They describe the sadness you feel when people change and the things that used to mean so much to both no longer exist and all that's left is a very empty feeling.

After having two incredibly mild winters, we have had a horrible one this year—including record snowfalls and cold temperatures. Today in a minus-60-degree wind-chill factor, I went up to the roof and cleared off the three-foot snowdrift that had accumulated. I must have strained myself lifting the shovelfulls because the hemorrhoids that I have as a result of bearing three children are making themselves known in a very painful way. (Ye gads, bet they would be hanging

232

down to midcalf if I had those eight kids Mike wanted.) It struck me that on this occasion having Mike around would have been one of those rare times when he would *not* have been a pain in the ass.

The big question on Lake Minnetonka these days is, Will the ice be off the lake by next August? I'm either suffering from hemorrhoids or freezing my ass off. Do you think I may have an anal fixation?

Take care,
NANCY

P.S. I made my flight arrangements today for my trip to New York. I'll be glad to have a couple of weeks out of this pressure cooker—see you the end of the month.

Englewood, New Jersey
April 23, 1982

DEAR NANCY,

Seems a good time to drop you a line, since I'm relegated to my bedroom by Laurie's sweet-sixteen party downstairs. It was great having you visit last month. Old friends as good as you are tough to come by, and when we have a chance to visit, it's almost too frantic. Too much to say and do in too short a time.

The last couple of years have made me realize just how important some friends are. You and I can share things that other friends, with the exception of Marilyn Peterson Mosca, can't begin to understand. We've been through the mill together, so to speak.

Sorry that Alice and I had opera tickets on Saturday night, but I'm sure Sam, my pseudo-brother and housemate, kept you entertained. Actually it's about time that Alice and I splurged and bought a series of tickets. For years we had talked about treating ourselves to something and finally had a chance for some good discount tickets so I could discover opera. Since neither of us has been especially active socially, the timing was right.

The only people I know who are romantically involved right now are Laurie and Burt, who is quite taken with an engaging young woman. (I still almost wrote "girl." She's in her mid-twenties, and that seems like a girl to me.) Laurie is driving me up the wall with her young-love problems. She's either up or down, making up or breaking up, crying all night or thrilled because its their four-month, two-week anniversary. I can't stand it! Heaven help me through these teenage years!

On the plus side for Laurie: She made up with her father. Jim invited her to stay over while I went to spend Easter weekend in D.C.

with Michael. I thought the psychic had missed on that one, just as April 17 had been uneventful after all, but Easter was work-things-out time for Laurie.

One reason why they made up might be because Jim and Paula are getting married in June. When Laurie told me, I had a knot in the pit of my stomach, but it quickly vanished. The marriage doesn't matter to me—no way in the world would Jim and I ever be together again. I just worry about the kids, in case anything happened to Jim. Also, there's probably some jealousy since I haven't been interested in anyone in ages. Michael is all "psyched up" about the wedding, says it will be a really big bash. I just hope Jim will reach out to his folks and make up with them before the wedding.

We've been holding classes in holistic health in my house, and one of the things I'm aware of is that I still do have some anger toward Jim bottled up inside. Before I can start another good relationship, I have to cleanse myself of the old one. My new teacher, Cindy Barger, says it's like wallpapering over old paper. In order to do a good job, you must first scrape off the old stuff. I know she's right about me, and I think I'm mellowing and that I can deal better with Jim now. Meditation and relaxation techniques are helping me feel better, and I highly recommend them to you.

Brad had his senior prom last night. It was fun helping him get ready and taking pictures. I was sorry that his mother missed out on this and that I've missed similar events with my boys. They really grow up too soon. Fortunately, Dave has been stopping over more often, partly because of the hockey play-offs. It's nice to have a big group of friends over on hockey nights—my social event for the week.

Fortunately, I've been working quite a lot lately. Even had a long-term job as math specialist (loved it). Unfortunately, it doesn't look as if there will be any job openings for next fall. Well, it's early yet.

I've been trying to find a class in biofeedback to take in some local college. In fact, I'd really like to get my master's in behavioral science or a related field, but I can't seem to zero in on the exact classes. Meanwhile, I'm taking holistic health classes and reading everything I can on the subject.

I'm also decorating my bedroom and knitting. I wore a sweater to school that I'd just finished the other day and had a lot of compliments. It dawned on me that this was the first sweater I had knitted for myself since Laurie was born. Everything I made was for the kids or Jim or gifts. Boy, have I got some lost time to make up for, and I'm digging out some patterns and buying some yarn. Don't forget to send me the pattern of the sweater you were finishing.

Hope things have calmed down for you. Must admit I slept most of the day after you left. You take it easy, too.

Love,
BOBBIE

DEAR BOBBIE,

Sure enjoyed my two weeks with you in Englewood. For some inexplicable reason, since I've been home, I seem to have been enveloped by a cloud of peace. Could it be I'm through the "pit" stage of the divorce process?

I'm sure a lot of it has to do with the time we spent working through the past eighteen years. It doesn't make any sense to have gone through all this turmoil and not to have learned anything from it. I hope all our introspection pays off.

I enjoyed meeting so many of your friends at the wine and cheese party. It's nice to be able to put faces to names now. I was particularly pleased to be able to talk at great length with Marilyn Peterson Mosca. We were able to talk so openly about our lives that I felt as if I had known her for years. The point we kept coming back to time and time again was "How did a couple of small-town girls like us end up like this?"

She told me she envied our writing. Seems she hasn't quite rid herself of all the garbage from those years. I wonder if, when she reads our book, she'll lose some of it vicariously. Wouldn't that be nice?

I told her that whenever I start wallowing in my pity pile, I think about what life would have been like had I married the only other man that I was ever serious about. I haven't seen him for years, but an old buddy of his told me recently that he is a real stuffed shirt now. Rough as our lifestyle has been at times, it has rarely been dull.

Then there was Sam! I think I've met my match. The man definitely has a free spirit. It will be interesting to see how the girls react when he comes to Minneapolis to visit. I'm looking forward to seeing him jog around the neighborhood in his red union suit. Did that man make me laugh! And didn't that feel good!

Things have been a bit crazy since I've been back. Our entire staff at the travel agency, some twenty-five people, flew to Montreal just to have dinner. Travel agents are notorious for having a good time and this group was no exception. By the time the evening was over, the whole group was throwing food all over the place, the maître d' climbed on top of our twenty-foot-long table and stripped, and my boss tied me to a support post and all the people in the restaurant pelted me with the napkins. And that's the mild stuff! If my children ever behaved as I did that night, I would ground them for life. This has all the makings of one of those nights it may take me a long time to live down.

Since we still have insurance benefits through the major league benefit plan, I decided to have my tubes tied. Inasmuch as I am petrified to be put to sleep, it was a tough decision. Considering I'm not even dating, let alone going to bed with anyone, I'm not sure why I bothered. The only thing I was in danger of delivering was a litter of index fingers.

Actually, I'm hoping the day will come when I'll be sufficiently put together emotionally to consider coming out of the convent. I'm not sure I can explain why I had the surgery. I think I just wanted control of my own body, and as long as there was even the chance of getting pregnant, that couldn't occur. Does that make any sense?

Since my parents were here for a two-week stay, I took advantage of them as baby-sitters and flew out west for one day and one night. Got up one morning and decided to use that pass that was burning a hole in my purse. I suspect there might be more than one or two people who would consider my doing that irresponsible, but I like to think of it as spontaneous! In addition to having thirty-six of the best hours I've had in a long time, I also missed one helluva snowstorm, including seventy-mile-an-hour winds. Someone's looking after me, I swear.

One of those someones is my lawyer. We were back in court for the third month in a row just recently. This divorce is going to be nothing but messy and difficult, but Alan is so calm about everything that it makes my life a lot easier. I can call him and be absolutely livid, and within thirty seconds he'll settle me down. He's been so supportive of me that no matter how it all turns out, I'll always call him friend.

And you, too.

Always,
NANCY

While I was in New York Bobbie and I spent hours sitting cross-legged on her twin beds hashing over the manuscript of our book word by word. When we were reading her letter describing Jim's telling her he was leaving, I suggested to Bobbie that it wasn't good enough to simply say, "I was hurt." What we really needed to hear was how she

236

felt, what she was thinking, how she reacted, what she said to him. She agreed and starting revising her work.

After we had been working quietly for several minutes, I looked over at Bobbie and found she had crawled into bed and had the covers pulled over her head. I walked over and looked at the paper she was working on. She had listed several specific things Jim had said that day, then there was a big empty space, and finally at the bottom of the page she had written, "I've blocked it all out."

At the time I thought Bobbie was escaping by diving under the covers, that it was too painful for her to think about that part of her life. It wasn't until six months later that I ever said anything to her about it. Only then did I find out how badly I had misinterpreted her actions.

When she was a small child, whenever she wanted to think, she would remove the cereal boxes from under the kitchen sink, crawl in, and close the door. It seems she had gone undercover to think. There's a good lesson here about making judgments about other people's actions.

N.M.

My mother worked to support the family, so I baby-sat with my younger brother and sister a great deal. Reading was my passion, and to have some privacy to read or think or fantasize, I'd hide in the cabinet under the sink.

It was easy to move the boxes to the oven to make space in the cupboard for me. Then I'd crawl in with a flashlight and a bunch of peanut butter crackers. Sometimes I'd hear my sister Janet or brother Dennis call, but unless it sounded urgent, I'd stay inside my cubbyhole. They never did discover my special place.

Even now, when I need to think or want to get rid of a headache, I'll crawl in bed and throw the comforter over my head. Fortunately, I can now read without being disturbed, and a favorite place is the front-porch swing. The outside spot I used as a kid was to hide under the hydrangea bush. You could say I've come up from the bushes.

B.B.

Englewood, New Jersey
August 1, 1982

DEAR NANCY,

Since I last dropped you a line, things have sure been up and down —maybe I should say up and down and up. I'm feeling great right now; things have been coming around full circle.

237

In July I took Alice on a singles hike. None of my female friends had been available to join me before, but going alone hadn't bothered me. (Sam went once.) We arrived at the parking lot with about sixty people milling around, and this time it was Alice who wanted to back out and leave. I wouldn't let her and later stepped up my pace and visited with other people met on previous hikes. Since it was her first sojourn, I kept an eye on her and came over during lunch. But, basically, left her alone and she was fine, as I knew she'd be.

On the way home, I reminded her of three years ago when she took me to a singles concert and I wanted to leave. It took me only three years to build a little confidence.

I started hiking because it's good exercise and fun. It also turned out to be a great no-pressure way to meet people. In fact, I met someone. His name is Phil; he's a professor, a physicist, and lives in Englewood. He's tall and lithe and looks like Pernell Roberts on "Trapper John, M.D." We went out for dinner on Friday, then hiked by ourselves on Sunday and just hit it off so well that we didn't want to part. He called the next day to say he had trouble writing equations on the board because he kept seeing my smile. We've been seeing each other steadily for more than a month, and we still hate to say goodbye.

The down things have been with Jim and Laurie again—back to square one. Laurie went to Greenwich Village, and while there, she witnessed a murder. She wasn't supposed to be there; it seems she has a knack for finding trouble. Needless to say, it was traumatic all around. Jim declined to become involved unless he could bring Paula. He said, "We are a team and do everything together." I lost my cool and replied that I wasn't trying to break them up—they probably deserved each other—but I felt outnumbered and thought the two of us could deal with Laurie's problems.

To make a long story short, Laurie testified for the police. She was so emotionally drained that after the interview she could hardly walk. Fortunately, she wasn't needed in court.

She later received an envelope addressed to "Lori" Bouton; it contained a copy of the *New York Times* article on the funeral of the youth she saw killed—no signature. I was quite upset and asked Jim if he knew anything about it; he said no. When I told him I was calling the police, he said, "I'll check and call you back." Later, he admitted that they had sent the clipping. They were concerned by Laurie's apparent lack of empathy and didn't think it would be misinterpreted as a threat. Sending a clipping with disguised handwriting did not seem to me to be the way to handle the problem.

Fortunately, Laurie did attend her father's wedding. With much pushing from me and her psychologist, she apologized for her behavior during an argument she had with Jim about the incident in the Village. Unfortunately, Jim's parents were not invited to the ceremony.

Shortly afterward, in one of our "family" sessions at the psychologists, Paula told us that Jim is ill. He has some disease that makes it difficult for him to digest his food. She said this is due to stress, and the stress is mainly from Laurie and his financial obligations to me. They are not going to continue to attend the "family" session with us. Paula feels Jim's health is more important than helping Laurie. She even has to rock him to sleep in her arms because he's in so much pain. Paula concluded: "We will no longer have any contact with Laurie. *Finis!*" Then she said she felt sorry for me, told the doctor he was terrific, and shook his hand; Jim followed her out the door.

You know, I feel sorry for him. Talk about full circle. I never dreamed I'd again feel any sympathy for him. He doesn't look well, but he's seemed gaunt for the last couple of years. He's also had kidney stones and other health problems. I can't believe that not seeing Laurie will help him feel better. In fact, I suspect the opposite. He hasn't had any contact with his parents in almost two years, and it must be bothering him. Laurie is his daughter. It's often hard for me to deal with her, but even though she's messing up, it would be impossible for me to completely turn my back on her. It must be very difficult for him to rationalize this move.

Paula said Laurie was "controlling" everyone, and they would no longer be controlled. Maybe I'm still susceptible to being controlled. (I had given in and agreed to include Paula at the psychologist's, much as I dreaded it.) I hope that, with time and help, others won't control me as much as before.

Laurie and I will be going to Michigan this week with my mom. She was going to stay with Jim when I went, but now she'll have to come along. I'm looking forward to seeing my family, but I will miss Phil. Did I tell you he canceled a bike trip so that he could take me out on my birthday? Yay! Hope you have some yays.

Love,
BOBBIE

DEAR BOBBIE,

Don't know when I'll get the chance to write you again. It's not that I'm short on desire, but time is a real problem these days.

I've been in law school for a month now and love every—well—almost every minute of it. I don't think I'm giving it the time that I should, but it's not exactly the only thing I'm doing.

Kerry spent last weekend with Deborah at St. Olaf College. Deb sent a poster home to me that has a woman carrying books, an adding machine with the roll of paper coming undone, and "in" and "out" mailboxes with letters flying out of them. The caption read: PLEASE, I CAN ONLY DO TWELVE THINGS AT ONCE. Apparently, that's the image I'm giving to my kids these days.

I was feeling very guilty the other day about not being home very often to fix dinner for the girls. If we all sit down to eat together once a month, it's a miracle. When Mike was still living with us, there was mandatory attendance at the dinner table each night. Kerry said to me, "Don't feel bad. We used to all eat together, but we fought all the time. Now we never eat together, but we're closer to each other than we've ever been."

Mike is pushing me to sell the house. I'm willing, but only if I have his guarantee that I'll get my half so that I can buy a small place for the girls and me. I've already had all the apartment living I need for one lifetime. The dog and cat are very important to the kids, so a house it must be. Of course, he's not willing to give me the time of day, so I'm not hustling my buns to sell the house.

Speaking of the dog, did your papers carry the latest saga of Mike Marshall? It seems (I wasn't there, so I'm only relaying what the girls told me) the dogcatcher drove her truck onto our private easement road for the purpose of talking to Mike about our dog, Jesse, running loose. Apparently, from the newspaper reports, she had talked to him about it before, and he never bothered to tell her Jesse wasn't his dog. He told her she was on private property and should leave. He was quoted in the paper as saying he told the woman that if she didn't leave, he couldn't be responsible for any damage to her property. Sometime after this, she alleges he threw a baseball and hit her truck! They disagree about where he hit it. She also claims he threw rocks at her truck.

The South Minnetonka police have charged Mike with fourth-degree assault and disorderly conduct. I've been taking a poll. I've asked several people what they would do if they wanted to get the dogcatcher off their property. So far, everyone has said that the first thing they would do is throw a baseball at her. Anyway, Mike pleaded not guilty—his trial comes up in March.

Mike still isn't working, so maybe all this good publicity over the assault charge will convince some university that he's just the kind of man they've been looking for!

Actually, I think Mike is making a career out of getting this divorce. He's compiled notebooks full of "evidence"—most of it of his own creation. He seems to believe that if he puts something on paper, it's final. He writes me (he won't speak to me either face to face or on the telephone) little "missiles," as I call them. In one of his latest he accused me of wanting custody of the girls so that I could get more money and of having no motherly or moral concern for them.

I found the part about the moral concern rather amusing. I suspect Mike doesn't like getting up in the morning, looking out his window, and seeing a strange car in my driveway.

Don't think I've told you about that new variable in my life. I met a man in early July, eventually went out with him on my birthday, and have been seeing a lot of him ever since. Seems I sold my book, turned forty, and got coaxed out of the nunnery all on the same day! Not bad, huh?

The girls have accepted having Michael (I don't want to hear about it!) in our lives. He's single and happy to be that way, which is good news for me. I'm glad I didn't date for the past year. I needed the time to heal. Still, even though I'm better, I'm not nearly well enough to get really involved in a heavy-duty relationship. The best part is that he's great with the girls. He's quick to give Kerry a hug, and I like that.

When Mike pointed out to me that my having a man sleep at the house showed no moral concern for the girls, I couldn't help but wonder where the immorality applied—in the doing it or in the being honest and open with my children about doing it!

Before I started writing this, I reread your last letter and was struck one more time with the parallels in our lives, specifically Jim's decision not to have anything to do with Laurie. Kerry came home recently from an afternoon of bowling with her father and said Mike had told her he was tired of playing games with the girls (here we go with the games again) and didn't want them to call him or come out to the apartment to see him anymore. Or at least that was her interpretation of what he said. Since that time, Deborah claims Kerry misunderstood him, but so far he hasn't called her to clear up that "misunderstanding." Instead of dealing with her up front, he comes into the house when no one is home and rifles through her bedroom and reads her mail. Maybe it's time to start leaving some fictitious letters lying around for his eyes.

Becky found out last week that she was on the homecoming court. During the tea that the student council sponsored, I learned that the girls' fathers were to escort them onto the field during the halftime of the football game. When I asked Becky about it, she said she wasn't going to ask Mike to do it. After a session of tears, I finally talked her into asking him, and he accepted. The night of the game, after some badgering by Becky, I agreed to go and take pictures. When I got to the place where the girls were, Becky came up to me and said, "Dad won't let you take our picture. He's being a real asshole." I told her not to feel bad about it, that it was his problem, and took my camera off from around my neck and had one of the other fathers take their picture. When I looked over and saw this supposedly mature man with his back turned to us, I felt glad to be rid of that kind of anger and bitterness. I can still remember lots of good times and still have some good feelings about Mike. I'm relieved to be free from the control that all those negative feelings can have on a person.

Just as there was never enough I could do to convince Mike I cared for him, there isn't anything I can do to convince him I'm not a greedy, ungrateful woman whose sole goal is to take him to the cleaners. Fortunately, what he thinks of me is of little importance now. I'm just trying to raise the girls as best I can and at the same time move forward with my life in a constructive and positive manner.

Mike is taking me back into court for the fifth time. Basically, he is asking the court to forget everything that has happened so far and to start over. Of course, he's throwing in a couple of additional requests, the biggest being that he get custody of the girls.

Alan received notice that Mike's lawyer has withdrawn and has been replaced by Dr. Michael G. Marshall, Ph.D., *pro se*. That means he's representing himself. Sounds to me as if he finally has a lawyer with whom he can agree. Think he's ever heard that old adage that a man who is his own lawyer has a fool for a client?

Alan tells me it will be another nine months until we can get this before a judge for final disposition. There is no doubt in my mind, however, that it will be the turn of the century before it's over.

Even good ole calm, cool, and collected Alan has reached the end of his patience. I had lunch with him recently, and he told me that he is prepared to pay out of his own pocket to hire a marriage counselor to get us back together. I think my sick sense of humor is rubbing off on him.

You want to hear something really weird? Mad as Mike makes me when he dumps a pile of shit on me, I still kind of like him. I saw him outside the other day and actually wished I could go out and talk to him. I couldn't stand to ever live with him again, but I still see all kinds of good there.

According to the motion he filed with the court, he has applied for fourteen different university positions and not received one interview.

God, what a waste! I don't think there's a better or more dedicated teacher alive than Mike.

I've blabbered on forever and not even mentioned Phil. You know how pleased I am for you. You've always been destined to be a loving wife and mother. Hope he's the kind of man who appreciates that dedication.

I think we're going to be okay, kid.

NANCY

Englewood, New Jersey
October 20, 1982

DEAR NANCY,

As the end of this year approaches, I realize how much things have changed for me and—wonder of wonders—for the better! Even Laurie recently said, "Mom, you came out ahead in this divorce."

It's easy to see and feel the change of having Phil around. My life is much happier because of him, but I decided sometime ago that it isn't healthy to be dependent on anyone else to make your life happy. He is a special part of my life; however, we both have time to follow our own interests, and I wouldn't think of changing this balance.

Recently, a divorced friend realized that he had been too dependent on his ex-wife for his happiness. With his new introspection, he concluded that it had been too heavy a burden for her. When he mentioned this, it made me wonder if Jim felt too much pressure for being responsible for my happiness. This also tied in with something Alice's ex-husband told me shortly after Jim left. He said that one of the things that attracted him to his new wife was her independence.

Since I handled everything when Jim wasn't around, I thought of myself as independent, even though it wasn't true emotionally. What is that old Pennsylvania Dutch saying? "We get too soon old, and too late smart." Think I'll stick with, "It's never too late!"

In fact, can you believe that Phil and I are talking about living together? I can't. I've come a long way, baby! Something inside still bothers me about this possible move, but not having him here bothers me more. It just feels right having him around.

It's not that I don't want to marry; marriage was on my mind even a couple of years ago when I wasn't anywhere near ready. We both want more time to see how things go; besides, we couldn't afford it.

This relationship is the big positive change for me this year, but it's not the only one. Doing this book with you has been a once-in-a-lifetime project. It is an accomplishment that we've achieved by ourselves. We were lucky to have a terrific editor in Joyce and great friendly advice, but we did it, kid!

When you called with the idea, it was certainly fortunate timing for me. True, I was finishing my teacher's certificate, which was another positive accomplishment. However, I had been itching to do something more.

Thanks to you, I've learned more about myself by doing this book than through meditation and psychology. In Michael's English book, there's a quote from one of Thoreau's *Journals* (1841): "Nothing goes by luck in composition. It allows of no tricks. The best you can write will be the best you are. Every sentence is the result of a long probation. The author's character is read from title-page to end. Of this he never corrects the proofs."

Certainly we can't change our past, but we can be more aware in the future. I'm positive there are many more lessons for me to learn and more hurdles to jump, just as there are more books to read and more friends to meet and more experiences to be enjoyed.

Some roles are finished with, whereas others are opening up, and I want to be ready. My children are pretty well grown. I've read that, as people grow older, they will remember more of the good happenings in their life. I hope my children will remember all the times we went to the duck pond, when I helped them deliver their papers, and the cookies we baked and books we read, and forget the friction of a couple of years. In fact, the friction between the boys and me has been over for some time. Michael and I have grown even closer this year. When he has vacation time he is here as much as he's at Jim's. He also stays in touch better than most college kids. I'm happy with our relationship, though I still worry a little because Michael wants to be famous in some creative field and Jim's a tough act to follow.

David isn't the type who keeps really close contact, but it makes me feel good when he unexpectedly drops in or calls. We've made good progress with our rapport and Dave is maturing nicely.

Laurie's still a handful, but believe it or not she's shown some positive progress lately. Knock on wood!

I'm looking forward to the holidays. The boys will be home, Brad will visit, and Sam will be here at least part-time. I hope Phil's sons will join us—the more the merrier. (Phil is looking forward to helping trim the Christmas tree.)

Really enjoyed my visit to Lake Minnetonka. Seeing the girls again was a treat, and I enjoyed meeting your friends. It was easy to see why you succumbed to Michael's appeal. One word—*Indulge*.

I'm glad the atmosphere at the house wasn't suffering from the tensions you are currently under. It was good to see that your girls enjoy Michael's company; that's important. I know it would be difficult for me if Laurie and Phil didn't get along. You also seem to have a good time and a good relationship with the girls. Believe me, I know teens can be a handful.

I've been trying to think of some advice for current baseball wives, and I have a few hints. First of all, Be comfortable. How well I remember filling our station wagon to the brim and trying not to buy anything else when we rented. Now I would buy a few plants; so what if you had to leave them behind. I'd probably also take a colorful rug or painting to hang on the wall. Maybe not practical but cheery.

If I had it to do over, I would be less practical. Would definitely spend more money for myself—baby-sitters, cleaning ladies, tickets to plays, even clothes. This was a personal problem, and others may not need this advice, but it's good to be aware of yourself as a person who deserves things. Also, I would travel more with just my husband—no kids along!

It's good to read about baseball wives running charity fund-raisers. When Jim was playing, this was not a very common venture. It would be a positive way to channel energy. Also, some wives have started a baseball wives' magazine. Hurrah for them! There's even a play called *Baseball Wives.* Phil and I went and enjoyed it very much. I really could identify with it. Hope you get a chance to see it, too.

Another way I would channel energy would be physically. In my twenties and thirties, the extent of my exercising was meager, basically, walking, running after children, and later some family hiking. Now I feel better than ever, and I'm biking (including a recent 42-mile trip), hiking (even places with names like the crevice and precipice), jogging, and learning to play tennis.

This is minor advice compared to the problems involved in a baseball marriage. The big problem of handling the separations must be faced alone. I'd advise each wife to follow whatever makes her most comfortable. It seems there are pitfalls at every turn of a relationship; however, being open and honest with your spouse may help. Truthfully, I don't know if I could have handled really knowing about Jim's pursuits. At the time, the best I could do to deal with the possibility that he was occasionally unfaithful was to try not to think about it and enjoy the many positive parts of our relationship. This is what made me most comfortable then. Now it would be a different story.

Last but not least, a sense of humor may be the best help of all for survival. Even now it's a priority; for example, shortly before he left for college, Michael was talking to Phil. He said, "I haven't seen you lately, but I've heard you." Phil asked what he meant. "Well," said Michael, "the other night when I knocked on Mom's door [around

1:00 A.M.], I heard you say, 'Oh shit.' " Phil and I laughed for several minutes. Thank goodness neither of us was uptight; laughter is good medicine.

Speaking of laughing, I'll close with a joke that Burt's mom (who once said the only thing wrong with me was that I lacked piss and vinegar) told at his wedding. What's the difference between herpes and love? Herpes lasts a lifetime.

So do good friends,
BOBBIE

Shorewood, Minnesota
October 1982

DEAR BOBBIE,

Wish you could have stayed longer, but I'm glad you got to see Minneapolis and Lake Minnetonka. After promising you some spectacular sunsets, I was glad the horizon came through on your last night here.

I've been meaning to ask you if you saw the article in *Life* magazine about the Milwaukee Brewers wives. After reading the article, I realized that I'm glad to be out of that rat race. Seeing pictures of the wives standing around after the game, waiting for their husbands to get dressed, made me flinch. I did my share of standing and waiting, but looking back on it, I'm not sure that was a healthy thing to do. Going to a game now and then would be okay, but night after night? Isn't that a rather passive way to live?

The worst part of the article was Linda Molitor's statement that she went on as many road trips as possible to "shoo away the flies." Makes you wonder if she had any sense of self-worth other than being married to a big-name baseball player. Placing oneself in that kind of defensive, one-down position is demeaning, to say the least.

Years ago, when we were living in Los Angeles, I asked Don Sutton's wife, Patti, how she felt about being married to a professional athlete. She raved on and on about how wonderful it was. At the time, they had a beautiful home in L.A., she hadn't had to move around at all since Don had been there for a while, and he was making good money. Don and Patti are both very attractive people and were frequently invited to be on various television game shows. Life was very glamorous for the Suttons.

Last spring they did an article for *People* magazine in which they talked candidly about how their marriage had deteriorated until they eventually separated; they also discussed their efforts to put it back together. I recently called Patti and asked her if she remembered how she had responded to my question years ago. She said she recalled it very well and knew now that she had been living in a fairy-tale world back then. She said that although the lifestyle gave them the financial ability to live comfortably and allowed them to meet some very interesting people, it was all in all a hard life.

In talking about their problems, Patti recalled that when she tried to discuss them with Don, he would tell her that she would never leave him because she was a clinger and he was a survivor. That reminded me of the times Mike would avoid tackling a problem by telling me that if I didn't like his lifestyle, I should get out. Don and Patti were lucky. They went for counseling and put their marriage back together.

Patti and I talked about what we would advise young women who are new to the game. We decided we'd tell them to avoid the fairy tale and recognize the reality. We'd tell them that the odds are good that their husbands will be unfaithful to them, but to recognize that as being part of the lifestyle and not to be destroyed by it. We'd tell them to make lives for themselves outside their husbands' careers. We'd tell them that the same ego that enables their husbands to perform well on the field may prevent them from performing well in their relationships. We'd tell them to be wary of letting all the attention and notoriety their husbands get detract from their own feelings of self-worth. We'd tell them all those things and more, but we agreed that they probably wouldn't understand. Do you think *we* would have listened?

I've gotten to know one of my professors at William Mitchell quite well. Whenever I need a morale boost, I stop in his office to chat. He's so positive and enthusiastic about life that he's contagious. I always feel great when I leave his office.

He knows that I'm going through a difficult divorce, finishing our book, being a single parent, and going to law school, so periodically he gives me a pep talk. Recently, he told me that if I don't let all of it get me down, I'll come out of this in much better shape then before. I already know that's true and can't wait to see how good things will be a year from now.

I've been fortunate to have so many people supporting me through all this. The girls have been my biggest blessing.

And Michael. The man seems to know intuitively when I'm getting ready to wallow in my pity pile and kicks me in the butt. On the other hand, he's always there with support when I need it most. I don't know if a year from now he'll still be in my life, but I do know I'll always love him for helping me learn to trust again.

I have to admit to you, girl, that I'm not looking forward to the shit hitting the fan when the book is published. My brother told me that he thinks I should either write it under a ghost name or wait until Mom and Dad are no longer living. Too late.

Remember how the psychic told you that you will write three books? Well, I want you to promise to devote the second one to unraveling the mystery of how my body found its way to the bottom of Lake Minnetonka.

Take care,
NANCY

After the Ball

After the ball is over, after the break of morn;
After the dancers' leaving; after the stars are gone;
Many a heart is aching, if you could read them all;
Many the hopes that have vanished after the ball.

—Charles Harris

About the Authors

Bobbie Bouton was born in Allegan, Michigan. She was graduated from Western Michigan University in 1961 and married Jim Bouton, whom she met in college, in 1962. She now lives in Englewood, New Jersey, with her three children and teaches special education at a local high school.

Nancy Marshall was born in Adrian, Michigan. She attended Eastern Michigan University for two and a half years until she married Mike Marshall early in 1963. She was graduated from Michigan State University in 1977. She now lives in Shorewood, Minnesota, with her three daughters and is attending law school.